Els Breugelmans

Investigating Consumer Behavior in an Online Grocery Context

Els Breugelmans

Investigating Consumer Behavior in an Online Grocery Context

The Impact of the Adopted Stock-out Policy and Virtual Shelf Placement

VDM Verlag Dr. Müller

Impressum/Imprint (nur für Deutschland/ only for Germany)
Bibliografische Information der Deutschen Nationalbibliothek: Die Deutsche Nationalbibliothek
verzeichnet diese Publikation in der Deutschen Nationalbibliografie; detaillierte bibliografische
Daten sind im Internet über http://dnb.d-nb.de abrufbar.

Coverbild: www.purestockx.com

Verlag: VDM Verlag Dr. Müller Aktiengesellschaft & Co. KG
Dudweiler Landstr. 125 a, 66123 Saarbrücken, Deutschland
Telefon +49 681 9100-698, Telefax +49 681 9100-988, Email: info@vdm-verlag.de
Zugl.: Antwerp, University of Antwerp, Dissertation, 2005

Herstellung in Deutschland:
Schaltungsdienst Lange o.H.G., Zehrensdorfer Str. 11, D-12277 Berlin
Books on Demand GmbH, Gutenbergring 53, D-22848 Norderstedt
Reha GmbH, Dudweiler Landstr. 99, D- 66123 Saarbrücken
ISBN: 978-3-639-09504-3

Imprint (only for USA, GB)
Bibliographic information published by the Deutsche Nationalbibliothek: The Deutsche
Nationalbibliothek lists this publication in the Deutsche Nationalbibliografie; detailed
bibliographic data are available in the Internet at http://dnb.d-nb.de.

Cover image: www.purestockx.com

Publisher:
VDM Verlag Dr. Müller Aktiengesellschaft & Co. KG
Dudweiler Landstr. 125 a, 66123 Saarbrücken, Germany
Phone +49 681 9100-698, Fax +49 681 9100-988, Email: info@vdm-verlag.de

Produced in USA and UK by:
Lightning Source Inc., 1246 Heil Quaker Blvd., La Vergne, TN 37086, USA
Lightning Source UK Ltd., Chapter House, Pitfield, Kiln Farm, Milton Keynes, MK11 3LW, GB
BookSurge, 7290 B. Investment Drive, North Charleston, SC 29418, USA
ISBN: 978-3-639-09504-3

ACKNOWLEDGEMENTS

Writing a dissertation is time-consuming and trying, but at the same time exciting, instructive and a big challenge. Without the help, support and encouragement of many individuals, I would never have been able to finish this dissertation successfully. Standing at the crossroads of my academic career, I would like to thank several persons that have contributed to the realization of this dissertation.

First and foremost, I would like to express my sincere gratitude to my supervisors, Katia Campo and Els Gijsbrechts, for their continuous support, patience and encouragement. It has amazed me several times how they could understand each other with half a word or sentence and how they gave (sometimes literally, independent of each other) the same constructive remarks, suggestions or advice. As for Els, I would like to thank her for giving me the chance to take up doctoral research and for her valuable comments and guidelines throughout the process. As for Katia, I am grateful for the many times that we sat together and discussed some (more practical) problems. I always found the interactions very helpful and rewarding. I have learned a lot from my supervisors and would not have been able to complete this dissertation successfully without their help!

My thanks also go to the members of the doctoral committee, Annouk Lievens and Walter van Waterschoot, for reading previous versions of this work and providing me with many valuable comments aimed at improving the quality of it. I especially thank Annouk Lievens for chairing my jury, for believing in me and for her encouragement. She made me feel confident to overcome every difficulty I encountered! I further thank Walter van Waterschoot for his critical reflections that have definitely improved the theoretical part in my dissertation. I also sincerely thank the members of the examination committee, Patrick De Pelsmacker, Gilles Laurent, Patrick Van Kenhove and Philippe Verbeeck. I consider it a real honour that they were willing to join my jury! I am grateful for their careful reading and thoughtful comments and realize that they have improved my dissertation. I am also much indebted to Bart Bronnenberg, Karen Gedenk, Christian Lutzky, Koen Pauwels, Joffre Swait, Harald van Heerde and Jianan Wu. Their answers on my questions, detailed suggestions and broader reactions have definitely helped to shape this dissertation.

i

As with any scientific research, the role of empirical data is invaluable. I am therefore grateful to anyone who helped in making my experiment succeed. To start with, I thank Marc Bauhertz, Michel Choquet, Willem Timmermans and Willy Noterman of Caddyhome, Delhaize for answering my practical questions and for their authorization to use their site in an experimental setting. I also thank dhr. Mellaerts (Delhaize Brasschaat) for making it possible to take pictures of product packages in his office. The experiment would never have been possible, however, without the help of software company Hypervision that developed the computer experiment. A special word of thanks goes to Mieke Calliau, Bart De Coster, Hans Palmers and Stijn Jacquemyn. I would also like to acknowledge the support of DataBaseManagement and the staff of the university for making the e-mail addresses available. Finally, I am much indebted to both the respondents (colleagues, family and friends) that pre-tested the experimental design and the respondents that participated in the research.

My sincere thanks go to Fund for Scientific Research, Flanders (FWO-Vlaanderen) and to the University of Antwerp. Without their support and financial help, it would not have been possible to complete this research. I particularly thank current but also former members of the marketing department at the University of Antwerp. I thank the head of the department, Marcel Weverbergh, and the secretary, Els Jordaens, for making my life easier and arranging (or agreeing on) a number of practical/financial things. I especially want to thank my predecessor Bram Foubert whom I have asked a millions of 'small questions'. He was always willing to answer them and I will always remember the talks we had on research and other elements of (academic) life. I wish him all the best at the university of Maastricht and hope that I can still pop in in his office when I start working there. I also thank Patricia Nisol for helping me to find my way in the programming language Gauss. Finally, I want to express my gratitude to current Ph D students of the marketing department, Joeri De Haes, Nathalie Dens and Wim Janssens, for their permanent support and nice words! I wish them all the best with the completion of their own dissertation.

Very warm thanks go to all my friends, for constantly reminding me of what is really important in life. Ann, Charlotte, Wendy, Ellen, Ilse, Vicky, Lies and Sandy: thank you many, many times! There are two people I need to mention especially, Sandy and Lies, who found the time to proofread my dissertation in such a short period. Sandy and Lies, I think that the completion of my dissertation can be considered as a legitimate reason to celebrate with chocolate cake... And Sandy, I would be glad to proofread your dissertation soon!

I also want to thank my family. Their understanding and love encouraged me to work hard and helped me to finish my dissertation. Knowing that they would be proud of me was an important stimulator to do my best! The two most important persons in my life are my sister, An and my boyfriend, Dave. *Zusje, dank je wel voor al je lieve woorden en aanmoedigingen op momenten dat ik het moeilijk had!* Last but far from least, I can not express in words my feelings of gratitude for my boyfriend. His love, patience, understanding and encouragement without any complaint (even when he was, again, pre-testing the experiment/questionnaire or when proofreading my dissertation) has enabled me to complete this Ph D project. The 'new man' really exists and does almost everything of the housekeeping. Yet, I do hope to do a bit more of my part in the near future! I first wanted to make the promise that evening- and weekend-work would be a thing of the past but I prefer to make promises that I can keep... therefore, I promise to do *less* evening- and weekend-work.

Els Breugelmans, Antwerp, August 2005.

Er zijn wel eens van die dagen
Dat het wat minder goed gaat
Even een dipje gehad
Het gevoel dat alles tegen slaat.

Juist op zo'n dag moet je denken
Aan de mooie dingen in het leven
Aan je familie, vrienden en vriendinnen
Die jou liefde geven
(Anoniem, Internet)

TABLE OF CONTENTS

INTRODUCTION

RESEARCH JUSTIFICATION

Electronic grocery shopping offers consumers the possibility to order groceries electronically. With the increasing popularity and commercial use of computers in our lives, online shopping has become a well-accepted and convenient way of ordering products. At this moment, electronic grocery shopping is evolving at an exponential rate. The electronic shopping environment differs on a significant number of aspects from the traditional shopping environment. These typical online environment characteristics not only influence the online consumer's shopping behavior, they also offer more flexibility for online retailers to implement merchandising actions.

Although the primary function of an e-channel is typically communication, making products available to consumers is notwithstanding an important (yet perhaps secondary) function. A commonly occurring failure in the distribution function of supermarkets are stock-outs. Due to more severe forecasting problems and strongly fluctuating demand, stock-outs are even a more daunting problem for virtual grocers than for traditional ones (e.g. Fitzsimons, 2000; Van Elburg – Emerce, 2001). What is more, recent research has shown that product unavailability rates second in the top 3 of irritations with online shopping, making online retailers especially vulnerable to stock-out losses in the long term (Marketing online, 9/11/2004). Despite their importance, stock-outs have not yet been investigated systematically in an online grocery context. Nevertheless, because of differences between the virtual and traditional supermarket environment (and, resultantly, between online and offline shopping behavior), online stock-out reactions might differ from offline stock-out reactions.

Moreover, doing the research in an online grocery context is especially valuable as online environment characteristics offer opportunities for merchandising actions that are not or difficult to implement in a traditional grocery store. Indeed, the merchandising costs or the costs retailers incur when making physical changes to the shopping environment are lower for an online retailer than for a traditional one.

RESEARCH OBJECTIVES

The first, global objective of this dissertation is to map the differences between an electronic and a traditional shopping environment and to indicate how these typical online environment characteristics affect online purchase behavior. The focus of this dissertation is on online purchase behavior in regular choice environments but especially in choice environments disrupted by stock-outs. In this respect, an overview of the most striking differences between an electronic and traditional grocery shopping environment (from a consumer's point of view) is developed and a state-of-the-art of out-of-stock related knowledge (in traditional shopping environments) is generated. Based on these overviews, it is derived how shopping behavior and stock-out reactions might differ between an online and offline shopping environment. These insights help to develop a conceptual framework that allows to assess how consumers make online purchase behavior decisions in a regular as well as in a disrupted (by stock-outs) online choice environment.

The second objective is to investigate how online purchase behavior decisions are affected by an e-tailer's merchandising actions. In this dissertation, the following two merchandising actions that online retailers can adopt, were identified:
(1) Implementation of active stock-out management to explicitly deal with the negative effects of stock-outs (the online stock-out policy);
(2) Implementation of in-store, shelf-related management (the virtual shelf placement).

1st Project: Opportunities for active stock-out management in an online store

The first project focuses on the impact of a number of active policies that online retailers can adopt to alleviate the consequences of service failures like stock-outs. More specifically, this project investigates the effects of the following three out-of-stock policies on online stock-out reactions (choice and incidence behavior):
(1) a 'visible, no-replacement' stock-out policy, i.e. a policy where stock-outs are visible for everyone and no replacement items are suggested (benchmark);
(2) a 'non-visible' stock-out policy, i.e. a policy where stock-outs are only visible for the buyers of the product (after clicking, a pop-up tells the buyer that the product is currently not available) (prominence-reduction);
(3) a 'replacement' stock-out policy, i.e. a policy where a replacement product is suggested for each out-of-stock product (compensation).

2

In traditional supermarkets, stock-outs are typically visible (empty shelf space) and no replacement items are suggested. The visible, no-replacement policy was therefore used as the benchmark case in our research. The selection of the other policies was based on the current practices of e-supermarkets. Both the benchmark as well as the other two policies are the ones that are most frequently adopted by existing online grocery stores. In addition, we selected policies where online retailers have, compared to traditional retailers, a noticeable 'implementation advantage'. First, while an out-of-stock in a traditional store is visible for all clients, an online retailer may choose to notify only buyers of that particular product (i.e. after clicking). Online retailers can, in contrast to traditional retailers, use a typical online environment feature like a pop-up to make stock-out failures less prominent. Second, an online retailer can more easily compensate for the inconvenience a stock-out causes by suggesting a replacement product for each out-of-stock product. Whereas traditional retailers first have to notice stock-outs and then have to physically reorganize the shelves, online retailers can use a technical process that ensures that suggestions are made immediately each time an out-of-stock occurs. One of the core issues when adopting a replacement policy is how to select an appropriate substitution product. In this respect, we will investigate if and to what extent the price of the suggested replacement items moderates the main effect of the replacement out-of-stock policy.

2ⁿᵈ Project: The visual salience of a product in an online store

The second project investigates whether and how consumers' choices in an online shopping context are influenced by the location of products on the virtual shelf. More specifically, this project investigates the impact of the following two aspects of virtual shelf placement on online choice decisions:
(1) the location of the products within a display (visibility, placement as such);
(2) product adjacencies (proximity, placement relative to other items).
For the latter aspect, the stock-out situation was used as a case in point to investigate if and to what extent consumers confronted with a stock-out for their favorite item, tend to focus on a particular, narrow, section of the shelf when choosing a replacement item.

Investigating virtual shelf placement is important. Although it was suggested that shelf management was no longer an issue in a virtual store (e.g. an unlimited/endless virtual space and a dramatic decrease in consumer's search costs), recently, more realistic sounds indicate that online stores do face (their own) shelf management problems. It is pointed out that the amount of information that can be presented on a single screen is limited ('screen space' constraint) and that products are more or less visible depending on their position on the virtual shelf. What is more, online retailers not only seem to have their own shelf management problems, they also have more opportunities to influence consumer's choices (and thus stock-out reactions) by better managing their existing shelves. Indeed, whereas offline retailers have to physically reorganize the shelf for each adjustment, online retailers can literally press one button to change the placement of products on a shelf. In addition, this project sheds further light on how assortment size strengthens the use of these shelf-related (visibility and proximity) tactics as task-simplifying choice heuristics. Focusing on the moderating effect of (online) assortment is justified as traditional literature has suggested that consumers are more responsive to the in-store environment in case of large assortments.

The research questions of this dissertation, per project are summarized in table 1.

Table 1: Research questions, per project

	Project 1: Stock-out policy	Project 2: Virtual shelf placement
Objectives	* How do consumers make purchase behavior decisions: - in a regular online choice environment? - in an online choice environment disrupted by stock-outs?	
	* What is the effect of different stock-out policies: (1) stock-outs visible for everyone (visible policy) versus stock-outs only visible after purchase attempts (non-visible policy)? (2) not suggesting a substitution product (no-replacement policy) versus suggesting a substitution product (replacement policy)? (2a) suggesting a substitution product of a higher price versus suggesting a substitution product of the same/lower price (moderating impact of a higher-priced suggestion)?	* What is the effect of virtual shelf placement: (1) products visible on the first screen versus products not visible on the first screen (visibility)? (2) products adjacent to a favorite out-of-stock product versus more distant products (proximity)? (3) the probability that consumers are more likely to rely on virtual shelf placement effects in large compared to small assortments (moderating impact of assortment size)?
Dependent variable	- category purchase incidence (logit incidence) - product choice (two-stage choice model)	- product choice (multinomial logit model)

4

The scope of both projects is limited to purchase behavior for grocery products in an electronic grocery shopping context. The data for both projects are collected by means of one realistic, online computer-simulated shopping experiment. In both projects, traditional purchase behavior models are adjusted so that they are able to capture the effects of the stock-out policy (project 1) and virtual shelf placement (project 2). While stock-out policy might affect both the category purchase incidence as well as the choice decision, shelf placement is typically considered as an in-store tactic used by retailers to affect (choice) decisions once consumers are in the store. For this reason, the focus is on the purchase incidence and the two-stage choice model (consideration plus choice stage) in the first project and on the choice (item selection) decision in the second project.

OUTLINE OF THE DISSERTATION

This dissertation consists of five chapters. In the first chapter, electronic grocery shopping is defined and the most important differences between an online and offline shopping environment and, as a result, between online and offline shopping behavior are highlighted. In the second chapter, a review of the marketing literature on retail stock-outs (in a traditional grocery shopping environment) is provided. This chapter zooms in on how stock-outs affect the consumer's decision making process and indicates how online stock-out reactions might differ from those in brick-and-mortar settings. In this chapter, we give a complete overview of all the possible factors that could influence stock-out reactions. Yet, in practice, consumer reactions are not necessarily affected by all these factors. In addition, it should be noted that these factors are not necessarily traded off in an explicit, compensatory process. It is possible that some of them work more 'unconsciously' or are integrated in simplifying heuristics. The empirical study will help us understand how factors come into play when consumers make purchase decisions in an (online) stock-out situation. The data collection method, an online computer-simulated shopping experiment, is described in chapter 3. After giving an overview of the research methodologies used in prior studies on stock-out reactions, the advantages of using an online computer-simulated shopping experiment in our research are stipulated. Next, the experimental design, the treatment of the manipulated variables and the data collection method are described. The two projects are discussed in chapter 4 and 5, respectively. The investigation of the impact of the stock-out policy on online stock-out reactions is discussed in chapter 4, while the impact of the visual salience of a product on online choice decisions is studied in chapter 5. This dissertation ends by summarizing the main findings (thereby stipulating the academic and managerial contributions) and by providing directions for future research.

CHAPTER 1: ELECTRONIC GROCERY SHOPPING

INTRODUCTION

In the late '90s, new Internet-based consumer business channels emerged in almost every industry sector. Although home ordering is not an entirely new service in the grocery sector (before the Internet-revolution, it was possible to order by fax or phone), new opportunities have emerged with the development of the Internet. The increasing popularity and commercial use of computers in society highlights the future potential of offering products on the Internet (Anckar, Walden and Jelassi, 2002; Geuens, Brengman and S'Jegers, 2003; Kämäräinen et al., 2001; Verhoef and Langerak, 2001). An e-channel is typically a hybrid channel with communication as its dominant function. Yet, together with the role of communication, e-stores typically have to deal with a number of distribution aspects. In this dissertation, we focus on stock-outs, a commonly occurring failure in the distribution function of the e-grocery channel (see next chapter, section 2.3).

In the next section, we define e-grocery home delivery services, describe the e-grocery market and identify the profile of current online grocery shoppers. Next, we give an overview of the most striking differences between electronic and traditional grocery shopping from a consumer's point of view, thereby indicating the most important advantages and disadvantages of e-grocery shopping. Afterwards, we indicate how virtual store characteristics might affect the consumer's purchase behavior process.

1.1 DEFINITION

Electronic commerce of groceries refers to *"consumers' ability to order groceries electronically"* (based on Verhoef and Langerak, 2001, p.275). Although most consumers will order groceries from home, our definition is more generic and also captures situations where consumers order groceries from other places than home (e.g. from the office, from a cybercafé or even within the store outlet itself). In the first section, we give an overview of the practices of online grocery retailers (i.e. different e-grocery models or types). Afterwards, we outline the online grocery market and describe the profile of the current online grocery shopper.

1.1.1 Practices of online grocery retailers

Two types of online grocery retailers can be distinguished: 'pure-play' retailers (pure online grocery retailers) and 'brick-and-click' retailers (multi-channel grocery retailers) (Morganosky and Cude, 2000). Pure-play retailers are virtual supermarkets, existing only online. Examples include Allosupermarche (www.allosupermarche.be, a Belgian website) and Netgrocer (www.netgrocer.com, a US website). Brick-and-click retailers are brick-and-mortar (traditional) stores that additionally offer an online grocery shopping service. Examples include Caddyhome (www.caddyhome.be, the online shopping site of Delhaize) and Peapod (www.peapod.com, the oldest online grocery shopping service in the US, owned by the international food provider Royal Ahold).

From a consumer's point of view, most e-grocers operate according to the same business model (see figure 1.1): after placing an order, professional shoppers ('pickers') fill the order and the e-tailer makes sure that the consumer receives the order. Most online grocery stores charge extra costs, such as a monthly and/or a picking and/or a delivery fee for these picking and/or delivery services (Ring and Tigert, 2001). Some e-grocery stores do not charge any costs as long as the order exceeds a minimum requirement. So, when the order is large enough, these consumers only pay for the ordered grocery items. While most e-grocery stores have common characteristics, differences between e-grocery stores in the three steps exist (Morganosky and Cude, 2001). In the following paragraphs, we briefly review the various options as they are currently operational.

Figure 1.1: Electronic grocery model

| Placing the order | → | Assembling the order | → | Delivering the order |

Next to *taking orders* online, some grocery retailers also take orders by telephone and/or fax (Morganosky and Cude, 2001; Verhoef and Langerak, 2001). In this research, we focus on orders that are placed via the web.

Once the consumer has placed the order, grocery pickers select the merchandise to *fill the order*. An online grocer can assemble orders via a warehouse model or via a store model. In the first model, retailers pick items from a warehouse or central distribution centre. In the second model, retailers contract with existing (self-owned or other) local retail stores and grocery pickers select merchandise at these stores to fill orders. Pure-play retailers typically fill orders from merchandise stored in a warehouse (e.g. Netgrocer, Streamline) while brick-and-click retailers tend to use either of the models (e.g. Tesco uses an in-store picking up model, Sainsbury and Caddyhome/Delhaize use a central distribution centre model). It seems to be commonly accepted that the warehouse model dominates the in-store model because it is more cost-efficient (as long as demand is sufficient): picking efficiency and space utilization can be improved and losses due to pilferage or spoilage can be reduced (Boyer and Hult, 2005b; Cude and Morganosky, 2000; Kämäräinen, Saranen and Holmström, 2001; Kämäräinen et al., 2001; Morganosky and Cude, 2000; Murphy, 2003; Roberts, Xu and Mettos, 2003; Saranen and Småros, 2001).

E-grocers also differ in the *delivery service* they offer (Morganosky and Cude, 2000). Some retailers offer consumers the possibility to either pick up the order at a pre-determined place (i.e. a place that the retailer believes to be convenient for the consumer, such as the grocery store, a petroleum station or a tobacconist) or have it home-delivered. Other retailers adopt one of the two delivery services. For instance, Colruyt offers Collivery (www.collivery.com, the home-delivery version) and Collect & Go (www.collectandgo.com, the pick-up version) while Caddyhome (the online shopping service of Delhaize) only offers a home-delivery service. A study of Morganosky and Cude (2002) based on longitudinal data revealed that respondents prefer home delivery over picking up the groceries. With respect to the home-delivery service, two versions exist: either attended reception/delivery (where the consumer has to be at home) or unattended reception/delivery (where a consumer-specific insulated box containing the goods is delivered to the consumer and attached securely in a locking device bolted on a building wall) (e.g. Kämäräinen et al., 2001; Punakivi and Tanskanen, 2002; Punakivi, Yrjölä and Holmström, 2001). At this moment, most retailers adopt an attended home-delivery, requesting the customer to be at home at the moment of delivery. Besides the chosen delivery mode, e-grocers also differ on other delivery aspects, such as the lead time (i.e. the minimum time difference between order and delivery/pick-up) and the available delivery time window (i.e. how long the customer has to stay at home waiting for the delivery) (see Kämäräinen et al., 2001; Punakivi et al., 2001; Saranen and Småros, 2001).

1.1.2 The grocery e-tailing market

During the dot.com bubble, (most of) the first pure-play (Internet-only) grocery retailers disappeared. After the bubble, a second stream of Internet grocery retailers with more profit potential appeared, namely stores that combine traditional and electronic grocery shopping (Tanskanen, Yrjölä and Holmström, 2002; Marketing Online, 31/03/'03). These second-wave, brick-and-click, stores have learned from the first-wave, pure-Internet, grocery retailers and have taken over the best parts of their former challengers' businesses (Tanskanen et al., 2002). Moreover, brick-and-click stores have a number of advantages over Internet-only stores such as the possibility to extend the brand name reputation and to leverage the existing shopping experience online, the possibility to offer a complete line of products, including perishables and the possibility to exploit existing grocery knowledge (Kempiak and Fox, 2002; Marketing online, 31/03/'03; Murphy, 2003).

Recent evidence has shown that online (grocery) retail revenues increase, with double- (or even triple-) digit growth figures being the rule rather than the exception (Andrews and Currim, 2004; Boyer and Hult, 2005a; McGree and Boyer, 2005; Straziuso, 26/05/2004; Wiersma, 2004a; Wiersma, 2005). Moreover, at this moment, electronic grocery retailers tend to expand their operations, thereby enlarging the geographic service area covered. The growth of electronic grocery shopping has been fastest in the UK, with Tesco claiming to be the largest e-supermarket in the world, covering almost 96% of the country (Boyer and Hult, 2005b; Wiersma, 2004b). Recent figures of credit card provider Visa, for instance, indicate that Britons have more than doubled the amount of money they spend online in the first quarter of 2004, compared to the same period in the previous year. One of the biggest winners was the online grocery industry (Hotelmarketing, 2004). E-grocery shopping has also grown in the US and in other parts of Europe (Tanskanen et al., 2002). For instance, Albert.nl, the electronic delivery service of the Dutch supermarket Albert Heijn, has recently expanded its operations and experienced an increase of 30% in its online turnover (Wiersma, 2004a).

Together with recent improvements in, for instance, the delivery service (e.g. offering unattended reception/delivery; Punakivi et al., 2001), the size and composition of the assortment (e.g. expanding the product offer; Netgrocer, 2004), the shopping application and ordering systems (Netgrocer, 2004) and website design and navigation (e.g. Kmart.com – Biz.yahoo, 23/03/'05), electronic grocery shopping is likely to exhibit strong growth in the future (Czarnowski, 2001; Marketing online, 22/03/'05; Punakivi, 2003; Van Elburg – Emerce, 2005). Indeed, industry watchers say that is no longer a question of whether electronic grocery shopping will be successful or not, but rather how big it will become (Straziuso, 26/05/2004). AMR research, for instance, has forecasted that supermarkets will be able to attain 5% of their turnover via the Internet, within five years (Marketing Online, 31/03/'03; see also AcNielsen, 08/03/2004; Marketing Online, 19/04/'05).

1.1.3 Current profile of the online grocery shopper

Current online grocery buyers can be categorized into two major groups: (1) hi-tech, time-starved consumers and (2) older/physically challenged consumers (McGree and Boyer, 2005; Morganosky and Cude, 2000). The first group typically consists of busy, time-pressed consumers that are very familiar with the Internet and e-commerce. Couples with double incomes and/or many and/or small children prefer to spend their spare time with their families instead of going to a grocery store (Bellman, Lohse and Johnson, 1999; Degeratu, Rangaswamy and Wu, 2000; Keh and Shieh, 2001; Småros and Holmström, 2000). The second group includes people who have disabilities related to age and/or health that make it difficult to go grocery shopping in an offline store (i.e. necessity users; Anckar et al., 2002; Morganosky and Cude, 2002). Research by Morganosky and Cude (2000) has revealed that the first group is the largest segment of the current online grocery population, while the second group is a smaller, yet non-negligible segment. Due to the differences in the segment sizes and as shown in table 1.1, online grocery shoppers tend to be relatively young, are more likely to have small children[1] and are more 'upscale' (i.e. better-educated and more affluent) than traditional grocery shoppers. In line with traditional grocery shopping, women make up the majority of the current online grocery shopping population (Andrews and Currim, 2004; Degeratu et al., 2000; Morganosky and Cude, 2002; Raijas and Tuunainen, 2001; Rohm and Swaminathan, 2004; Verhoef and Langerak, 2001; Zhang, 2001).

---

[1] Note that, compared to traditional grocery shoppers, the average household size of online grocery shoppers is larger. This implies, at the same time, that single households are less likely to shop for groceries online. Ordering groceries via the Internet typically pays off for larger households as they tend to have a large shopping basket. In contrast, the relatively high fixed costs, together with the rather small shopping basket of single households, makes the net price relatively high and might make single households reluctant to engage in online grocery shopping.

In addition to these 'typical' demographic online grocery shopper characteristics, many online grocery shoppers are characterized by their dislike of grocery shopping (i.e. shopping avoiders). Research has shown that over a quarter (28%) of adult men and women strongly dislike grocery shopping and that more than 60 percent like to decrease the time spent on grocery shopping (Key Findings, 1999; Yröjla, 2001). The convenience offered by electronic grocery shopping makes grocery shopping more bearable for those consumers who dislike it very much (Kutz, 1998; Keh and Shieh, 2001; Morganosky and Cude, 2002; Småros and Holmström, 2000; Wydra and Martin, 1997).

Socio-demographic trends in society might lead to a higher demand for electronic grocery shopping in the future. First, the number of dual-incomes is expected to increase as more and more women become active in the labor market. Such households, especially those with young children, become more pressed for time and might prefer their groceries to be delivered directly to home. Second, there is a strong increase of the ageing population. Seniors are one of the fastest-growing segments in our society. Together with the increase in the acquisition of personal computers and the increase of knowledge of and familiarity with e-commerce, these socio-demographic trends further underscore the future potential of e-grocery shopping (e.g. Anckar et al., 2002; Burke, 1997; Keh and Shieh, 2001; Morganosky and Cude, 2000; Rohm an Swaminathan, 2004; Verhoef and Langerak, 2001).

Table 1.1: Demographic profile of online grocery shoppers

Dimension	Raijas and Tuunainen (2001)		Morganosky and Cude (2002)	Degeratu, Rangaswamy and Wu (2000)		Rohm and Swaminathan (2004)
	Non-users of EGS	Users of EGS		% of US population (18+)	% of Peapod members	
Sample size	44	47	243			429
Country	Finland	Finland (2 online stores)	US (10 markets)	US	US (1 online store)	US (1 online store)
Gender	66% women	75% women	82.3% women			72% women
Household composition	18% 1 person 23% 2 persons 57% with children	2% 1 person 9% 2 persons 87% with children	19.9% 1 adult 63.2% 2 adults 16.9% > 2 adults 16.9% 0 children 27.3% 1 child 35.7% 2 children 20.1% > 2 children	34% children	53% children	19% 1 person 37% 2 persons 20% 3 persons 21% 4-5 persons 2% > 5 persons
Age	54% 18-35 years 30% 36-45 years 16% > 46 years	38% 18-35 years 53% 36-54 years 9% > 46 years	33.8% < 34 years 34.6% 35-44 years 22.5% 45-54 years 9.2% > 55 years	33% 18-34 years 39% 35-54 years 28% > 54 years	37% 18-34 years 51% 35-54 years 12% > 54 years	27% < 30 years 63% 30-49 years 10% > 50 years
Education			8% high school or less 34.3% high school graduate with some college education 57.7% college graduate	52% high school or less 26% some college education 15% college graduate 7% post-graduate	9% high school or less 25% some college education 39% college graduate 27% post-graduate	0% high school or less 2% high school graduate or equivalent 7% some college, no degree 33% college graduate 58% post-graduate
Income	20% < 25000 € 27% 25000 € - 33000 € 19% 33001€ -50000 € 34% > 50000 €	9% < 25000 € 13% 25000 € - 33000 € 38% 33001 € -50000 € 48% > 50000 €	11.8%<29999 $ 14.1% 30000 $ - 49999 $ 23.6% 50000 $ - 69999 $ 50.5% >70000 $	65% < 50000 $ 26% 50000 $ - 99000 $ 9% > 99000 $	18% < 50000 $ 41% 50000 $ - 99000 $ 41% > 99000 $	3% < 15000 $ 5% 15000 $ - 29999 $ 13% 30000 $ - 49999 $ 19% 50000 $ - 74999 $ 15% 75000 $ - 99999 $ 35% >100000 $
Social status	17% leading position 61% white collar 10% student	9% leading position 73% white collar				

Own representation, based on:

Raijas, A., and Tuunainen, V.K. (2001). Critical factors in electronic grocery shopping. *The International Review of Retail, Distribution and Consumer Research*, 11 (3).

Morganosky, M.A., and Cude, B.J. (2002). Consumer demand for online food retailing: Is it really a supply side issue? *International Journal of Retail and Distribution Management*, 30 (10).

Degeratu, A.M., Rangaswamy, A., and Wu, J. (2000). Consumer choice behavior in online and traditional supermarkets: The effects of brand name, price, and other search attributes. *International Journal of Research in Marketing*, 17 (1).

Rohm, A.J., and Swaminathan, V. (2004). A typology of online shoppers based on shopping motivations. *Journal of Business Research*, 57 (7).

1.2 DIFFERENCES BETWEEN TRADITIONAL AND VIRTUAL GROCERY CHANNELS

Table 1.2 gives a summary of the differences between a traditional and a virtual shopping environment. Based on this table, we can define the most important advantages and disadvantages of electronic grocery shopping for a consumer. While the advantages can be considered as enablers of Internet retailing growth, the disadvantages can be considered as factors hindering the growth and success of Internet retailing (cf. Grewal, Iyer and Levy, 2004). For this table, we assume that online retailers fully utilize the opportunities that are achievable within the virtual shopping environment. However, at this moment, not all online stores fully exploit these opportunities. Therefore, the extent to which consumers can benefit from each of the advantages depends on the way a company chooses to operate (Anckar et al., 2002).

1.2.1 Advantages of electronic grocery shopping

The most cited advantage of online grocery shopping by the customer and the most often emphasized benefit by e-tailers is **convenience** (e.g. Andrews and Currim, 2004; Boyer and Hult, 2005a/b; Geuens et al., 2003; Keh and Shieh, 2001; Morganosky and Cude, 2002; Raijas and Tuunainen, 2001; Småros and Holmström, 2000). Convenience results from the fact that people can access merchandise that is unavailable in their local markets, can order their products from home or another place at any time and, in the case of home delivery, can receive their products at home. Related to convenience, are time savings due to less planning time, transportation time (no traffic jams) and waiting time (no crowds) (Hansen, 2005; Ring and Tigert, 2001; Verhoef and Langerak, 2001).

Second, an often-mentioned benefit of online retailing for consumers is the possibility to **search and compare products and product-related information more easily and with greater depth** than in a traditional, brick-and-mortar store (Alba et al., 1997; Ariely, 2000; Bakos, 1997; Lynch and Ariely, 2000; Rohm and Swaminathan, 2004). For one, the Internet leads to lower search costs for comparing prices and products across e-tailers because of an electronically-open marketplace (Alba et al., 1997; Grewal et al., 2004; Keh and Shieh, 2001). In addition, due to the convenient arrangement of products on a small computer screen, it is easier to compare products in an online than in a traditional store (e.g. Bakos, 1997; Childers, et al., 2001; Lynch and Ariely, 2000; Menon and Kahn, 2002; see also studies using/investigating computer-simulated shopping experiments: Burke et al., 1992; Campo, Gijsbrechts and Guerra,

14

1999). Third, the Internet adds value to the online retail experience because of its capability to deliver dynamically-updated information/product offers tailored to the needs of the consumer (one-to-one marketing; Alba et al., 1997; Hoffman and Novak, 1996; Rohm and Swaminathan, 2004). Online retailers not only have the possibility to target information/product offers to specific individuals, they also have the possibility to create personalized, dynamically-updated, customer interfaces (Häubl et al., 2004). What is more, online retailers offer consumers the possibility to customize the shopping environment themselves. This includes, for instance, the ability to sort the alternatives according to specific attributes or the opportunity to use a predefined personal shopping list. Such a list consists of a consumer's most frequently purchased items, items purchased on a previous purchase occasion or items selected on other self-determined criteria (such as a 'party-list') (Andrews and Currim, 2004; Danaher, Wilson and Davis, 2003; Degeratu et al., 2000). These features make it easier for a consumer to search and/or compare alternatives in an online than in a traditional store (McGree and Boyer, 2005).

Another important benefit of Internet shopping is the **availability** of a large number of **alternatives** on the one hand and the access and depth of (product and price) **information** on the other hand. First, because competitors are just one click away, consumers can more easily gain access to the product offerings and product and price information of other competitors (Alba et al., 1997; Brynjolfsson and Smith, 2000). Second, compared to a traditional store which is limited by floor/shelf space, an online retailer has the possibility to offer a larger product assortment on the screen[2] (Verhoef and Langerak, 2001) and/or a very specialized assortment with hard-to-find products (Alba et al., 1997; Anckar et al., 2002). Moreover, whereas store-based retailers face more difficulty retaining knowledgeable salespersons and experience higher costs when making physical changes to the shopping environment (such as price changes, inserting promotional displays,...), online retailers use central databases which can be considered as 'super sales associates'. Such an associate will never be sick or moody, is able to

---

[2] The availability of an unlimited collection of (physical) alternatives is only valid with respect to the communication function of the e-channel. From the viewpoint of the linked distribution function, the e-channel does impose limits with respect to the availability of alternatives. For one, many online retailers (initially) restrict their services to one, a few or even a small part of the country. Second, despite the lack of a space constraint on the virtual shelf itself, online grocery retailers do have to physically stock their products somewhere.

remember many things, never forgets and learns quickly (facilitating changing of and adding information to the environment) (Alba et al., 1997).

1.2.2 Disadvantages of electronic grocery shopping

One of the major disadvantages of electronic grocery shopping relates to the **absence of hedonic shopping characteristics** (Babin, Darden and Griffin, 1994; Rohm and Swaminathan, 2004). Compared to a traditional environment, the online environment is more sterile, lacking the sensory stimulation or entertainment value present in traditional stores. First, in an Internet environment, consumers can not communicate with other customers, nor ask questions to an employee (Ring and Tigert, 2001; Verhoef and Langerak, 2001). Some e-tailers try to compensate for this loss in shopping enjoyment by using a webcounter (showing the number of visitors of the online store), an interactive service where consumers can (directly) contact sales personnel via mail or phone and/or a forum that serves as a surrogate for the social factor[3] (Eroglu, Machleit and Davis, 2001; Kolesar and Galbraith, 2000). Second, online retailers have difficulty replicating the sensory stimuli that are available to consumers in a physical store (e.g. touch, smell or sound) (Degeratu et al., 2000; Hansen, 2005; Rohm and Swaminathan, 2004). In order to compensate for the lack of sensory search attributes, online retailers typically stress the guarantee of high product quality (Boyer and Hult, 2005a/b; Raijas and Tuunainen, 2001; Tanskanen et al., 2002). Whereas some researchers have indicated that entertainment-related criteria are less important in a goal-oriented purchase context (e.g. Zeithaml, Parasuraman and Malhotra, 2002), others have empirically shown that even in goal-driven shopping environments, like online grocery stores, hedonic aspects of the shopping experience do come into play (Childers et al., 2001).

Other typical disadvantages of online grocery shopping are, in case of home-delivery, related to the necessity to be at home when products are **delivered**, the lead time needed to deliver the products and/or the available delivery time window. Especially consumers that require instantaneous delivery of their products will prefer a traditional grocery

---

[3] Other more advanced – and hence less used by electronic grocery shopping – techniques that online retailers can use to enhance the hedonic aspects of the shopping experience are chat rooms, bulletin boards, communities and discussion groups (Verhoef and Langerak, 2001). In addition, it should be noted that hedonic shopping characteristics are also partly present when consumers order products in the presence of other persons (e.g. in a cyber-café).

store over an electronic one. Yet, as mentioned above, online grocers have tried to look for solutions, such as an unattended delivery box or a reduction in delivery time, to lessen these shortcomings as much as possible (Keh and Shieh, 2001; Rohm and Swaminathan, 2004). In addition, most online retailers charge the costs of picking and/or delivering merchandise in small quantities to consumers (see previous section, cf. Alba et al., 1997). Some consumers consider this as an additional barrier that refrains them from shopping online.

Finally, issues of **privacy** (the protection of personal information) and **security** (the protection from fraud and financial loss) remain important reasons why consumers are reluctant to buy online (Parasuraman, Zeithaml and Malhotra, 2005). Through technological advances (such as encryption or network security), these concerns can be diminished in the (near) future (Cude and Morganosky, 2000; Kempiak and Fox, 2002; Van den Poel and Leunis, 1999). Moreover, while there exist well-established techniques in brick-and-mortar channels, recent evidence indicates that confidential customer information held by brick-and-mortar merchants might be more vulnerable to fraud than data held by Internet merchants (Internet Retailer, 22/03/'05).

Table 1.2: Comparison of traditional and virtual supermarkets

Characteristic	Traditional supermarket	Virtual (web-based) supermarket	Enable/limit e-growth
Convenience (time & effort-savings)	* Reach usually limited by geographic location * Restricted by opening hours * Requires physical handling * Requires transportation * More potential of wasted time (getting dressed, traffic jams, deal with crowds)	* Reach usually not limited by geographic location * Open 24 hours a day, 7 days a week * Requires less physical handling * Requires less/no transportation * Saves time (not getting dressed, no traffic jams, no crowds)	Enable
Ease of use (searching and comparing)	* Difficult to make cross(competitive)-comparisons * Arrangement of products on physical shelves * Product offer & information targeted at aggregate consumer segments * Product display designed to aggregate consumers * Product offer, information and display static * Not possible to customize shopping environment	* Less difficult to make cross(competitive)-comparisons * Arrangement of products on a computer screen * Product offer & information targeted at individual consumers * Product display designed to individual consumers * Product offer, info and display dynamically updated * Possible to customize shopping environment	Enable
Availability of alternatives & information	* More friction in market * Limited floor/shelf space * Salespersons	* Competitors one click away * Endless shelf space * 'Super sales associate' (central database)	Enable
Hedonic shopping characteristics	* Receive sensory stimulation from the environment * Possible to communicate with personnel or other shoppers * Suitable for products with sensory attributes	* Sterile environment * Difficult to engage in communication with others * Less suitable for products with many sensory attributes	Limit
Delivery	* Instantaneous delivery	* Products always require lead time for delivery * Necessity to be at home when goods are home-delivered * Charging extra picking and/or delivery costs	Limit
Privacy and security	* Costs are not directly charged to consumers * Well-established techniques to ensure the security and privacy	* Relatively new channel where transactions are done via a public domain	Limit

Based on:

Alba, J., Lynch, J., Weitz, B., Janiszewski, C., Lutz, R., Sawyer, A. and Wood, S. (1997). Interactive home shopping: consumer, retailer and manufacturer incentives to participate in electronic marketplaces. *Journal of Marketing*, 61 (3).

Djevizova, K., and Atanassova, Y. (2004). eStrategies for promotion of end-use efficiency products and services in the local market. Available at http://www.acadjournal.com/2004/V12/Part6/p1/.

Grewal, D., Iyer, G.R., and Levy, M. (2004). Internet retailing: enablers, limiters and market consequences. *Journal of Business Research*, 57 (7).

Rohm, A.J., and Swaminathan, V. (2004). A typology of online shoppers based on shopping motivations. *Journal of Business Research*, 57 (7).

1.3 ONLINE GROCERY SHOPPING BEHAVIOR

Because of the peculiarities of the online shopping environment, the way consumers shop in an online store may be different from the way they shop in a traditional store (Grewal et al., 2004). In this section, we describe how typical online environment characteristics affect consumers' search costs and their purchase decision strategies (cf. Degeratu et al., 2000).

1.3.1 Differences in search costs

One of the main differences between the online and offline environment is centered on the ability of the online environment to make product attribute information more accessible and easy to search across and within online stores. Yet, many e-tailers act as a stand-alone site. Therefore, the costs of conducting cross-store comparisons increase (cf. Alba et al., 1997; Lynch and Ariely, 2000). Second, also search costs within an online store might be lower for some attributes but higher for others as the online environment lacks *sensory* search attributes[4]. Degeratu et al. (2000) partitioned search attributes into four primary categories: (1) brand name, (2) price, (3) non-sensory attributes (i.e. *"attributes that can be conveyed well in words"*) and (4) sensory attributes (i.e. *"attributes that can be directly determined through the senses"*). Online search costs are lower for the first three categories because these attributes can be easily assessed in an online environment while they are higher for sensory attributes. As a result, the importance of sensory attributes will be lower in an online store while the importance of non-sensory attributes will be higher. When attribute information is missing (not available in memory) or when it is costly to obtain (expected benefits vanish compared to search costs), the brand name becomes a surrogate cue. Hence, for product categories with some (few) sensory search attributes, the importance of the brand name is increased (reduced) in the online compared to the offline environment (cf. Danaher et al., 2003; Degeratu et al., 2000). Finally, literature has shown that the ability of online stores to provide more product information on attributes other than price reduces the online consumer's price sensitivity for (supermarket) products (Andrews and Currim, 2004; Degeratu et al., 2000; Lynch and Ariely, 2000; Zhang, 2001).

---

[4] There are no differences between the online and offline supermarket with regard to experience attributes (e.g. taste) and credence attributes (e.g. health benefits). In both channels, information has to be inferred by consumers (e.g. from own memory) (e.g. Degeratu et al., 2000).

1.3.2 Differences in purchase decision strategies

As indicated by the previous section, convenience is an important reason for consumers to engage in e-grocery shopping. Such convenience-oriented consumers typically do not like to spend much time and effort to shop for groceries and are willing to pay the extra (picking and/or delivery) costs in return for time and effort savings. As such, they are typically more likely to be focused on a quick and distraction-free transaction, rather than on the shopping experience itself (AcNielsen, 08/03/2004; Andrews and Currim, 2004; McGree and Boyer, 2005). As a result, online shoppers are, compared to traditional grocery shoppers, even more likely to adopt simple decision rules that allow them to make a satisfactory decision while minimizing cognitive effort.

Second, many online stores have the opportunity to tailor the product offer, the information and the interface to individual consumers and allow consumers to customize the shopping environment themselves. In the realm of convenience, consumers are likely to value and/or make use of these services (cf. Andrews and Currim, 2004; Degeratu et al., 2000; Häubl et al., 2004). The usefulness of these services depends on the effort necessary to calibrate the mechanisms and the accuracy and appropriateness of the resulting outcomes (Alba et al., 1997). These mechanisms typically aim at helping consumers to more effectively and efficiently screen alternatives and, thereby, reduce the number of alternatives that are taken into consideration. For instance, literature has shown that consumers using personal lists are more state dependent as they are less likely to select items that are not on the list (Andrews and Currim, 2004; Danaher et al., 2003; Degeratu et al., 2000; McGree and Boyer, 2005; Zhang, 2001). Similarly, consumers engage in less product search with personalized product recommendations as these services typically provide a list where products are sorted in descending order according to the predicted attractiveness for the consumer which is based on other buyers' behavior or on consumers' stated preference (Häubl et al., 2004).

Third, because of an electronically-open marketplace and unlimited shelf space, a large number of alternatives becomes available to consumers shopping in an Internet environment. Yet, while this might be appealing for some consumers, others may find it too tedious and stressful to process and acquire information on all these products.

Therefore, despite the fact that the online environment has the capability to increase the universe of potential options, there are reasons to expect that a significant majority of consumers do not inspect the complete set of options (Alba et al., 1997; Shankar, Smith and Rangaswamy, 2003; Wu and Rangaswamy, 2003).

Finally, because the picking and/or delivery costs are typically substantial and because most e-grocery services require consumers to be at home each time grocery products are delivered, consumers are stimulated to make multiple-item sales from only one online retailer. Ordering more items with one e-tailer alleviates the necessity to wait at home (or to make an extra trip to pick them up) and reduces the extra costs and, thereby, the net price (Alba et al., 1997). Empirical evidence has shown that online consumers, on average, buy more per purchase occasion than offline consumers (Andrews and Currim, 2004).

SUMMARY

Electronic grocery shopping has always been recognized as a promising phenomenon. The growing pains that hindered a success story from the start of the Internet-revolution are overcome and, at this moment, electronic grocery shopping is evolving at an exponential rate. Electronic grocery shopping is very valuable for time-starved people and/or necessity users (having physical limitations) and/or those that dislike grocery shopping very much. Some unique aspects associated with the online environment will further enable the spread of Internet retailing. From a consumer's point of view, online stores offer the convenience of being able to select merchandise from a wide, easily searchable selection anywhere, anytime and – in case of home-delivery – have the products delivered at the doorstep. In contrast, shopping via the web also has some important disadvantages that might limit its success: less hedonic shopping characteristics, attended delivery requirement and privacy/security issues. These typical online environment characteristics have the potential to influence a consumer's purchase behavior process. Search costs for attribute information differ between an online and offline environment, making consumers more or less likely to use specific attributes in their online choice decisions. Next, being motivated by the convenience resulting from e-grocery shopping services, online consumers are more likely to adopt task-simplifying decision rules. Also other typical online environment features (such as personal lists or personalized product recommendations) reduce consumers' degree of searching and help them to more effectively and efficiently screen alternatives. Finally, online consumers typically engage in multiple-item purchases because it allows them to lower the shipping costs (and net price) and reduces the necessity to stay at home to wait for or to make an extra trip to pick up the grocery products.

CHAPTER 2: Retail Out-of-Stocks

Introduction

Stock-outs are a commonly occurring failure in the distribution function of supermarkets. Out-of-stock rates vary depending on a variety of factors (e.g. variations among store outlets, regions, categories or time of day or week). Yet, the majority of the rates tend to fall in the range of 5-10% (Gruen, Corsten and Bharadwaj, 2002). Despite advances in Efficient Consumer Response, Category Management and inventory tracking that improve the supply chain, stock-out problems tend to stay an important problem (Gruen et al., 2002; Sloot, Verhoef and Franses, 2005). At present, the overall average out-of-stock rate worldwide is around 8% (Anderson Consulting, 1996; Gruen et al., 2002; Peckman, 1963; Sloot et al., 2005; Verhoef and Sloot, 2005).

In the first section, we define a stock-out situation and give an overview of the marketing literature on retail stock-outs in a traditional shopping context. In the second section, we distinguish the main reactions consumers can adopt when they are confronted with a stock-out situation. In this section, we also present the framework of Campo, Gijsbrechts and Nisol (2000) that explains the underlying mechanisms (cost components) of stock-out reactions. Afterwards, we give a brief overview of the antecedents of these costs and, hence, stock-out reactions. Up till now, no study has investigated how offline stock-out reactions might differ from online stock-out reactions. Yet, differences between the online and offline shopping environment (see chapter 1) might cause differences in the stock-out reactions (section 2.3). In section 2.4, we briefly review consumers' purchase behavior in 'regular' low-involvement choice settings and indicate how 'disruptions' in the choice context affect routinized response behavior. Stock-outs are a typical example of such disruptions. Yet, they differ from other disrupting events – such as promotions – in that they are essentially negative in nature and may *force* consumers to change their planned purchase decisions (Campo, Gijsbrechts and Nisol, 2004). Finally, because we aim at improving the understanding of the impact of merchandising actions on stock-out reactions, section 2.5 zooms in on how stock-outs affect the consumer's decision making process (product category incidence and choice).

2.1 STOCK-OUTS

Stock-outs typically are unexpected, disturbing events that force consumers to react on the spot[1]. After giving a definition of a stock-out situation, we give an overview of the most important articles that investigate the stock-out problem in a traditional, offline, context.

2.1.1 Definition

An out-of-stock situation in a store can be defined as *a situation where a stock keeping unit (SKU) that was previously available, is temporarily unavailable, i.e. no longer available at a place that is accessible to the consumer* (based on Beuk, 2001, p.5).

Using this definition implies that there is an out-of-stock situation when *an SKU* is no longer available, irrespective of the presence of other alternatives that only differ in size, in variety, in brand or in a combination of these (and other) attributes (Beuk, 2001). Hence, we focus on an item instead of a brand stock-out. In the latter case, all items (all varieties and all sizes) of a brand are missing whereas only a single SKU, i.e. one specific combination of attributes of a brand, is missing in the former case. This distinction is important because customers that are confronted with a brand stock-out will, by definition, not have the possibility to switch to an alternative size or variety of that brand (e.g. Peckman, 1963; Sloot et al., 2005). Second, the definition implies that a product has to *belong* to a retailer's *regular assortment*, being available before and after the out-of-stock occurrence. So, when a customer looks for but can not find a product that does not belong or no longer belongs to the assortment offered by the retailer, one can not speak of an out-of-stock situation (Beuk, 2001; permanent assortment reductions: Campo et al., 2004). Finally, a product is out-of-stock if it is *not on the shelf*, even if it is in the warehouse of the store because the latter is a place not open to customers (Beuk, 2001).

---

[1] It should be noted that not all stock-out occurrences are unexpected/surprising to the same degree. For example, depending on the time of day and/or day of week, consumers expect stock-out situations to be more or less likely to occur (e.g. Gruen et al., 2002). In this research, we do not focus on forward-looking consumers that take systematic patterns in retailer stock-out occurrences into account when making a purchase decision (cf. Campo, Gijsbrechts and Nisol, 2003).

2.1.2 Previous out-of-stock research

In the marketing literature, out-of-stocks are a subject of research since the 1960s. Table 2.1 gives an overview of the most important (academic) articles that investigate stock-outs in a brick-and-mortar setting[2]. Studying stock-outs can involve a number of different components. The first, basic, element that can be explored, is the *frequency of stock-outs* observed for items sold in supermarkets. Although (early) consultancy work (e.g. Progressive Grocer study, 1968a/b) typically focuses on measuring the extent of stock-out occurrences, most (early) academic studies *describe and measure consumer reactions* when they are confronted with an out-of-stock situation. Recently, the increase in attention for Efficient Customer Response, Continuous Replenishment Planning and Category Management initiated a new boost. This renewed interest has produced theory-based models that *explain* stock-out reactions by linking them to a number of product-, category-, store-, situation- and/or consumer-related characteristics. A fourth component that can be researched, are the *financial consequences* resulting from stock-outs. Authors can thereby take the viewpoint of the retailer, the manufacturer, or both. Some authors focus on (explaining) consumer reactions as their main point of view and determine the financial consequences of a stock-out situation for the retailer and/or manufacturer as an implication (e.g. Campo, Gijsbrechts and Nisol, 2003; Peckman, 1963). Others mainly focus on the financial consequences that are related to different stock-out reactions (e.g. Walter and Grabner, 1975). In the second column of table 2.1, we indicate the components that are studied in each article.

Table 2.1 shows that most studies have focused on explaining and predicting the short-term effects of an out-of-stock (column 4). In addition, almost all the research has taken place in an offline grocery context (column 5, exceptions are Fitzsimons, 2000 – CDs in a simulated web environment; Zinn and Lui, 2001 – small appliances, home decoration items, furniture and jewellery in a retail store and Anderson, Fitzsimons and Simester, 2004 – bedding and bath products for a national mail order catalog). Table 2.1 (columns 6 and 7) further shows that most studies concentrate on a small number of product categories and typically limit their attention to one particular retail format and/or store (Sloot et al., 2005). In the next section, we discuss the main out-of-stock reactions distinguished in these studies (column 3).

---

[2] In this overview, we only focus on marketing-oriented articles. We did not insert studies that focus on measuring stock depletion costs or that are from a logistic point of view.

Table 2.1: Overview of out-of-stock studies

Author(s)	Objective†				Main out-of-stock reactions measured	Time frame (ST, MT, LT)	Research setting		
	Measure occurrences	Describe reactions	Explain reactions	Assess financial consequences			Product type	# of categories	# of retail chains & stores
Peckman (1963)	(X)	X		(X) (manufacturer & retailer)	Size switch Brand switch Postponement	ST	Grocery products	14	No exact info: different chains and stores
Shycon & Sprague (1975)				X (manufacturer)	n.r.	ST & LT	Grocery products	No info	No info
Walter & Grabner (1975)		(X)		X (retailer)	Size switch Brand switch Store switch Postponement	ST	Grocery products	1 (liquor products)	1 retail chain 1 store
Charlton & Ehrenberg (1976)		X			Brand switch	ST & MT	Grocery products	1 (detergent)	n.r.
Schary & Becker (1978)				X (manufacturer)	n.r.	ST & LT	Grocery products	1 (beer)	Whole market
Schary & Christopher (1979)		X	(X)		Size switch Brand switch Category switch Store switch Postponement Cancel	ST	Grocery products	No info	1 retail chain 2 stores
Motes & Castleberry (1985)		X			Brand switch	ST, MT & LT	Grocery products	2 (potato chips and cereals)	n.r.

Author(s)	Objective†				Main out-of-stock reactions measured	Time frame (ST, MT, LT)	Product type	Research setting	
	Measure occurrences	Describe reactions	Explain reactions	Assess financial consequences				# of categories	# of retail chains & stores
Emmelhainz, Stock & Emmelhainz (1991)		X	(X)		Item (variety / size) switch Brand switch Category switch Postponement Store switch Special trip	ST	Grocery products	5 (frozen orange juice, toothpaste, peanut butter, coffee, tomato sauce)	1 retail chain 1 store
Corstjens & Corstjens (1995)		X	X		Substitute to alternative SKU (brand, size, flavor) Store switch Postponement Cancel	ST	Grocery products	n.r.	n.r.
Verbeke, Farris & Thurik (1998)		X	X		Brand switch Category switch Postponement Cancel	ST	Grocery products	5 (soft drink, cooking margarine, coffee creamer, rice, detergent)	1 retail chain 7 stores
Bell & Fitzsimons (1999)		X			Decision satisfaction SKU switching behavior	ST	Grocery products	1 (granola bar) 1 (yoghurt)	n.r. 5 retail chains 1 store
Fitzsimons (2000)		(X)	X		Decision satisfaction Store switching	ST	Grocery products, CDs	Granola bar CDs	Offline (Granola bar) Online (CDs)

| Author(s) | Objective[†] | | | | Main out-of-stock reactions measured | Time frame (ST, MT, LT) | Research setting | | |
	Measure occurrences	Describe reactions	Explain reactions	Assess financial consequences			Product type	# of categories	# of retail chains & stores
Campo, Gijsbrechts & Nisol (2000)		(X)	X		Size switch Item (brand / variety) switch Store switch Postponement Cancel	ST	Grocery products	2 (cereals, margarine)	1 retail chain 1 store
Beuk (2001)		X	(X)		Variety switch Brand switch Category switch Store switch Postponement Consumer satisfaction	ST	Grocery products	1 (Coca Cola)	1 retail chain 4 stores
Zinn & Liu (2001)		(X)	X		Substitute (brand, size, variety) Delay purchase Leave store	ST	Non-grocery products	4 (small appliances, home decoration, furniture, jewellery)	1 retail chain (discount) 4 stores
Gruen, Corsten & Bharadwaj (2002)	X	X	(X)	X (manufacturer & retailer)	Size switch Variety switch Brand switch Store switch Postponement Cancel	ST & LT	Grocery products	18	No info
Campo, Gijsbrechts & Nisol (2003)	(X)	X	X	X (manufacturer & retailer)	Incidence Quantity Choice	ST & MT	Grocery products	2 (cereals, margarine)	1 retail chain 1 store

Author(s)	Objective[†]				Main out-of-stock reactions measured	Time frame (ST, MT, LT)	Product type	Research setting	
	Measure occurrences	Describe reactions	Explain reactions	Assess financial consequences				# of categories	# of retail chains & stores
Corsten & Gruen (2003)	X	X	(X)	X (manufacturer & retailer)	Variety switch Size switch Brand switch Store switch Postponement Cancel	ST & LT	Grocery products	n.r.	n.r.
Anderson, Fitzsimons & Simester (2004)	(X)	X			Future demand	LT	Non-grocery products	2 (bedding and bath products)	National mail order catalog
Kucuk (2004)		X	X		Brand switch Store switch	ST	Grocery products	1 (Coca Cola)	1 retail chain 3 stores
Sloot, Verhoef & Franses (2005)		(X)	X		Item (variety / size) switch Brand switch Category switch Store switch Postponement Cancel	ST	Grocery products	8 (eggs, milk, margarine, detergent, cigarettes, salty snacks, beer and cola)	8 retail chains 12 stores

[†] We distinguish between the main and secondary goals, by using parentheses for the latter.

Based on Sloot, Verhoef and Franses (2005). The impact of brand and category characteristics on consumer stock-out reactions. *Journal of Retailing*, 81 (1).

2.2 OUT-OF-STOCK REACTIONS

In this section, we first discuss the main stock-out reactions that consumers tend to adopt when they encounter an out-of-stock situation. Next, we present the framework of Campo, Gijsbrechts and Nisol (2000) explaining the driving forces (captured by economic costs) that interact and cause consumers to take one response over another. Subsequently, we give an overview of the antecedents (i.e. observable characteristics) of these costs and, thus, stock-out reactions.

2.2.1 Main out-of-stock reactions

Based on table 2.1 (column 3), we can distinguish two major stock-out reactions: consumers either decide to choose another alternative in the category or decide not to buy in the category when confronted with a stock-out[3] (cf. Verhoef and Sloot, 2005). These two main reactions can be further divided[4]. Choosing another alternative in the category involves package size switching (switching to another format of the same brand), variety switching (switching to another flavor of the same brand) or brand switching (switching to another brand). Deciding not to buy in the category includes category switching (switching to another product that fulfils the same needs[5]), store switching (going to another store), postponement (delaying till a subsequent shopping trip) or cancellation (dropping the purchase).

Table 2.2 (right part) gives, for a number of stock-out studies, the frequency of occurrence for the different out-of-stock reactions. It has to be noted that these studies typically do not consider all responses simultaneously. Moreover, different definitions are used by different researchers. For instance, Sloot et al. (2005) define item switching as *'switching to another format or variety of the same brand'* (p.19) whereas Campo et al. (2000) define it as *'purchasing another item (brand and/or variety)'* (p.223). In

---

[3] As shown in table 2.1, most of the previous studies concentrate on the impact of stock-outs on choice and category purchase incidence decisions, ignoring the quantity decision. Campo et al. (2003) have shown that quantity effects might be at play – although only to a limited extent as they could only find a (small) significant out-of-stock effect on quantity for one of the two examined categories.

[4] In academic research, more than 15 possible consumer out-of-stock reactions were distinguished (e.g. Emmelhainz, Stock and Emmelhainz, 1991). In this dissertation, we have opted to discuss the primary responses (cf. Beuk, 2001; Campo et al., 2000; Gruen et al., 2002; Sloot et al., 2005).

[5] An inherent problem with this stock-out response is the definition of the product category. For instance, if a consumer switches to a one-litre bottle of mineral water when a one-litre bottle of Coca Cola is unavailable, this is undoubtedly a category switch whereas a switch to a one-litre bottle of Fanta is more dubious. Yet, when categories are correctly identified, one can expect that this type of out-of-stock reaction is rather exceptional (Beuk, 2001).

addition, Zinn and Liu (2001) define 'leaving the store' as a composite indication of store switch and cancellation whereas others separately investigate these reactions. On the whole, the table shows that the alternative switching reaction (brand, size, variety either measured separately or simultaneously) is the most frequently occurring option and that deciding not to buy in the category (captured by category switching, store switching, cancellation and deferment) is much less dominant but stays a non-negligible reaction (Campo et al., 2003).

It is generally accepted that each of the stock-out responses might lead to negative outcomes (Gruen et al., 2002). Two types of losses can be distinguished: direct losses, i.e. on category/brand sales and profit (e.g. Campo et al., 2003; Schary and Christoper, 1979) and indirect losses, i.e. via retail/brand satisfaction, loyalty and image (e.g. Bell and Fitzsimons, 1999; Fitzsimons, 2000; McGoldrick, 2002; Zinn and Liu, 2001) (Gruen et al., 2002). Note that stock-outs occurring at a competitive manufacturer or retailer offset these (direct and indirect) losses to some extent (cf. Peckman, 1963; Corsten and Gruen, 2003).

Depending on the specific out-of-stock reaction, the negative consequences on *sales or profit* are more severe for the retailer or the manufacturer. As retailers are largely concerned about the total category sales within the store, buying the product at another store is the most problematic reaction for a retailer. For a manufacturer, the largest direct loss results when consumers switch to an alternative of the competitor. Both retailers and manufacturers bear a direct loss when consumers decide to cancel the purchase. When consumers decide to postpone the purchase, no direct losses result but the cash flow (for retailers and manufacturers) is negatively affected and demand becomes less certain (hence making forecasting and replenishment more difficult). When consumers decide to switch to another package size and/or variety of the same brand, losses for a retailer and a manufacturer are limited and only occur when consumers switch to a smaller or cheaper alternative (Campo et al., 2003; Gruen et al., 2002). Table 2.2 (left part) gives an overview of the direct losses that both manufacturers as well as retailers incur with the different out-of-stock reactions.

Next to direct losses, both the retailer and the manufacturer experience additional *indirect losses*. Out-of-stock research has shown that stock-outs have a negative effect on satisfaction with the retailer (e.g. Beuk, 2001; Fitzsimons, 2000) and/or the brand (Verbeke, Farris and Thurik, 1998), possibly leading to a decrease in retailer and/or brand loyalty. What is more, as trial precedes adoption (Asseal, 1998; Schary and Becker, 1978), giving consumers the opportunity to try another store/brand might lead to permanent store/brand switching (Beuk, 2001; Gruen et al., 2002; Schary and Becker, 1978).

Table 2.2: Overview of empirical studies that measure consumer responses to out-of-stocks

Out-of-stock reaction		Direct loss†		study 1	study 2	study 3	study 4	study 5 (***)					study 6		study 7	study 8	study 9
		Retailer	Manufacturer					Soft-drink	Margarine	Coffee cream	Rice	Detergent	Cereals	Margarine			
CHOICE	Switch size	Partial (~ specific product bought)	Partial (~ specific product bought)	52%	19.3%	4.8%	41% (*)	n.r.	n.r.	n.r.	n.r.	n.r.	n.r.	15%	n.m.	62% (*)	18% (*)
	Switch variety	Partial (~ specific product bought)	Partial (~ specific product bought)	n.m.	n.m.	n.m.		n.r.	n.r.	n.r.	n.r.	n.r.	44% (*)	51% (*)	4.2%		
	Switch brand	Partial (~ specific product bought)	Yes	30%	64.1%	5.0%	31.5%	65%	47%	62%	50%	31%			35.5%		34%
CATEGORY INCIDENCE	Switch category	Partial (~ specific product bought)	Yes	n.m.	n.m.	12.4%	0.5%	Low	Low	Low	Low	Low	n.m.	n.m.	5.2%	n.m.	2%
	Switch store	Yes	No	18%	14.1%	47.9%	13.7%	14%	34%	20%	28%	23%	3.3%	2%	22.6%	22.9% (**)	19%
	Defer purchase	No (cash flow, demand fluctuation)	No (cash flow, demand fluctuation)		2.5%	11.1%	12.3%	21%	19%	18%	22%	46%	49%	30%	32.4%	15.1%	23%
	Drop purchase	Yes	Yes		n.m.	18.7%	n.m.	n.m.	n.m.	n.m.	n.m.	n.m.	3.7%	2%	n.m.	Part of **	3%

† Based on Gruen, Corsten and Bharadwaj (2002) *Retail out-of-stocks: A worldwide examination of causes, rates and consumer responses*. Washington D.C.: Grocery manufacturers of America.

Legend: Study 1: Peckman (1963) (with size unavailability), study 2: Walter and Grabner (1975), study 3: Schary and Christopher (1979), study 4: Emmelhainz, Stock and Emmelhainz (1991), study 5: Verbeke, Farris and Thurik (1998), study 6: Campo, Gijsbrechts and Nisol (2000), study 7: Beuk (2001), study 8: Zinn and Liu (2001), study 9: Sloot, Verhoef and Franses (2005)

n.m. = not measured, n.r. = not relevant

* Some authors measure variety and size switching as one stock-out reaction (e.g. study 4: Emmelhainz et al., 1991; study 9: Sloot et al., 2005), others measure brand and variety switching as one stock-out reaction (study 6: Campo et al, 2000) while still others measure variety, size and brand switching as one stock-out reaction (study 8: Zinn and Liu, 2001).
** Zinn and Liu (2001) (study 8) define 'leaving the store' as either forgoing the purchase (canceling) or searching for the item elsewhere (store switching).
*** Verbeke et al. (1998) (study 5) removed a brand's complete line of SKUs, thereby making switching SKUs within the same brand not possible.

33

Campo, Gijsbrechts and Nisol (2000), inspired by work of Corstjens and Corstjens (1995), have built and tested a conceptual framework that incorporates the mechanisms driving customer stock-out reactions. In this model, it is assumed that each out-of-stock reaction entails specific costs. The trade-off between these costs causes the consumer to prefer one action over the other (e.g. Campo et al., 2000; Corstjens and Corstjens, 1995). The conceptual framework discerns three major cost types (see table 2.3): substitution costs, transaction costs and opportunity costs. Substitution costs refer to the difference in utility between the preferred (out-of-stock) product/store and an alternative product/store. Transaction costs stem from costs made to acquire the alternative item. This involves search costs to find a suitable alternative, holding/handling costs and, when switching stores, shopping costs including transportation costs, time and effort to visit the alternative store. Finally, opportunity costs concern the reduction in consumption utility when canceling or postponing the purchase.

Table 2.3: Consumer cost components driving consumer out-of-stock reactions

Out-of-stock reaction		Substitution costs	Transaction costs			Opportunity costs
			Search	Holding	Shopping	
Choice	Package size switching	√	√	√		
	Variety switching	√	√			
	Brand switching	√	√			
Incidence	Category switching	√	√			
	Store switching	√	√		√	
	Purchase deferment				√	√
	Purchase cancellation					√

Based on Campo, Gijsbrechts and Nisol (2000). Towards understanding consumer response to stock-outs. *Journal of Retailing*, 76 (2).

These costs differ across reactions in response to a stock-out situation. Selecting another alternative (brand, variety and package size switching) involves a loss in utility because one has to switch to a higher-priced and/or less-preferred alternative product (substitution costs) as well as an increase in time and effort necessary to find a suitable alternative (search costs). Package size switching entails holding costs in addition to these substitution and search costs. Costs associated with switching towards a different category are very similar to costs associated with brand or variety switching and entail substitution and search costs resulting from the necessity to consume and find a (less preferred) substitution product in another category. Switching to a different store involves next to search and shopping costs, also substitution costs following from the fact that one has to buy in another store than the preferred one. Postponing the purchase not only results in a shopping cost when customers have to return earlier than planned, it also gives rise to opportunity costs associated with the risks of running out of the product. Also canceling the purchase involves opportunity costs, because there is no consumption at all.

Depending on the levels of each of these cost components, the most likely reaction of a consumer can be deduced. For instance, if the opportunity cost is very low, consumers are more likely to postpone or cancel the purchase. On the other hand, when the opportunity cost is high (e.g. running out of diapers), consumers will be more likely to switch to another alternative or store in order to get the product (cf. Campo et al., 2000; Gruen et al., 2002; Corsten and Gruen, 2003). In the next section, we discuss a number of characteristics that influence the magnitude of these costs and, therefore, cause consumers to prefer one out-of-stock reactions over another.

2.2.3 Antecedents influencing out-of-stock reactions
In order to better understand consumer stock-out reactions, researchers have linked differences in these reactions (driven by differences in the magnitude of the costs underlying these reactions) to a number of explanatory characteristics (e.g. Beuk, 2001; Campo et al., 2000; Corstjens and Corstjens, 1995; Emmelhainz, Stock and Emmelhainz, 1991; Fitzsimons, 2000; Kucuk, 2004; Peckman, 1963; Schary and Christopher, 1979; Sloot et al., 2005; Zinn and Liu, 2001). The identification of these explanatory factors gives important insights into the direction and magnitude of stock-out effects and helps retailers and manufacturers to get a better understanding of stock-out reactions. In this research, we focus on the main effects of the explanatory characteristics and do not consider possible interaction effects (see Sloot et al., 2005 who investigate the interaction between brand equity and product type).

In table 2.4, we divide the explanatory factors in five clusters and indicate per factor the type of costs and the out-of-stock reactions they affect and whether or not there exists empirical support for the hypothesized effect(s). In this table, we focus on how cost changes resulting from antecedents produce <u>direct</u> shifts in stock-out response probabilities. As such, we exclude compensatory/indirect shifts. For instance, for item loyalty, we only report the direct (negative) effects on alternative (brand, variety or size) switching and do not explicitly state that this effect is compensated by an indirect shift towards the other stock-out responses (cf. Campo et al., 2000). The following five clusters are distinguished (cf. previous research: Campo et al., 2000; Sloot et al., 2005):

- **Product-related characteristics**: i.e. characteristics that relate to the specific product that is unavailable. Important variables are item loyalty (the tendency to stay with the favorite item), the nature/type of the product (i.e. private label versus national brand) and brand equity[6] (the strength of a brand in terms of price level, awareness and quality).

- **Category-related characteristics:** i.e. characteristics that point to the specific product class in which the stock-out occurs. Factors that have been put forward as potential antecedents are the nature of the category (hedonic versus utilitarian), assortment size and composition (the number of acceptable, available, alternatives), the organization of the shelf, the importance of the category (or the related concept of involvement; Beuk, 2001) and buying frequency (or the level of habitual buying) in the category. At this moment, no confirmatory results are available for the latter three factors.

- **Store-related characteristics**: i.e. characteristics that relate to the store or the retail chain in which the stock-out occurs. Important store-related antecedents which are empirically confirmed are store loyalty (the tendency to concentrate purchases in one store) and the type of the store (EDLP versus HiLo). No empirical evidence is available for the number of acceptable, alternative stores in the neighborhood of the store where the stock-out occurs and the distance between two stores (the number of minutes needed to reach a competitive store).

- **Situation-related characteristics**: i.e. (time-dependent) characteristics that relate to the specific shopping trip in which the stock-out occurs. A number of studies have shown that buying urgency (related to the risk of running short of the product before the next shopping trip) and the part of the week (early versus late in the week) are important antecedents for stock-out reactions. In contrast, mixed findings are available for the moderating impact of the shopping trip (fill-in/minor versus major) while no empirical findings are available for the moderating impact of personal usage (buying a product for own usage versus buying a product for other persons in the household or for visitors).

---

[6] Sloot et al. (2005) argue that not the distinction between private label versus national brand but, instead, brand equity is an important explanatory factor. Both manufacturer and retailer (private label) brands can have high or low equity (Ailawadi, Lehmann, and Neslin, 2003). Yet, Sloot et al. (2005) could only find a significant effect in a model where brand equity alone was added. From the moment that brand loyalty was included, no significant effects were found for brand equity, indicating that brand equity and brand loyalty are probably strongly correlated (cf. Verhoef and Sloot, 2005).

- **Consumer-related characteristics**: i.e. characteristics that relate to the consumer (shopper) who is confronted with the stock-out. Important consumer-related antecedents include the sensitivity of a consumer for promotions (deal proneness), the extent to which consumers engage in impulse buying (the tendency to make unplanned purchases) and consumers' tendency to focus on the price or quality level. Whereas no empirical evidence is available for deal proneness, the explanatory impact of the other three consumer-related antecedents is empirically confirmed. In addition, mixed findings are available for the attitude towards shopping (positive versus negative) and the time pressure (the degree of hurriedness) while no empirical evidence is present for the impact of shopping frequency (average number of shopping trips/week) and mobility (availability of car or not).

Table 2.4 suggests that the most important clusters are the product- and category-related ones, indicating that out-of-stock reactions are mainly influenced by product- and category characteristics. In contrast, store-, situation- and consumer-related antecedents seem to be less important (cf. Sloot et al., 2005; Verhoef and Sloot, 2005).

Table 2.4: The impact of explanatory characteristics on costs driving stock-out reactions

Antecedent	Characteristic	Expected effect (+, -, +/-) via cost type[†]	Expected (direct) effect (+, -, +/-) on stock-out reaction[†]	Empirical support
Product-related	Item loyalty	Substitution costs, item (+); Transaction costs, search (+)	Alternative switch (-)	Yes
	Brand type (PL vs NB)	Substitution costs, store (+)	Store switch (-)	No
	Brand equity	Substitution costs, item (+)	Brand switch (-)	Yes
Category-related	Nature of category (hedonic vs utilitarian)	Transaction costs, shopping (-)	Variety & size switch/store switch/postpone (+); Store switch (+); Postpone (-/+)	Yes
	Availability of acceptable alternatives	Transaction costs, shopping (-); Opportunity costs (+)	Alternative switch (+)	Yes
	Shelf organization	Substitution costs, item (-); Transaction costs, search (-)	Alternative switch (+/-)	No
	Importance of category	Transaction costs, search (+/-); Opportunity costs (+)	Postpone/cancel (-)	No
	Buying frequency	Transaction costs, search (-)	Alternative switch (+)	No
Store-related	Store loyalty	Substitution costs, store (+); Transaction costs, search (+)	Store switch (-)	Yes
	Store type (EDLP vs HiLo)	Substitution costs, store (+)	Store switch (-)	Yes
	Availability of acceptable stores	Transaction costs, shopping (-)	Store switch (+)	Mixed
	Distance	Transaction costs, shopping (+)	Store switch/postpone (-)	No
Situation-related	Buying urgency	Opportunity costs (+)	Postpone/cancel (-)	Yes
	Part of the week (early vs late)	Opportunity costs (+)	Postpone/cancel (+)	Yes
	Shopping trip (minor vs major)	Opportunity costs (+)	Postpone/cancel (+)	Mixed
	Personal usage	Opportunity costs (-)	Postpone/cancel (+)	No
	Promotion sensitivity	Substitution costs, item (-); Transaction costs, search (-)	Alternative switch (+)	No
Consumer-related	Impulse buying sensitivity	Opportunity costs (+)	Postpone/cancel (+)	Yes
	Price sensitivity	Substitution costs, item (-)	Alternative switch (+)	Yes
	Quality sensitivity	Substitution costs, item (+); Transaction costs, shopping (-)	Store switch/postpone (-)	Yes
	Attitude towards shopping	Transaction costs, search (+)	Alternative switch (-)	Mixed
	Time pressure	Transaction costs, shopping (+)	Store switch/postpone (+)	Mixed
	Shopping frequency	Opportunity costs (+)	Postpone/cancel (+)	No
	Mobility	Transaction costs, shopping (-)	Store switch/postpone (+)	No

[†] '+' refers to cost increases and direct shifts *towards* the reported stock-out response; '-' refers to cost decreases and direct shifts *away from* the reported stock-out response; '+/-' refer to situations where both positive as well as negative effects can result (e.g. depending on the shelf organization, search costs can increase as well as decrease).
Based on Campo, Gijsbrechts and Nisol (2000). Towards understanding consumer response to stock-outs. *Journal of Retailing*, 76 (2) and on Sloot, Verhoef and Franses (2005). The impact of brand and category characteristics on consumer stock-out reactions. *Journal of Retailing*, 81 (1).

2.3 ONLINE OUT-OF-STOCK REACTIONS

Recent evidence suggests that stock-out problems are not limited to traditional supermarkets (see previous sections), but constitute a far more daunting problem for virtual e-grocers (e.g. Bhargava, Sun and Xu, 2005; Danaher, Wilson and Davis, 2003; Melany Smith – ClickZ-today, 2004; see also online grocery sites like Netgrocer, Caddyhome). Compared to traditional stores, online stores experience more severe forecasting problems because of a more strongly fluctuating demand (e.g. Fitzsimons, 2000; Van Elburg – Emerce, 2001). What is more, online retailers may be especially vulnerable to stock-out losses for their long term success as recent research has shown that product unavailability rates second in the top 3 of irritations with online shopping (Marketing online, 9/11/2004).

Despite their importance, stock-outs have not yet been investigated systematically in an online (grocery) context (see table 2.1). Nevertheless, because of differences between the virtual and traditional shopping environment (see chapter 1), online stock-out reactions might differ from offline stock-out reactions[7]. Consumers confronted with an out-of-stock situation when ordering via the Internet can choose similar stock-out reactions as before. Yet, the online environment does neither change the costs of switching to an offline store, nor affects the costs of postponing the purchase to a next, offline shopping trip. In addition, we do not expect that the online environment changes the magnitude of the opportunity costs (i.e. decreases in utility incurred when consumption in the category is reduced or dropped). In the next sections, we indicate how virtual store characteristics affect the impact of stock-outs on the incidence decision (switching to another store and postponing the purchase to a later purchase occasion) and on the choice decision (switching to another alternative within the category).

2.3.1 Deciding not to buy in the category

First, compared to a conventional brick-and-mortar store, the reach of an online store is not limited by the geographic location. As a result, more acceptable, alternative stores

---

[7] In this research, we aim to investigate how the shopping mode itself (the e-channel) – and not the type of persons that use the e-channel – affects stock-out reactions. In order to correct for such selection biases, we only focus on the impact of online channel characteristics on consumer's stock-out reactions and not, for instance, on typical demographics or characteristics of current online grocery shoppers (cf. Danaher et al., 2003; Degeratu et al., 2000).

are available and it becomes easier to **substitute to another online store**. Because competitive online stores are just one click away, the time necessary to switch to another online store decreases. Yet, this is only valid from a communication point of view. From the viewpoint of the linked distribution function, e-channels can (and do) restrict the geographic delivery area (McGree and Boyer, 2005). Switching to another online store is therefore only possible if there are competitive stores that deliver in the area where someone lives. In addition, the monetary costs and effort that arise from switching to another online store might offset the time-saving benefits. First, most online stores charge extra costs per delivery, such as a picking and/or a delivery fee (Ring and Tigert, 2001) and, in case of home-delivery, require consumers to be at home (Punakivi, Yrjölä and Holmström, 2001). In order to avoid these negative burdens, consumers try to make multiple-item sales from only one online retailer (cf. Alba et al., 1997). Grouping the purchases not only decreases the extra costs and, thereby, the net price but also reduces the necessity to be at home (or the necessity to install different reception/delivery boxes in case of unattended delivery or to drive around to different places in case of picking up the products). Second, in many online stores, the product offer, the information and the display is tailored/customized to individual consumers (e.g. personal lists). As such, online grocery shoppers might become even more reluctant to switch to another online grocery shop.

So, although online store characteristics both decrease as well as increase the costs underlying the store switching reaction, we expect that the disadvantages related to switching to another online store more than overcompensate the time-saving benefits – especially when the site is customized/tailored to suit consumers.

Second, **postponing** the purchase and returning to the same (online) store earlier than planned in order to purchase the out-of-stock product triggers two opposing effects. On the one hand, the convenience of being able to shop anywhere (from home or another place), anytime decreases shopping costs. Compared to a traditional store, revisiting an online store earlier than intended requires less planning and transportation. Due to this increase in flexibility, consumers can more easily return to an online store and, thus, are more likely to defer the purchase to an accelerated shopping trip. Yet, on the other hand, as argued before, consumers might be more reluctant to pay the extra costs and/or to stay at home waiting for the delivery of (or to make an extra trip to pick up) a single product (cf. Alba et al., 1997).

2.3.2 Deciding to buy another alternative in the category

As mentioned in the previous chapter, the online environment offers unparalleled opportunities to compare and locate alternatives. In general, this implies that the costs to **find a suitable replacement item within the category** are expected to be lower in an online versus an offline environment (Bakos, 1997; Childers, et al., 2001; Lynch and Arlie, 2000). Yet, because the online environment lacks sensory search attributes, search costs might be lower for some attributes but higher for others. Resultantly, asymmetric switching shifts within the category (or the specific substitution action chosen) might be different in an online versus an offline environment (e.g. Burke et al., 1992; Campo, Gijsbrechts and Guerra, 1999; Degeratu, Rangaswamy and Wu, 2000). While the search costs of non-sensory attributes typically are lower in an online than in a traditional store, the search costs of sensory attributes are higher. Hence, compared to offline consumers, online consumers are more likely to focus (and thus switch) to alternatives with specific non-sensory attributes. In contrast, the available information (and thus importance) of sensory attributes is lower in an online store, making consumers less likely to switch to alternatives with specific sensory attributes. In the latter case, not only search costs but also substitution costs are affected. Because of the difficulty to correctly replicate sensory stimuli in the online environment, consumers perceive more risks when switching to alternatives with many sensory attributes (Degeratu et al., 2000; Rohm and Swaminathan, 2004). Furthermore, in a situation where less information is available to facilitate the choice process, consumers are more likely to focus on risk-reducing indicators, such as the brand name as an indication of product quality (Campo et al., 2003; Degeratu et al., 2000).

Second, compared to traditional stores, online stores have the potential to offer a larger number of alternatives as well as more (non-sensory) product information for each of these alternatives. More available, acceptable alternatives increase the probability of switching to a replacement item because both substitution and search costs tend to be lower. Providing consumers with more (non-sensory) product information helps to reduce the uncertainty resulting from the out-of-stock situation and further increases the probability that consumers select another alternative.

2.3.3 Overall differences between online and offline out-of-stock responses

Based on the previous arguments, it is evident that online environment characteristics change the underlying costs associated with stock-out reactions and, thereby, make it more or less likely to select one of the stock-out reactions. First, compared to a traditional store, search costs (for non-sensory attributes) substantially decrease and more acceptable alternatives are available in a virtual store. Together with the necessity to pay extra costs and/or to stay at home waiting for the delivery (or to incur extra transportation costs to pick up the product) when ordering earlier or with another e-grocer, we expect that e-shoppers, compared to traditional shoppers, are more likely to stay in the online store and select another alternative within the category when confronted with a stock-out situation. In the next sections, we present the conceptual framework that was developed to indicate how stock-outs influence consumers' routinized response behavior and the consumer's purchase decision process in an (online) grocery context.

2.4 CONSUMER PURCHASE BEHAVIOR FOR GROCERY PRODUCTS

The purchase of a grocery product is, in contrast with more durable goods, typically a low-importance and low-risk decision. In such a situation, consumers very often are low-involved and lack the time, the resources and/or the motivation to engage in central-route processing. Instead of carefully and thoughtfully evaluating all the arguments/alternatives in the environment, consumers are more likely to process the information peripherally, using simple/peripheral cues. Peripheral processing is an 'easy way' to think about things and allows one to make a quick decision (Petty and Cacioppo, 1984; Petty and Cacioppo, 1986). In the literature, it is shown that the time consumers spend when shopping for grocery products is far too short to allow them to engage in central-route processing. Laundry detergent shoppers, for instance, spend on average 13 seconds when purchasing in the category, including the time to walk to the desired product (Hoyer, 1984). Dickson and Sawyer (1990) found a similar result: the average shopping time was less then 12 seconds and about 42% of the investigated shoppers spent 5 seconds or less.

Second, grocery shopping is a familiar task that must be done on a regular basis. Consumers have made these decisions a numerous times in the past and, therefore, have well-defined and structured choice criteria (stabilized rules of thumb) (Hoyer, 1984;

Leong, 1993; Howard and Sheth, 1969). When buying frequently-purchased items in a *regular* choice environment, consumers engage in <u>routinized response behavior</u> (or product concept utilization). This stage is typically characterized by little or no information seeking and by quick decisions (Howard, 1989; Howard and Sheth, 1969; van Waterschoot and Gijsbrechts, 2003). *Disruptions* in the choice environment might interrupt routinized response behavior at a particular point in time. In this dissertation, we focus on stock-outs as a disrupting event. Other disruptions that might occur in the choice environment include, for instance, price changes, promotions or new products (e.g. Andrews and Srinivasan, 1995; Dickson and Sawyer, 1990). In contrast to most other 'shocks', stock-outs are essentially *negative* in nature. By limiting the choice variety, stock-outs may *force* consumers to change routinized response behavior (Campo et al., 2004). To cope with these disruptions (i.e. to respond to 'shocks' in the environment), consumers often adopt a <u>limited problem solving</u> (LPS) process (or product concept attainment). Like in routinized response behavior, consumers engaging in limited problem solving can rely on a previously-formed set of evaluative criteria. However, the disruption in the environment makes them uncertain about which of the alternatives is the best and, compared to the previous stage, causes consumers to spend more time and effort when choosing a product (Howard, 1989; Howard and Sheth, 1969). It should be noted that limited problem solving is the stage that is *most typical* when consumers are confronted with a disruption. Yet, we can not exclude that consumers engage in routinized response behavior or in an extensive problem solving stage when disruptions occur. For instance, when promotions frequently occur in the product category, consumers might not consider them as disruptive and might engage in routinized response behavior. On the other hand, when consumers are, for instance, faced with 'new' (previously not used) benefits in the category, they might include these new benefits in their decision. As such, they engage in an extensive problem solving or product concept formation process (cf. Howard, 1989; van Waterschoot and Gijsbrechts, 2003).

2.5 THE CONSUMER'S DECISION MAKING PROCESS AFFECTED BY STOCK-OUTS

In this section, we describe how stock-outs affect the consumer's decision making process. We focus on the category purchase incidence and the choice decision. For both decisions, we first discuss which criteria consumers use in a regular choice environment and then zoom in on how stock-outs influence the decision making process. In this conceptual framework, we integrate the most important antecedents that were described earlier.

2.5.1 The incidence decision

Previous research has shown that the incidence (buy or do not buy) decision depends on the perceived attractiveness of the product category, household-specific variables (such as usage rates and in-home inventory levels) and preference uncertainty (e.g. Bucklin and Gupta, 1992; Bucklin and Lattin, 1991; Dhar, 1997).

Out-of-stocks increase preference uncertainty and reduce the attractiveness of the product category, as previously available alternatives can no longer be chosen. These outcomes may turn a buy-decision into a non-buy-decision depending on the 'severeness' of their effects. The latter is largely governed by the consumers' preference for the missing items *(item loyalty)* and the presence of other, suitable replacement items in the assortment *(availability of acceptable replacement items)*. First, consumers that are more loyal towards a specific item have the tendency to stay with the preferred item rather than to seek variation (e.g. McAlister and Pessemier, 1982). As such, the drop in category attractiveness is higher for item-loyal consumers. In addition, item-loyal consumers have relatively limited purchase and consumption experience with other items of the category, making them more uncertain about which product to select in a stock-out situation. In sum, the more loyal consumers are towards a specific item, the less likely they are to make a purchase in the category when confronted with a stock-out (cf. Beuk, 2001; Campo et al., 2000; Corstjens and Corstjens, 1995; Emmelhainz et al., 1991; Kucuk, 2004; Schary and Christopher, 1979; Sloot et al., 2005; Zinn and Lui, 2001). Second, also the number of acceptable, available alternatives has an effect on the tendency to buy in the category when confronted with a stock-out. When many acceptable alternatives are available, both the perceived risks of switching to another item as well as the difficulty of finding a suitable replacement item reduce. As a result, consumers confronted with a stock-out are more likely to buy another alternative when more acceptable, available alternatives are offered (cf. Boatwright and Nunes, 2001; Broniarczyk, Hoyer and McAlister, 1998; Campo et al., 2000; Campo et al., 2003; Sloot et al., 2005).

In addition, purchase incidence effects will depend on the overall consequences of not making any purchase in the category. When consumers need a specific product immediately or when they have almost no stock of the product at home *(buying urgency)*, they are more likely to select another alternative within the category when a stock-out occurs (Campo et al., 2000; Emmelhainz et al., 1991; Sloot et al., 2005; Zinn and Lui, 2001).

2.5.2 The choice decision

When selecting an alternative in a regular choice context, consumers have been found to simplify their choice decisions in two ways: (1) by reducing the complete set of alternatives in a category to a better-manageable subset of alternatives (consideration set formation) and (2) by using simple choice rules or tactics. Both heuristics allow consumers to cope with complex choice decisions and help them in making quick and effortless decisions.

First, there is ample support that consumers do not take the universal set of alternatives into account each time they choose a low-involvement product. Instead, they simplify the decision process by using a more restricted subset of alternatives, called the consideration set, from which they make their final choice (e.g. Andrews and Srinivasan, 1995; Bronnenberg and Vanhonacker, 1996; Roberts and Lattin, 1991; Shocker et al., 1991; Wu and Rangaswamy, 2003). The concept of consideration set formation is grounded in both consumer behavior (or psychological) theory (i.e. limits on the cognitive ability to process all information on all alternatives or limited information-processing ability) as well as in the information search theory (i.e. limits on the ability to search for all information on all alternatives or limited information-acquisition ability) (Manrai and Andrews, 1998; Mehta, Rajiv and Srinivasan, 2003; Roberts and Lattin, 1991; Roberts and Latin, 1997; Siddarth, Bucklin and Morrison, 1995; Wu and Rangaswamy, 2003). Although the two-stage choice process (captured by the evoked set concept) is a commonly accepted notion, Howard (1989) and other authors (such as Kotler, 1991) have indicated that the notion can be refined. Typically, the following concepts are distinguished (cf. Kotler, 1991; Shocker et al., 1991; Wu and Rangawamy, 2003): the awareness set (*"the subset of alternatives that a consumer knows"*), the consideration/evoked set (*"the subset of alternatives that meet initial buying criteria"*) and the choice set (*"the subset of alternatives that remain as strong contenders"*). The sets and the definitions introduced by Kotler (1991) are not universal and often are used interchangeably (cf. Shocker et al., 1991; Siddarth, et al., 1995). In addition, the use of fuzzy words in operational definitions, such as *'seriously* considered', 'in the *near* future' and '*immediately prior* to choice' further point out the vagueness surrounding these concepts (Wu and Rangaswamy, 2003). Recent literature has proposed a 'fuzzy set' representation, indicating that the screening process need not be binary and that there is considerable overlap between the different concepts. In this approach, consideration sets have a graded structure and alternatives vary in the degree to which they are member of the consideration set (Bronnenberg and Vanhonacker, 1996; Fortheringham, 1988; Wu and Rangaswamy, 2003). The consideration set membership of an alternative may, for example, increase because environmental stimuli, such as aisle displays or other point-of-purchase materials, make it more desirable. Contrary, some less desirable environmental stimuli, such as an out-of-stock situation or a price increase, may reduce the consideration set membership of an alternative (cf. Wu and Rangaswamy, 2003).

Second, previous research has proposed that consumers use simple tactics or cues when making repeat purchase decisions for low-importance, low-involvement products in a regular choice environment (cf. Hoyer, 1984; Leong, 1993). Specifically, decision making in low-involvement categories is found to be driven by four main indicators: (1) preferred product characteristics, (2) acceptable price, (3) in-store elements that highlight products and (4) recency of purchase. First, consumers often have a focal attribute when choosing in a product category (e.g. Bell and Fitzsimons, 1999; Kamakura, Kim and Lee, 1996), which they primarily rely on when making a decision. For example, when flavor is the salient (most important) attribute for a consumer, especially alternatives with a desirable attribute level (e.g. preferred flavor) will be taken into account (cf. performance-oriented choice tactic; Hoyer, 1984). Second, consumers typically have a reservation price and are more likely to consider alternatives that are below that reservation price (Jedidi and Zhang, 2002) (cf. price-oriented choice tactic; Hoyer, 1984). Third, in-store elements that highlight an alternative positively influence the degree of attention for that alternative (Chandon, Hutchinson and Young, 2001; Nedungadi, 1990; Simonson, 1993). For example, placing a product at eye- or hand-level, increases its visibility and, therefore, its choice probability (Chandon et al., 2001; Corstjens and Corstjens, 1995; Drèze, Hoch and Purk, 1994) (cf. in-store related tactics; Hoyer and Cobb-Walgren, 1988). Fourth, the most recently purchased product may either receive more attention (in case of reinforcing behavior, Roberts and Lattin, 1991) or less so (in case the consumer is variety-seeking, McAlister, 1982)

(Bronnenberg and Vanhonacker, 1996) (cf. affect-related tactics; Hoyer, 1984). Once consumers have identified alternatives warranting greater consideration, they engage in a more detailed analysis where, for instance, also other (non-focal) attributes will come into play (e.g. Andrews and Srinivasan, 1995; Bronnenberg and Vanhonacker, 1996; Gensch, 1987; Gilbride and Allenby, 2004; Hoyer, 1984; Laroche, Kim and Matsui 2003; Manrai, 1995; Shocker et al., 1991).

As argued before, we expect that consumers confronted with a **stock-out situation** typically (although not exclusively) engage in a limited problem solving process. The disruption makes them undecided about which of the remaining alternatives is the best (Howard and Sheth, 1969). Obviously, out-of-stock alternatives can not be selected, reducing their choice probability to 0% (cf. Campo et al., 2003). In contrast, the choice probability of the remaining alternatives increases because they can act as a replacement. The extent to which a stock-out increases another item's choice probability will depend on the degree to which these alternatives will catch a consumer's eye. As mentioned before, when making a choice decision in a disrupted choice environment, consumers typically rely on a similar (previously-formed) set of evaluative criteria. More specifically, the attractiveness of the remaining items is a function of (1) shared (especially focal) attributes with the stock-out item *(availability of acceptable replacement items & consumer's sensitivity to specific attributes)*, (2) the difference in price level *(consumer's sensitivity to price)*, (3) in-store elements that highlight the item *(e.g. shelf organization)*, and (4) whether and how long ago the alternative item has been purchased before *(item loyalty)*. First, Campo, Gijsbrechts and Nisol (2003) have shown that stock-outs typically induce asymmetric (non-IIA) choice shifts (disproportionate shifts to items with specific attributes). Using attributes as cues facilitates the replacement decision while keeping substitution risks low. For instance, consumers may focus on items of the same brand because they expect them to be of the same quality level or buy a product of the same flavor expecting that it will provide similar consumption experiences The costs of finding a suitable replacement item depend on consumer's tendency to stay with specific attributes and the availability of SKUs with this level in the assortment (Boatwright and Nunes, 2001; Broniarczyk et al., 1998; Campo et al., 2000; Campo et al., 2003; Sloot et al., 2005). Second, price-conscious shoppers are more sensitive to price, being less likely to switch to higher-priced replacement items in case of a stock-out (Sloot et al., 2005). Third, the organization of the shelf has an impact on the time and effort needed to find a suitable replacement item (impact on search costs) (Kucuk, 2004). Finally, depending on the variety-seeking nature of consumers, they are more or less likely to turn to previously purchased items when confronted with a stock-out (Beuk, 2001; Campo et al., 2000; Corstjens and Corstjens, 1995; Emmelhainz et al., 1991; Kucuk, 2004; Schary and Christopher, 1979; Sloot et al., 2005; Zinn and Lui, 2001).

SUMMARY

Stock-outs have been investigated in the traditional grocery context with different degrees of detail, from various angles and with different objectives. Traditional out-of-stock research has suggested that consumers confronted with a stock-out either decide to choose another alternative in the category or decide not to buy in the category. Stock-out problems are not limited to traditional supermarkets, also virtual e-grocers will not escape from it. Because of differences between the online and offline environment, online stock-out reactions differ from those in brick-and-mortar settings. We hypothesized that, compared to offline consumers, online consumers that are confronted with a stock-out situation are more likely to stay in the online store and choose another alternative.

In this research, we focus on purchases of grocery products in an online grocery context. Grocery products are characterized by their low-importance, low-risk decision making process. In such low-involvement situations, consumers typically engage in peripheral route processing. To this end, they adopt a number of time- and effort-reducing heuristics such as a consideration set formation process and the use of simplifying (performance-, price-, in-store- or affect-oriented) tactics. These heuristics allow consumers to make quick decisions in a regular choice environment (routinized buying behavior). Yet, disruptions in the choice environment typically cause consumers to adopt a limited problem solving process, using previously-established choice tactics to reach a satisfactory decision while minimizing processing time and effort. Stock-outs are a typical example of such disruptions. In contrast to other disrupting events (such as promotions), stock-outs are essentially negative in nature and may force consumers to change routinized response behavior.

CHAPTER 3: Research design

Introduction

In order to collect data for our empirical studies, we used one online, computer-simulated shopping experiment. Using such a computer experiment is especially well-suited given the setting (online grocery shopping) and the manipulation of the variables of interest. When studying online purchase behavior, the computer environment is the true choice environment. The setting in which the data is collected, matches the lifelike setting very closely. In the first section, we discuss the research methodologies (study designs and data collection methods) used in prior studies on stock-out reactions and indicate why a computer-simulated shopping experiment is the most appropriate research design for our research. In section 3.2, we describe the experimental design, the treatment of the manipulated variables and the data collection method. In section 3.3, we present some general characteristics of the sample and the collected data set.

3.1 Overview of research methodologies

Table 3.1 gives an overview of the different research methodologies that are applied in previous out-of-stock studies. The research methodology differs on two major dimensions: the research design and the data collection method. The research design goes from an uncontrolled to a highly controlled research environment. In an uncontrolled setting, the researcher observes a choice environment that is not the result of his suggestions or manipulations (i.e. a situation where stock-outs happen by accident). In a controlled setting, researchers manipulate the variables of interest (explicitly introducing stock-outs for a number of pre-selected alternatives) in an attempt to more precisely measure their effects on consumer reactions. The data collection method goes from techniques measuring actual purchase behavior in a stock-out situation (revealed behavior) to techniques that ask consumers what they did or would do in a stock-out situation (stated behavior) (cf. Nagle and Holden, 1995). Table 3.2 classifies the various marketing research techniques according to these two dimensions. In table 3.3, we contrast the uncontrolled (quasi field) experiment with the experimentally controlled research designs and summarize the strengths and weaknesses of each of the different designs.

Table 3.1: Overview of the research methodology used in previous out-of-stock studies

Author(s)	Research methodology	
	Research design (true or hypothetical stock-outs)	Data collection method
Peckman (1963)	Survey (hypothetical)	Personal interviews (n = 1173)
Shycon & Sprague (1975)	Case studies (hypothetical)	n.r.
Walter & Grabner (1975)	Survey (hypothetical)	Written questionnaires (n = 1433)
Charlton & Ehrenberg (1976)	In-home experiment (hypothetical)	Personal interviews (n = 158)
Schary & Becker (1978)	Quasi field experiment (true)	Aggregate sales data
Schary & Christopher (1979)	Quasi field experiment (true)	Personal interviews (n = 1167, 29.4% was confronted with out-of-stocks)
Motes & Castleberry (1985)	In-home experiment (hypothetical)	Personal interviews (n = 241)
Emmelhainz, Stock & Emmelhainz (1991)	Controlled field experiment (true)	Personal interviews (n = 2810, 375 were confronted with out-of-stocks)
Verbeke, Farris & Thurik (1998)	Controlled field experiment (true)	Telephone surveys (n = 590)
Bell & Fitzsimons (1999)	Controlled laboratory experiment (hypothetical)	Written questionnaires (n = 164)
	Quasi field experiment (true)	Scanner panel data (n = 356, 12594 choices)
Fitzsimons (2000)	Controlled Laboratory experiment (3) Computer (simulated web) experiment (1) (hypothetical)	Written questionnaires
Campo, Gijsbrechts & Nisol (2000)	Survey (hypothetical)	Written questionnaires (n = 449 margarine; n = 544 cereals)
Beuk (2001)	Controlled field experiment (true)	Written questionnaires (n = 599)
Zinn & Liu (2001)	Quasi field experiment (true)	Written questionnaires (n = 283)
Gruen, Corsten & Bharadwaj (2002)	Meta-analysis	Published / Publicly available studies
	Quasi field experiment (true)	Personal interviews (USA, 23040) Personal interviews (outside USA, > 48000)
	Quasi field experiment (true)	Scanner panel data Retail audit data
Campo, Gijsbrechts & Nisol (2003)	Quasi field experiment (true)	Scanner panel data
Anderson, Fitzsimons & Simester (2004)	Quasi field experiment (true)	Scanner panel data
Kucuk (2004)	Survey (hypothetical)	Personal interviews (n = 544)
Sloot, Verhoef & Franses (2005)	Survey (hypothetical)	Personal interviews (n = 749)

n.r. = not relevant
Based on Sloot, Verhoef and Franses (2005). The impact of brand and category characteristics on consumer stock-out reactions. *Journal of Retailing*, 81 (1).

Table 3.2: Classification of research methodologies

		RESEARCH DESIGN	
		Uncontrolled	**Experimentally controlled**
DATA COLLECTION	**Revealed purchase behavior**	Aggregate sales data Retail audit data Consumer panel data	Controlled field/in-store experiment Computer-simulated shopping experiment Laboratory shopping experiment In-home shopping experiment
	Stated purchase behavior	Survey/personal interviews (real stock-out situation)	Survey/personal interviews (hypothetical stock-out situation)

Based on Nagle, T. and Holden, S. (1995). *The strategy and tactics of pricing: a guide to profitable decision making*. Englewood Cliffs, N.J, Prentice Hall, p.266.

Table 3.3: Overview of strengths and weaknesses of research designs

Criteria	Uncontrolled research design	Experimentally controlled research design				
	Quasi field experiment (past sales date & survey) (real)	Controlled field (in-store) experiment	Computer-simulated experiment	Laboratory experiment	In-home experiment	Survey / Questionnaire (hypothetical)
Time	Very slow (by accident)	Slow	Fast	Relatively fast	Relatively fast	Very fast
Costs	Rather expensive	Expensive	Rather expensive	Rather expensive	Rather expensive	Very inexpensive
Implementation problems	Yes (by accident)	Yes (retailer resistance)	No	No	No	No
Internal validity	Very low	Moderate	High	High	Moderate	Moderate
External validity	Very high	High	Moderate	Moderate	Very low	Very low
Noise in data	Yes	Yes	No (automatic recorded and stored)	Reporter bias	Reporter bias	Reporter bias

Based on Burke, R.R. (1996). Virtual shopping: Breakthrough in marketing research. *Harvard Business Review*, 74 (2).

In the next paragraphs, we first discuss the uncontrolled (quasi field) experiment and indicate how both stated as well as revealed purchase behavior coming from such an experiment can be used to investigate stock-out effects. Next, we discuss the advantages and disadvantages of using an experimentally controlled survey design where consumers are asked what they would do when confronted with a hypothetical stock-out situation. Afterwards, we give an overview of the controlled experiments which have the potential to offset some of the disadvantages associated with both the uncontrolled experiment as well as the simple survey design. These controlled experiments typically give rise to a (newly-created) dataset of revealed purchase behavior (although other data collection methods capturing stated behavior can also be used). After indicating why a computer-simulated shopping experiment is the most appropriate research methodology for our research, we assess, in the last section, how the validity of such an experiment can be safeguarded.

3.1.1 Uncontrolled field experiment

In <u>uncontrolled or quasi field experiments</u>, out-of-stocks happen 'by accident' as a result of an interruption in the supply. Events such as material shortages, strikes and other supply system failures might cause stock-out situations (e.g. Anderson, Fitzsimons and Simester, 2004; Bell and Fitzsimons, 1999; Campo, Gijsbrechts and Nisol, 2003; Gruen, Corsten and Bharadwaj, 2002; Schary and Becker, 1978; Schary and Christopher, 1979; Zinn and Lui, 2001). The biggest advantage of this design is the high external validity because of the natural, real-world environment in which the research takes place (investigation of true stock-out occurrences). The biggest problem, however, is the lack of control over the variable(s) of interest (e.g. the specific alternatives that are unavailable) and the lack of control over other, extraneous, variables that influence a purchase decision. In addition to the very low internal validity, also other disadvantages may limit the use of quasi field experiments. Because out-of-stocks happen by accident, it is a very slow and rather expensive process. Moreover, the total sample size needed has to be substantial in order to get a large-enough sample of respondents that encountered a stock-out.

In order to collect data in an uncontrolled (quasi-field) experiment, researchers can use questionnaires/surveys. In this case, supermarket shoppers are *interviewed* immediately after leaving the supermarket. They are asked whether they encountered a stock-out and what they did when the product s/he wanted was not available in the store (e.g. Schary and Christopher, 1979; Zinn and Lui, 2001). Most questionnaires are complemented with additional questions in an attempt to better understand shopping behavior and to get a grasp on how stock-outs work.

Researchers can also investigate true stock-out occurrences by analyzing *past sales data*, such as aggregate sales data (aggregate sales data per alternative over different stores within a pre-specified region), retail audit data (aggregate sales data per alternative for an individual retail outlet) and scanner panel data (individual purchase reports from members of a consumer panel) (cf. Nagle and Holden, 1995). The most important advantage of past sales data is the fact that it offers insights in realistic, revealed, purchase behavior. Yet, disadvantages with each of the three types of past sales data hinder their usage. First, aggregate sales data sum sales in many different chains/outlets (mixing observations of a stock-out situation in one store with a non-stock-out situation in other stores). Second, in both aggregate sales and retail audit data, it is very difficult to disentangle stock-out periods from non-stock-out periods as data is often collected by quarter, month or week. Neither aggregate sales data, nor retail audit data are often used to deduce stock-out effects. An exception is the study of Schary and Becker (1978) who use market share information resulting from a strike affecting the complete market. Because of the peculiarities of this situation, they were able to avoid some of the limitations inherent in aggregate sales data. Scanner panel data meet some of the problems associated with aggregate sales and retail audit data as it consists of *individual* data of respondents who have agreed to provide information at specified intervals (*daily* reports) over an extended period (Malhotra, 1999). Yet, scanner panel data also have a number of important disadvantages (which are also present for aggregate sales and retail audit data). First, past sales data lack natural data variation, especially for category management stimuli such as the stock-out policy, shelf and assortment (Campo and Gijsbrechts, 2005). Second, past sales data typically miss a systematic and sufficiently detailed registration of these category management stimuli. For instance, available out-of-stock data is often incomplete and unreliable (Campo and Gijsbrechts, 2005), making it necessary to develop tracking procedures to identify stock-out situations (e.g. Campo et al., 2003). Third, no information about consumer perceptions and evaluations is available. Hence, it is quite difficult to trace why consumers act the way they act and how they would act if they are exposed to a stock-out of a different product and/or on a different shopping trip (Campo and Gijsbrechts, 2005).

3.1.2 Controlled experiment – hypothetical purchase behavior
In an exploratory survey design, respondents are asked, through the use of *questionnaires/personal interviews*, about their intended behavior when confronted with a hypothetical stock-out in the store (e.g. Campo, Gijsbrechts and Nisol, 2000; Peckman, 1963; Sloot, Verhoef and Franses, 2005; Walter and Grabner, 1975). The most important advantages are the relatively rapidity and low costs of these interviews. Indeed, a survey design allows to keep the number of necessary interviews at a tractable level. Yet, asking respondents how they would react to a hypothetical out-of-stock situation has important limitations. First, the lack of realism (lack of marketing stimuli, lack of competitive context,…) places significant burdens on the results (Burke, 1996).

Some authors try to enhance the realism of the task by showing respondents a picture with the store's shelf layout (e.g. Campo et al., 2003). Second, there might exist significant differences between intended/stated and actual/revealed behavior (Campo et al., 2000; Schary and Becker, 1978). Moreover, consumers are often not consciously aware of their motives to select specific products and, therefore, may be unwilling or unable to give the desired information (Malhotra, 1999). Indeed, it has been shown that most people believe that they are not influenced by seemingly unimportant factors but – in practice – do become affected by the 'steering power' of these variables (cf. impact of shelf on purchase behavior: e.g. Drèze, Hoch and Purk, 1994; Simonson, 1999; Simonson and Tversky, 1992; Tversky and Simonson, 1993). Third, surveys often artificially draw the attention of a consumer to the unavailability of a product (Campo and Gijsbrechts, 2005). Indeed, a survey design takes the implicit assumption that customers have the intention to purchase in the category, that they notice the out-of-stock and that their favorite item is unavailable (Campo et al., 2003; Sloot et al., 2005).

3.1.3 Controlled experiments – actual purchase behavior

In controlled field (or in-store) experiments, researchers create, in the actual choice environment, an out-of-stock situation for specific products (by removing pre-selected alternatives from the shelf), while controlling other variables as much as possible (e.g. Beuk, 2001; Emmelhainz, Stock and Emmelhainz, 1991; Verbeke, Farris and Thurik, 1998). In an attempt to more precisely and cleanly observe stock-out effects, researchers conduct an experiment in the realistic choice environment without the consumers' knowledge (high external validity). Yet, the time and costs to set up such an experiment are high and controlling other, extraneous, variables is often not without problems. The greatest barrier of implementing a controlled in-store experiment is gaining the cooperation of retailers and/or manufacturers as controlled field experiments are often not without risks for them (Burke, 1996; Nagle and Holden, 1995). A number of constraints hamper the execution of a controlled field experiment such as supplier contracts that demand that specific alternatives are on the shelves, special instructions that must be given to remove alternatives at fixed times or the fear to pull successful products of the shelves. In essence, retailers and manufacturers worry about the potential loss in sales, visits as well as image and loyalty (Beuk, 2001; Schary and Becker, 1978; Verbeke et al., 1998).

Two studies have used <u>in-home shopping experiments</u> where respondents are visited at home during a number of weeks and are offered a number of (artificial) products to purchase – comparable to doorstep selling. On a specific week, they are told that the leading market share product is unavailable (e.g. Charlton and Ehrenberg, 1976; Motes and Castleberry, 1985). Clearly, this type of experiment lacks external validity (absence of store environment, competitive context, real-world marketing stimuli) and is very obtrusive. However, it benefits from the absence of retailer resistance.

In <u>laboratory experiments</u>, out-of-stocks are manipulated in an artificial setting that is rather low in external but high in internal validity. Laboratory experiments encompass a range of possibilities, going from very rudimentary to somewhat more realistic (Nagle and Holden, 1995). The rudimentary design used to investigate *offline* out-of-stock reactions presents stimuli in booklet format with each product category listed on a separate page and products described with their brand name, flavor, size,... and unit price. Both out-of-stock studies that use a laboratory experiment (Bell and Fitzsimons, 1999; Fitzsimons, 2000) have focused on such a rather rudimentary design as they did not replicate the store environment, nor included a (real-life) shelf. In contrast, a more realistic design incorporates full-size mock shelf displays using high-quality color copies of actual package shelf facings or – even more realistic – actual product packages. When investigating consumer's decisions in an *online* shopping environment, the computer environment can be considered as a laboratory. In this case, consumers are asked to make a number of (fictitious) purchase decisions in a choice environment that corresponds very closely to the realistic environment. For instance, neither in the <u>computer experiment,</u> nor on a realistic online shopping site, are consumers forced to wander physically through the store and to move, bend or stretch to get the products. Also the manipulation and representation of in-store marketing stimuli as well as the setting (e.g. store layout, atmosphere,...) match the natural shopping environment very closely. In addition, with the growing popularity of personal computers and the Internet, computer-simulated shopping experiments also offer new opportunities for testing the impact of an out-of-stock situation on *offline* purchase behavior (Burke, 1996; Needel, 1995). *'Computer-simulated shopping experiments open up new opportunities for marketing research, allowing researchers to collect purchase data in a tightly controlled yet realistic environment, at relatively low costs and with a high degree of flexibility'* (Campo, Gijsbrechts and Guerra, 1999).

Using a computer-simulated shopping experiment offers several advantages over other research methods, both the more realistic ones as well as the more simple ones (Campo et al., 1999). First of all, a computer-simulated shopping experiment integrates some of the clutter that is missing in a survey design. At the same time, it gives researchers the opportunity to control extraneous variables and to more carefully select the participants for the experiment (Burke, 1996; Nagle and Holden, 1995). The capability to closely control the experiment permits the researcher to draw conclusions with fewer purchases in much less time and with lower costs than would be possible with a (controlled) field experiment. It must be recognized that the technique won't be able to completely duplicate reality but, unlike most other less-realistic market research methods, it does allow shoppers to pay selective attention to products. Further, a computer-simulated shopping experiment allows researchers to conduct experiments in a very convenient way as corrections can be made very easily and quickly. Collecting data is also more rapid and faultless because the computer unobtrusively registers the outcomes of and the actions during the shopping process, e.g. the amount of shopping time in each product category, the items picked up or the amount of time used to examine packages and labels (i.e. statistical videotape; Burke, 1996). Yet, computer-simulated shopping experiments are not without limitations. Experiments can be time-consuming and are often expensive. Depending on the desired degree of sophistication and the desired degree of control, costs and time needed to set up and implement an experiment will be larger or smaller.

A controlled experiment (in-store, home, laboratory/computer-simulated) typically results in a new data set containing revealed purchase behavior that is manifested in the experimentally controlled out-of-stock situation. Yet, some researchers have also used (telephone) interviews to collect stated out-of-stock behavior (especially in a controlled, in-store experiment). In this case, consumers are asked whether they were able to find the SKUs they were looking for and if not, how they reacted. Some additional questions can be included to gain more insights in the resulting out-of-stock reactions. In laboratory/computer-simulated experiments, actual/revealed purchase behavior is often enriched by additional data coming from questionnaires before or after the purchase simulation exercise.

3.1.4 Safeguarding the validity of a computer-simulated shopping experiment

In a controlled, computer-simulated, experiment, the researcher manipulates one or more variables of interest (independent variables) and measures their effects on one or more dependent variables, while controlling extraneous or 'background' factors. As a result, the internal validity rises, increasing the potential of extracting valid inferences about the causal relationship between dependent and independent variables (Cook and Campbell, 1979; Malhotra, 1999). The benefits of a complex (more controlled and/or more realistic) experiment must be balanced against the costs of setting up such an experiment. In essence, when deciding on the experimental design, researchers often trade off internal versus external validity. A computer-simulated experiment is usually characterized by its high internal validity at the expense of lower external validity.

External validity refers to the assessment of whether the cause-and-effect relationships found in the experiment can be generalized to and across other universes (e.g. subjects, settings and contexts) (Cook and Campbell, 1979; Lynch, 1982; Malhotra, 1999). The first perspective of external validity concerns the generalizability *to* the target population (Cook and Campbell, 1979; Lynch, 1982). This relates to the representativeness of the sample and can be monitored by drawing appropriate samples. The second perspective of external validity relates to generalizability *across* other settings and populations. This includes two aspects: robustness and ecological validity. Robustness denotes whether a relationship found in an experiment can be replicated with different subjects, research settings and time intervals. Researchers can control this by replicating tests within a single study or across studies (e.g. using other subjects, research settings or time periods) (Cook and Campbell, 1979). Ecological validity (or realism) refers to whether the experimental choice environment is a realistic reproduction of the true choice environment. Researchers can control this by using a realistic research design – realistic tasks, settings, stimuli, manipulations and measures (Lynch, 1982; Winer, 1999). Implicitly, the idea exists that the more realistic the experiment, the more generalizable the results. A severe implication of this argument implies that any unrealistic representation of the experiment would render externally invalid results. However, unrealistic factors in an experimental design are only a threat to the external validity if one of these unrealistic features *interacts* with the treatment variable (Lynch, 1982). Results can still be generalizable if the unrealistic features do not have an effect on the investigated relationships (Campo, 1997). Hence, in the simulated environment, it is important to realistically duplicate those elements that influence purchase behavior in the real market (Pessemier, 1964).

Concerning external validity, there is growing evidence that computer-simulated shopping experiments, despite the presence of a number of possibly artificial features, provide highly realistic buying behavior data (Burke et al., 1992, Campo et al., 1999). This particularly holds in our study, where both the real and experimental choice setting were online, allowing us to recreate the 'actual' shopping environment even better.

Table 3.4 gives an overview of a number of points that should be taken into account when a computer-simulated shopping experiment is used to investigate online shopping behavior.

Table 3.4: External validity of a computer-simulated shopping experiment (csse)

Unrealistic aspect of csse	Points of interests
Experimental task	
Fictitious purchases	Exploratory behavior (choice)
Pre-imposed shopping decisions:	More extensive alternative evaluation
- fixed shopping frequency	Stronger purchase event feedback (higher incidence)
- fixed and reduced # of categories	
Reduced inter-purchase time	
Lack of real-life characteristics	
Absence of time constraint	More extensive alternative evaluation
Absence of budget constraint	Higher incidence, reduced price sensitivity
Absence of space constraint	Higher incidence
Absence of inventory	Bias in incidence
Absence of consumption experiences	Higher incidence, stronger purchase event feedback
Manipulations	
Out-of-stock frequency and conditions	Bias in out-of-stock effects (choice/incidence)
Other in-store stimuli	Bias in effects of other stimuli (choice/incidence)
Measures	
Choice	Exploratory behavior (choice)
Purchase timing	Higher incidence

Based on Campo, K., Gijsbrechts, E. and Guerra, F. (1999). Computer simulated shopping experiments for analyzing dynamic purchasing patterns: Validation and guidelines. *Journal of Empirical Generalisations in Marketing Science*, jg.4, p.22-61.

A first point of interest is the experimental task. Although consumers are typically specifically asked to mimic their regular shopping behavior as closely as possible, the fictitious shopping task has no real consequences. Because consumers do not experience realistic risk-burdens, they might show more exploratory behavior and engage in more risky purchases (e.g. more expensive items). Second, some shopping decisions in an experiment are pre-imposed by the researchers, such as the shopping frequency and the available product categories. Fixing these aspects is often needed for practical reasons (e.g. because of the limited budget available and to reduce respondents fatigue). When the fixed shopping frequency and/or the fixed (limited) number of categories cause consumers to deviate from their normal purchase behavior, the external validity is threatened. Third, most experiments require subjects to make multiple purchases in a single session. Such 'time compression' is also needed for practical reasons as it restricts the potential confounding effects of extraneous variables and limits internal validity threats (such as history, maturation and mortality effects[1]). On the other hand, the 'time compression' might threaten the external validity of the experiment because previous purchase decisions might have a stronger impact on subsequent decisions. Yet, previous research has already shown that time compressed settings do allow to realistically capture dynamic purchase patterns (Burke et al., 1992; Campo et al., 1999).

Second, an experiment is typically characterized by the absence of a number of real-life constraints, like time, space and budget (Burke et al., 1992; Campo et al., 1999). The time constraint typically differs between a simulated shopping experience and an actual one, potentially biasing consumer's purchase behavior. Yet, it can be expected that consumers that are pressed for time when shopping for groceries also have a larger time constraint when filling out a questionnaire. As such, we expect a natural match between the real and experimental shopping environment. The space and budget constraints are often lacking in a computer-simulated shopping experiment. In most of the experiments, respondents do not physically receive the products, nor do they have to make purchases using their own money. Literature has shown that it is very difficult to impose a realistic budget constraint as consumers will not take a budget into proper consideration unless it is their own money. As a result, consumers might purchase more frequently compared to what they normally would do and might become less price sensitive (Burke et al., 1992; Cohen and Gadd, 1996). Next, the lack of, for instance, a pantry where one is physically confronted with the current stock of the products might reduce external validity, making consumers more or less likely to purchase. To compensate for this drawback, Campo et al. (1999) introduced inventory cues that served as a memory aid. They inserted on the computer screen, information about the household inventory level

---

[1] History is defined as *'specific events that are external to the experiment but occur at the same time as the experiment'*, maturation is defined as *'an extraneous variable attributable to changes in the test units themselves that occur with the passage of time'* and mortality is defined as *'an extraneous variable attributable to the loss of test units while the experiment is in progress'* (Malhotra, 1999, p.220-221).

which was weekly updated by information on the household's reported average consumption rate and the purchases made in the simulated store. Finally, also the absence of consumption might threaten external validity as consumers do not have the opportunity to learn through consumption or to become satiated (Burke et al., 1992; Campo, 1997; Campo et al., 1999).

Third, the manipulations of the treatment variables (e.g. marketing mix manipulations like out-of-stock occurrences, out-of-stock policy, assortment and shelf placement – see section 3.2.3) should be replicated as realistically as possible. Unrealistic manipulations give rise to biases and, hence, interfere with the external validity (Burke et al., 1992; Campo, 1997; Campo et al., 1999). For instance, out-of-stocks should be portrayed and selected in a realistic way in order to be able to derive generalizable conclusions.

Finally, the impact of the fact that one is being observed should be taken into consideration (i.e. the impact of the measurement and measurement procedures). In such a high situational involvement, consumers exhibit more rational and socially acceptable behavior and try to please the researcher because they want to 'look good' and 'give the right answer' (Malhotra, 1999). Needel (1995) suggests that computer-simulated shopping experiments may overcome problems like social desirability and embarrassment because no interviewer is present or watching (i.e. unobtrusiveness). Yet, subjects of a computer experiment do know that they are participating in an experiment and, hence, know that actions and purchases are observed.

Based on the previous overview, it is evident that a number of elements should be taken into consideration when using controlled computer experiments. The extent to which potential validity threats will actually occur, depends on the consumer's ability and willingness to imitate actual purchase behavior in the artificial environment. The latter is determined by consumer's own experience with the examined categories, the realism of the experiment and the instructions given (Campo, 1997). First, a suitable sampling procedure should be used to select 'experienced' grocery buyers (i.e. consumers that have sufficient experience with grocery shopping in general as well as with buying products in the selected product categories) (see sampling procedure, section 3.2.5). Second, the experimental design should be made as realistically as possible (see the description of the online computer experiment, section 3.2.1). In this respect, researchers can insert cues that have been demonstrated to enhance the realism of the shopping task in previous computer experiments. Research of Burke et al. (1992), for instance, has suggested that adding constraints, such as an inventory/storage constraint, could reduce biases in purchase decisions. This is confirmed by research of Campo et al. (1999) who have demonstrated that the presence of an inventory cue can indeed be considered as a 'realistic' purchase constraint mechanism. Third, the researchers should use clear instructions (yet, they should be careful not to reveal the purpose of the experiment) and can decide to familiarize respondents with the procedure beforehand (see the description of the online computer experiment, section 3.2.1).

In sum, using a computer-simulated shopping experiment has important advantages over other research methodologies and is the most appropriate design for our research because it recreates the 'actual' look and feeling of an online supermarket while giving the opportunity to manipulate the variables of interest, to control extraneous variables and to collect additional, perceptual information (Burke, 1996; Nagle and Holden, 1995).

3.2 EXPERIMENTAL DESIGN
In this section, we first give a general description of the experiment. Subsequently, we discuss the product categories, the treatment of the manipulated variables (i.e. out-of-stock occurrences, out-of-stock policy, shelf layout and assortment), the assignment of these treatments and the sampling procedure.

3.2.1 Description of the online computer experiment
As argued in the previous section, we choose to collect data through a realistic, online computer-simulated shopping experiment. Our computer experiment consisted of three modules: (1) a short pre-purchase questionnaire to screen respondents and to collect some general information, (2) a purchase simulation module (and, if necessary, a between-purchase questionnaire) and (3) a post-purchase questionnaire to survey the experiences with the virtual store. The application was pre-tested by a convenience sample of 16 respondents. Some small changes to facilitate the questions, to simplify the navigation in the online shop and to shorten the experiment were implemented accordingly. See appendix 3.A for an overview of the final online store experiment.

In the **purchase simulation** module, we exposed respondents to a realistic, online store. Our online store was based on the site of an existing Belgian online grocery shopping service and was upgraded and adjusted to fit our experimental design[2]. Using the site of an existing online grocery store adds to the realism of the experiment (e.g. the 'actual' shopping environment was preserved as much as possible, marketing mix stimuli that were controlled – such as price – were replicated as accurately as possible,...). In our online store, consumers could self-select the layout of the shelf. They could choose between a verbal shelf (i.e. a verbal list with descriptions of products) or a pictorial shelf (i.e. scanned pictures of real products placed on an actual shelf) (see appendix 3.A for a figure). In both cases, consumers could choose between a shelf arranged by brand or by flavor (for more information: see 3.2.3.3). We only allowed respondents to make a purchase from the online store by browsing the aisles and did not offer them, for instance, the possibility to create a personalized shopping list or to construct lists based on other self-determined criteria. Respondents did have the possibility to zoom in on one of the items (obtaining a picture in the verbal store and a larger picture in the pictorial store), get more information regarding the product (i.e. information that is printed on actual product packages such as ingredients, nutritional value and consumption information) and price (e.g. price per package or per kilo). In order to increase the realism of the experiment, each week was preceded and followed by a moving animation (a picture of a shopper entering or leaving the store, respectively) and after 'departing', each respondent received an overview of the products that were delivered at his (fictitious) doorstep.

Respondents were asked to make purchases for two product categories (margarine and cereals) during six successive, fictitious weeks. While such time compression might appear artificial, it has been shown to realistically capture dynamic purchase patterns[3] (Burke et al., 1992; Campo et al., 1999). In the task instruction (see appendix 3.A, module 2), respondents were explicitly asked to mimic their real shopping behavior as accurately as possible. For instance, they were asked to imitate their true purchase incidence pattern (e.g. they were not obliged to buy every week) and their true choice pattern (e.g. they were permitted to buy more than one package/product during one

---

[2] The software and the experimental site were developed by Hypervision, the software company responsible for the e-grocery site. For more information regarding Hypervision, see www.hypervision.be
[3] What is more, the 16 respondents that pre-tested the experiment had no problems with the time-compressed setting and did not consider it as disruptive.

week) (cf. Campo et al., 1999; Campo, 1997). Although we can not completely exclude that the instructions made respondents aware of the stock-out situations before the start of the simulation, there are reasons to believe that this has not been a problem. For one, Campo et al. (1999) has suggested that interview instructions may highlight certain response possibilities without biasing the results. They used examples in the interview instructions of their experiment to make variety-seeking behavior more rationally acceptable (by e.g. stressing the tendency to switch among items or to stay with the same items). Yet, they did not find a significant difference in variety seeking behavior between experimental and scanner data. Second, not all consumers indicated in the post-purchase questionnaire that they noticed stock-outs (see section 4.4.1 for the manipulation check). Third, we used a between-subject design for the stock-out policy and assortment manipulations (see section 3.2.4), making consumers unaware of the different experimental conditions. Next to providing consumers with clear interview instructions, we attempted to reduce biases in the category purchase incidence decision by displaying the household inventory at the top left-hand corner of the screen. The inventory was weekly updated using information on (1) the purchases made during the week and (2) the household's average consumption rate (collected in the pre-purchase questionnaire, see appendix 3.A, module 1) (cf. Campo et al., 1999; Campo, 1997). Although the presence of the in-home inventory cue might have biased purchase behavior, we expect these biases to be rather limited. For one, Campo et al. (1999) has demonstrated the validity of including such inventory cues as a 'realistic' purchase constraint. Second, it can be expected that consumers that normally do not pay attention to their in-home inventory also tend to neglect this piece of information in the course of the experiment.

In an attempt to help consumers, a demonstration before the purchase simulation was inserted. In this demonstration, a number of features of the online shop were explained such as the household's inventory level, the switching between the two product categories, the possibility to switch the mode (verbal versus pictorial) and/or organization (by brand versus by flavor), the purchase process (e.g. "placing products in the shopping cart", "going to the check-out") and the possibility to request more information (picture, product and price). In this demonstration, it was (again) stressed that respondents were not obliged to purchase during a specific week and could, in such a situation, leave the store without any problems.

Before and *after* the purchase simulation, **questionnaires** were used to collect additional information (see appendix 3.A, module 1 and 3). Table 3.5 gives an overview of the questions that were asked in the pre- and post-purchase questionnaires. For some variables (e.g. store loyalty, time pressure, shopping attitude and product importance), we decided to use single-item instead of multi-item scales. Single-item scales can be considered as an appropriate empirical justification when pragmatic considerations such as respondents fatigue necessitate the use of a shorter scale (Viswanathan, 2002). In addition, we only used single-item statements for variables that were not the main focus of the research. For these control variables, we selected, from existing multi-item scales, the statement that best captured the basic scale dimension, using the factor loadings that were reported by previous researchers (such as Campo et al., 2000; Van Trijp, Hoyer and Inman, 1996). Other, more important, variables (e.g. item loyalty, acceptable alternatives available, assortment variety and costs associated with finding and choosing products within an assortment) were measured using multiple statements. Cronbach alphas and principle component analysis confirmed the reliability and validity of these scales (see table 3.5).

Table 3.5 also specifies the purpose of each question. Questions that were necessary to screen respondents (e.g. grocery shopping experience, product category experience) and to initiate the purchase (e.g. average quantity consumed per week, home-inventory) were asked before the purchase simulation, while questions that could possibly have an impact on subsequent purchase behavior were asked after the purchase simulation (e.g. attitude towards product category, preference towards items, assortment evaluations). Some of the questions were needed to construct variables necessary in the model estimation (see next chapters: e.g. average quantity consumed per week, home-inventory, preference towards items). Pre- and post-purchase questions could also help to gain better insights into (purchase) decisions of a respondent. For instance, they could be used to better understand the results found in the subsequent chapters or to construct a profile of respondents that reacted in a particular way (e.g. a profile of respondents that dropped out during the experiment or a profile of respondents that changed the layout of the shelf).

Some of the respondents were also questioned *during* the purchase simulations. This was the case when they did not make a purchase in the product category and when their inventory level was insufficient to satisfy the consumption of the next week. In this situation, respondents did not make a purchase, despite the fact that – based on their, current, inventory level and their earlier indicated consumption rate – they should do so. We inserted this question to take into account that consumers might decide to go to another store when their preferred product is unavailable (see chapter 2, section 2.2.1 overview of the main stock-out responses). If relevant (i.e. if both conditions are satisfied), consumers were asked to indicate whether or not they would buy a product of the product category under consideration elsewhere and if so, how much they would buy. Data from our empirical study indicate that the number of people that would switch stores when confronted with an out-of-stock was rather small, comprising only 5% for margarine and 6% for cereals[4]. Yet, we recognize that, despite the use of the between-purchase questionnaire, we can not exclude that the store-switching reaction is partly underestimated[5]. Although we stressed that respondents were not obliged to make a purchase in the category each week, we can not rule out that the artificial setting might have partly biased the category purchase incidence decision. What is more, some of the store- and situation-related antecedents that directly impact the store-switching reaction (e.g. store loyalty, part of the week: see chapter 2, section 2.2.3) were very difficult to control/account for with the use of an experimental design.

---

[4] We found no consistent change in the purchase behavior of respondents before and after they received the between-purchase questionnaire, indicating that the disruptive nature of the question seems to be limited.

[5] We refer to the underestimation of the *online* stock-out reaction. Yet, it should be noted that, in general, the store switching reaction is expected to be lower in an online context than in an offline one (see section 2.3).

Table 3.5: Variables used in pre- and post-purchase questionnaires (see Appendix 3.A)

Pre-purchase questionnaire

Variable	Measurement instrument	Psychometric characteristics†		Purpose									
		Margarine	Cereals	Screen respondents	Initialize experiment	Sample profile	Construct variable (model estimation)	Ch 4: segm analysis	Ch 5: ass & cons diff	Drop-out profile	Shelf layout	switching profile	Control
Socio demographics													
Gender	Dichotomous question					X				X	X		
Age	Open question					X				X	X		X
Postal code	Open question												
Household composition	Multiple choice					X				X	X		
Number of children	Multiple choice, divided by age					X				X	X		
Work situation	Multiple choice					X				X	X		
Occupation	Multiple choice					X				X	X		
Education	Multiple choice					X				X	X		
Online shopping experience													
Internet experience	Multiple choice									X	X		X
Online shopping experience	Multiple choice									X	X		X
Reasons for not buying online	Multiple choice												X
Products bought online	Multiple choice												X
Propensity to purchase online (general & grocery products)	%							X	X	X	X		
Familiarity with Caddyhome	Multiple choice												X
Grocery shopping information													
Grocery shopping experience	Multiple choice			X				X		X	X		
Traditional shopping behavior	Multiple choice							X	X	X	X		
Store loyalty	1 statement (7-point likert scale) (Campo et al., 2000)							X	X	X	X		
Time pressure	1 statement (7-point likert scale) (Putrevu and Ratchford, 1997)							X	X	X	X		
Shopping attitude	2 statements (7-point likert scale) (Campo et al., 2000)	0.67	0.66					X	X				
Product category information													
Product category experience	Multiple choice			X	X								
Average quantity consumed/week	Number of packages used per week			X	X		X	X					
Inventory level	Number of packages at home			X	X		X						

Variable	Measurement instrument	Margarine	Cereals	Screen respondents	Initialize experiment	Sample profile	Construct variable (model estimation)	Ch 4: segm analysis	Ch 5: ass & cons diff	Drop-out profile	Shelf layout	switching profile	Control
		Psychometric characteristics†		Purpose									
Post-purchase questionnaire													
Revisit/repurchase intention (general & product category)	%							X	X				
Product perception and normal buying behavior													
Item loyalty	3 statements (7-point likert scale) (Campo et al., 2000)	0.7	0.65					X	X				
Acceptable alternatives available	3 statements (7-point likert scale) (Campo et al., 2000)	0.7	0.68					X	X				
Product importance	1 statement (7-point likert scale) (Van Trijp et al., 1996) Dichotomous question (brand versus type)							X	X				
Attribute importance	& indication of degree of importance (7-point scale)							X	X		X		
Assortment perceptions													
Variety (# and quality of products)	6 statements (7-point likert scale) (based on Donthu and Gilliland, 1996 and Morales et al., 2005)	0.84	0.81					X	X				X
Costs (finding and choosing products)	6 statements (7-point likert scale) (Menon, Raghubir and Schwarz, 1995 and Hufmann and Kahn, 1998)	0.89	0.87					X	X				X
Shelf organization	1 statement (7-point likert scale)							X	X		X		X
Satisfaction with purchase decision (general & product category)	3 statements (7-point likert scale) (Cole and Balasubramanian, 1993)							X	X				
Availability of favorite items & preferences towards items													
Items missing in assortment?	Selection of items respondents purchased in the past and that were unavailable in the online store they saw & indication of degree of preference (7-point scale)							X	X				X
Notice unavailability?	Dichotomous question							X	X				
Item preference	Selection of items respondents purchased in the past & indication of the share that the items take in the total shopping basket for that category (constant sum: 100 points)						X	X	X				X

† We report associated reliabilities (Pearson correlation for two items, Cronbach alpha for three or more items). The principal component analysis associated a separate factor with each scale.

3.2.2 Selection of the product categories

In this research, we are interested in frequently purchased products, more particularly grocery products, as this is an important market that is often confronted with stock-outs. When consumers confronted with a stock-out have to look for an acceptable replacement item within a large assortment (which is typically the case for grocery products), they face additional search costs. Especially for consumers that want to make an easy and effortless decision (which is particularly the case when shopping for grocery products online), such extra search costs might cause irritation and frustration. Therefore, doing the research in an online grocery context is likely to result in interesting findings. Yet, investigating stock-out, stock-out policy and virtual shelf placement effects for other (less frequently purchased) categories is certainly an interesting topic for future research.

We selected **margarine and cereals** as the two grocery categories for which consumers could make purchase decisions. The focus on only two categories was needed for practical reasons. It was infeasible to include all the grocery categories offered in an online store, given the budget made available for this research. What is more, asking consumers to make purchase decisions for a large number of product categories across different weeks would be very time-consuming and demanding. For both categories, we made sure that the online store offered all the information that is available in a brick-and-mortar store (e.g. ingredients, nutritional information,...). As such, there are no differences with respect to the availability of search attributes between an online and a brick-and-mortar store (cf. Degeratu, Rangaswamy and Wu, 2000; McGree and Boyer, 2005).

Both margarine and cereals are typically considered as low-involvement, low-risk categories (e.g. Leclerc and Little, 1997). They are regularly plagued with stock-outs and have been the subject of research in a number of previous out-of-stock studies (Campo et al., 2000/2003; Motes and Castleberry, 1985; Sloot et al., 2005; Verbeke et al., 1998). Moreover, consumer reactions towards a stock-out situation in these categories span the entire set of possibilities, going from switching towards another alternative to deciding not buy in category (cf. Campo et al., 2000/2003). We also controlled for the nature of the category by selecting two categories that differed in the type of products offered. While margarine is more likely to be perceived as an utilitarian/functional category, cereals is more likely to be perceived as a hedonic category (Campo, 1997; Campo et al., 2000). Finally, in order to obtain an adequate sample of respondents and enough observations per respondent, we focused on product categories with (1) a high percentage of users (high penetration rate) and (2) a high rotation (high purchase frequency) (e.g. Campo, 1997; Verbeke et al., 1998). The relatively low penetration of the cereals category was expected to be compensated by the high purchase frequency of cereals buyers. In addition, we used a sample where respondents a priori indicated that they (and/or other persons in their household) used cereals.

3.2.3 Treatment of the manipulated variables
In this section, we give a short overview of the stimuli that were manipulated during our experiment:

    (1) out-of-stock occurrences;
    (2) out-of-stock policy;
    (3) shelf layout (mode and organization);
    (4) assortment.

A more thorough discussion, justification and explanation of the out-of-stock policies is given in chapter 4. Shelf placement and assortment are discussed in greater detail in chapter 5. In our research, we decided to control other, extraneous, marketing mix stimuli (such as promotion and price), the competitive context and other aspects that cause clutter in the environment. Although it is possible that these aspects influence purchase behavior, we expect biases to be limited and decided not to explicitly include/manipulate them in this experiment because of budget constraints.

3.2.3.1 Out-of-stock occurrences
In this research, we decided to focus on item instead of brand stock-outs as it is the most often occurring problem. Because the first week is used as an initialization week, no stock-outs occurred during this week. We made sure that, on average, in the other experimental weeks (weeks 2-6), 8% of the products in the category were unavailable[6]. This figure is in line with previously reported stock-out rates (Anderson Consulting, 1996; Gruen et al., 2002; Sloot et al., 2005; Verhoef and Sloot, 2005). The occurrence

---

[6] Note that, in this research, there is no version of the online store without stock-outs. The absence of such a benchmark store makes it very difficult to assess if and how online stock-outs influence indirect losses.

of out-of-stocks was randomly distributed across items and experimental weeks, using the following rules of thumb:

- the distribution of stock-out situations across different weeks should be realistic but not necessarily equal. As a result, the number of stock-out items could differ between experimental weeks but these differences were kept to a minimum and it was ensured that in each week at least one alternative was unavailable (see the discussion of assortment, section 3.2.3.4, for the exact number of out-of-stock alternatives).

- a particular item had to be available at least once during the experimental weeks (except the first week where all items were offered). In addition, the occurrence of out-of-stocks was uniformly distributed over low- and high-share items, over national brand and private label items and over attribute levels (brands, tastes, types and/or sizes).

Although the random assignment of stock-outs might be a limitation, we do think that it is a realistic way of generating stock-out situations. For one, previous research of Campo et al. (2003) has indicated that stock-outs occur for a wide variety items. In their empirical application, stock-outs occurred over different brand types (national brand as well as distributor/generic brands) and over low- and high-share items. Second, current facts of existing online grocery shopping services also confirm that the random assignment is a realistic reproduction of reality. Explicit checks with the staff of the online grocery shopping service used in this dissertation revealed that stock-outs indeed occur randomly over different brand types and over low- as well high-market share items.

3.2.3.2 Out-of-stock policy

In this research, we focused on three kinds of out-of-stock policy: (1) *no-replacement* with out-of-stocks *visible* on the screen, (2) no-replacement with out-of-stocks *not visible* on the screen (only after clicking), (3) *replacement* with variations of the suggested substitution products according to different attributes. In the first out-of-stock policy, consumers immediately noticed that a product was unavailable (the stock-out situation was clearly indicated on the screen). In the second out-of-stock policy, product unavailability was only announced to potential buyers of the stock-out product at the moment they clicked on the item to activate their purchase. In the third out-of-stock policy, a replacement product was suggested for each out-of-stock product (see figure 3.1) (we will discuss the manipulation check in chapter 4).

Figure 3.1: Visual representation of the different out-of-stock policies

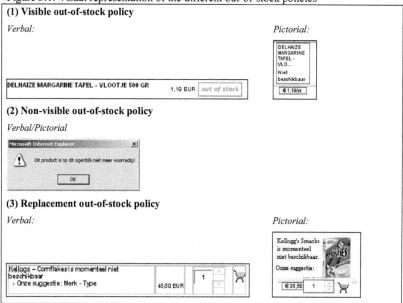

Depending on the focal attribute, different alternatives will qualify as the closest substitution item. In order to control this, we decided to focus on either flavor or brand when selecting the suggestion product, leading to two versions of the replacement stock-out policy. In a replacement stock-out policy with a focus on brand, substitution products of the same brand were suggested. In contrast, in a replacement stock-out policy with the focus on flavor, substitution products of the same flavor were suggested. Figure 3.2 shows the rules that were used when assigning the substitution products. The aim of the rule was to select those replacement products that were closest to the stock-out product with respect to the focal attribute (either brand or flavor).

Figure 3.2: Overview of the rules used to select substitution products

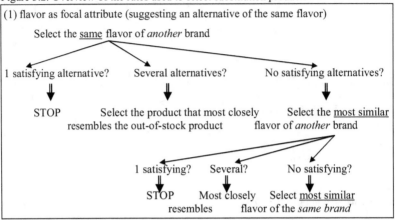

(1) flavor as focal attribute (suggesting an alternative of the same flavor)

Select the <u>same</u> flavor of *another* brand

1 satisfying alternative?   Several alternatives?   No satisfying alternatives?

STOP   Select the product that most closely   Select the <u>most similar</u>
resembles the out-of-stock product   flavor of *another* brand

1 satisfying?   Several?   No satisfying?

STOP   Most closely   Select <u>most similar</u>
resembles   flavor of the *same brand*

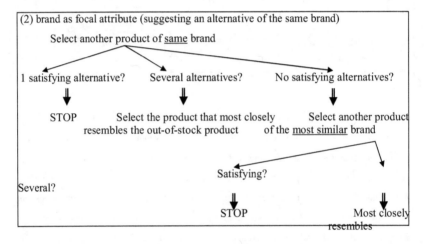

(2) brand as focal attribute (suggesting an alternative of the same brand)

Select another product of <u>same</u> brand

1 satisfying alternative?   Several alternatives?   No satisfying alternatives?

STOP   Select the product that most closely   Select another product
resembles the out-of-stock product   of the <u>most similar</u> brand

Satisfying?

Several?

STOP   Most closely
resembles

<u>3.2.3.3 Shelf layout</u>

In our experiment, consumers could self-select the most appropriate shelf mode and organization. In a demonstration preceding the purchase simulation exercise, consumers were shown how these features could be changed.

With respect to the shelf mode, consumers could opt for a verbal version, i.e. a list where alternatives are verbally described, or a pictorial version, i.e. a virtual shelf where photographic images of the front-packages of alternatives are displayed (cf. Burke et al., 1992). See appendix 3.A for a visual presentation.

With respect to the shelf organization, products were sorted by brand or by flavor. In order to be consistent across the two categories, we will use the term 'flavor' to describe (1) the different types of the category of margarine (i.e. margarine and minarine) and (2) the different tastes of the category of cereals (e.g. choco, honey, health, sugar,…). We used the criteria of proximity in the manipulation of the shelf organization (cf. Hoch, Bradlow and Wansink, 1999). In both the verbal as well as in the pictorial shelf, we started by grouping the products according to the focal organization attribute. Afterwards, if more than one possibility remained to position the products, other attributes came into play. As a result, in a shelf that is organized by brand (flavor), products of the same brand (flavor) were located next to each other. The shelf organization was made as realistic as possible and there was no systematic link between the position/place of a product on the shelf and its success (e.g. market share). We refer to appendix 3.B for more details with respect to the organization of products on the shelf.

3.2.3.4 Assortment

We also manipulated the offered assortment. We explicitly took into account that retailers can enlarge their assortment along different attributes. For instance, retailers can decide to add new flavors of existing brands or new brands of existing flavors. Therefore, we used the following three assortments: (1) a limited assortment, (2) an assortment extended with flavors and (3) an assortment extended with brands. The focus on only flavor and brand as possible extensions is a limitation of this research but was necessary to keep the number of treatments manageable. We selected these two attributes because previous research has indicated that they are two particularly important attributes for consumers when evaluating the assortment (e.g. Boatwright and Nunes, 2001).

Table 3.6 summarizes the attribute levels for each assortment for the 2 categories under consideration. Table 3.6 also indicates, per assortment, the number of alternatives and the total number of out-of-stock items (i.e. the sum of out-of-stock occurrences over the experimental weeks; see 3.2.3.1).

Table 3.6: Attributes levels for each assortment (margarine and cereals)

MARGARINE

Attribute	Assortment 1 (limited)	Assortment 2 (add new flavors of existing brands)	Assortment 3 (add new brands of existing flavors)
Brand	Becel control	Becel control	Becel control
	Benecol	Benecol	Benecol
	Delhaize margarine	Delhaize margarine	Delhaize margarine
	Derby	Derby	Derby
	Effi	Effi	Effi
	Roda	Roda	Roda
	Solo	Solo	Solo
	Vitelma	Vitelma	Vitelma
			Add new brands: * Alpro * Belolive * Bertolli * Planta
Flavor		Add minarine: * Becel essential * Becel pro-active * Benecol, light * Delhaize, minarine * Vitelma, minelma	
# alternatives	11	19	17
# out-of-stock items	6	10	9

CEREALS

Attribute	Assortment 1 (limited)	Assortment 2 (add new flavors of existing brands)	Assortment 3 (add new brands of existing flavors)
Brand	Kellogg's	Kellogg's	Kellogg's
	Others[†]	Others[†]	Others[†]
			Add new brands: * Private label * Nestlé
Flavor	Nature	Nature	Nature
	Choco	Choco	Choco
	Honey	Honey	Honey
		Add new flavors: * Sugar * Health	
# alternatives	21	32	46
# out-of-stock items	13	18	25

[†] We decided to collapse some low-share cereal items, such as Breakfast Club, Jordans and Weetabix, into one category because of estimation reasons. Yet, they are uniquely defined through the use of the other (taste/type) attribute variables.

In order to test if consumers really perceive differences in the variety of and satisfaction with these assortments, we pre-tested the three assortments. We decided to use a convenience sample consisting of undergraduates (instead of actual grocery buyers). Although it is true that undergraduate students typically are not the main grocery shopper of a household, we believe that the use of such a convenience sample is justified at this (pre-test) stage. Undergraduate students were exposed to one of the three assortments and were surveyed about their perceived variety of and satisfaction with the offered assortment. In order to increase consumer's attention for the offered assortment, they were asked to indicate which of the products they would select in the assortment. Results of this pre-test revealed that the manipulations had the expected effects: there were significant differences (in the expected directions) with the perceived variety as well as with the level of satisfaction between the three assortments. For example, the variety perceptions and the satisfaction with the limited assortment were significantly lower than the variety perceptions and the satisfaction with an assortment that was extended by brands/flavors (we will discuss the assortment evaluations in this research in chapter 5)[7].

3.2.4 Assignment of treatments

Subjects were randomly assigned to one of the four different out-of-stock policies (visible/no-replacement, non-visible, replacement – focus brand, replacement – focus flavor) and to one of the three different assortments (limited, extended – flavors, extended – brands). Moreover, in each scenario, 8% of the products were unavailable and consumers could choose between a verbal or a pictorial shelf and between a shelf arranged by brand or by flavor. In order to control for allocation biases, we split the default presentation layout, i.e. the layout that consumers see first and that is set by the online retailer/researcher. We use a split of $\frac{1}{3}/\frac{2}{3}$ for verbal/pictorial[8] and $\frac{1}{2}/\frac{1}{2}$ for brand/flavor, with all combinations, i.e. verbal-brand, verbal-flavor, pictorial-brand, pictorial-flavor, proportionally occurring at the beginning of the experiment.

The out-of-stock policy and the offered assortment are 'store-characteristics' and remained unaltered for a respondent during the complete experiment. Hence, in total, we had a 3 (assortment) x 4 (stock-out policy) between-subject design. The presentation

---

[7] The results of this pre-test were confirmed by real/experienced shoppers, i.e. we found similar results with respect to the variety perceptions between the different assortments with our final dataset. This shows that the use of a convenience sample of undergraduates was indeed justified and did not constitute a problem.

[8] We decided to use the division 1/3 and 2/3 in accordance with the current development of using more realistic interfaces in electronic grocery shopping services (cf. Chittaro and Ranon, 2002; cf. 3D Product representations – eLab Internet Research Hot topics). An exploratory research on a number of existing online grocery sites indeed revealed a tendency to present a pictorial version at the start (as the default option) while at the same time giving consumers the opportunity to switch towards a verbal version.

mode and organization, in contrast, could be changed by the respondents themselves. Results from our experiment show that switching behavior was rather limited (despite the fact that a demonstration preceding the shopping simulations explicitly showed how respondents could switch the mode and/or organization of the shelf). On average, in both categories, only 13% switched to another mode and only 7% switched to another organization[9]. This is in line with other research. For instance, Wu and Rangaswamy (2003) found that only 13% of the purchases involved a search on a specific attribute (i.e. only 13% re-arranged the products in a category on that attribute).

3.2.5 Sampling procedure

In order to get a representative sample, we used e-mail addresses coming from 2 mailing lists. Our sampling frame consisted of addresses from a list broker, complemented with addresses from the staff members of the university (including technical and administrative as well as academic staff). The list broker-addresses were hired from DataBaseManagement and were derived from the dataset of the Office of Consumer Preferences[10]. The office of consumer preferences is a life-style dataset. Members of this dataset fill in a questionnaire, capturing a set of accurate facts regarding a number of themes (such as interests, vacations, preferences with regard to communication, reading behavior, purchase intention in the long and short run, means of transport, IT usage, gifts, house and family). Persons are contacted yearly to update the questionnaire. The data is collected with respect for privacy and in compliance with the opt-in policy. The addresses of the list broker were selected based on demographic and purchase behavior information. To make sure that consumers could participate in the experiment, we decided to retain consumers that a priori indicated that they or someone else in their household used cereals. The addresses of the list-broker can be considered as the cross-section of the 'regular/traditional' shopping population (albeit

---

[9] In an attempt to better understand the underlying characteristics of people that changed the mode of the shelf, we compared the profile (capturing household characteristics, Internet experience and grocery shopping information) of respondents that switched and those that did not switch the mode, per category. We further refined this analysis by dividing the switching group into those that switched to a verbal setting and those that switched to a pictorial setting. A similar approach was adopted for shelf organization (dividing between those that switched to a brand or a flavor organization). There were very few significant differences between respondents that switched the mode (or organization) of the shelf and those that did not. When there was a (marginal) significant difference, this was typically only for one of the two categories. As such, there does not seem to be a systematic profile of 'switchers' in our dataset, neither for the mode, nor for the organization of the shelf.

[10] For more information regarding DBM, see www.databasemanagement.be and the Office of Consumer preferences (*'het Bureau voor Consumentengedrag'*), see www.postopmaat.be

with a bias towards cereals buyers). The e-mail addresses of university employees were inserted, not only because of sample size considerations but also to 're-direct' the sample towards a more highly-educated, higher-income population (cf. current profile of online grocery shoppers, see chapter 1). By using e-mail addresses and conducting an online research, we made sure that the chosen households were qualified for the study (cf. Hansen, 2005).

Respondents were invited to participate in the research by an e-mail that included a link to the online experimental site. To increase the response rate, we inserted a number of incentives: the possibility to win the first prize, i.e. a weekend in Disneyland®Resort Paris (worth 404 €), or one of eight Fnac-tickets (worth 20 €). For each mailing address, participation was requested of the household member typically in charge of grocery shopping. We decided to ask actual ('experienced') grocery buyers (instead of, for instance, a convenience sample of students) to participate in the experiment in order to capture realistic purchase behavior. As shown in the previous chapter, consumers that engage in routinized response behavior rely on task-simplifying heuristics stemming from previous shopping and consumption experiences. Respondents should therefore have sufficient shopping experience in order to capture realistic consumer reactions. In addition, respondents should not only have sufficient experience with grocery shopping in general, they should also have enough experience with the product categories under consideration (cf. Campo, 1997). Only respondents regularly consuming from a category were confronted with questions for that category. When consumers indicated in the pre-purchase questionnaire that they never used products of that product category or when less than 1 unit was used per month, the questions for that category were skipped. Taking this into account, we made sure that respondents that indicated that they never bought grocery products themselves or that neither used margarine, nor cereals were thanked for participating and excluded from the rest of the experiment.

3.3 CHARACTERISTICS OF THE SAMPLE AND DATA SET

In this section, we describe the response rate and provide reasons to understand why some of the respondents dropped out during the experiment. Next, we discuss household characteristics of the final sample and report a number of general characteristics of the experimental dataset.

3.3.1 Response rate

Table 3.7 gives an overview of the response rate and indicates where respondents ceased the experiment.

Table 3.7: Overview of the response towards the online computer experiment

	#	%
Total number of sent e-mails	12331	
Total number of undeliverable e-mails	1915	15.53%
Total number of delivered e-mails	**10416**	

	#	%[†]
Completed (finish whole experiment)	1655	15.89%
Sorry (low purchase frequencies for both products)	232	2.23%
Total (end)	**1887**	**18.12%**
Drop out – post-purchase questionnaire	111	1.07%
Total (end purchase simulations)	**1766[11]**	**16.95%**
Drop out – pre-purchase questionnaire	81	0.78%
Drop out – demonstration	182	1.74%
Drop out – shopping session 1	246	2.36%
Drop out – shopping session 2	71	0.68%
Drop out – shopping session 3	38	0.36%
Drop out – shopping session 4	27	0.26%
Drop out – shopping session 5	11	0.11%
Drop out – shopping session 6	8	0.08%
Total (drop out)	**775[12]**	**7.44%**
Total (start)	**2662**	**25.56%**

[†] = this % is calculated with respect to the total number of delivered e-mails

Table 3.7 indicates that 10416 respondents received an e-mail. In total 2662 started the experiment, constituting a response rate of more than 25%. This response rate compares favorably to other studies that ask consumers to participate in an online research by sending them an e-mail (e.g. 26.9% McGee and Boyer, 2005; 18.4% Verhoef and Langerak, 2001). 1766 respondents completed the purchase simulations (17%). The average time to complete the experiment took about 40 minutes. Most people (about 40%) finished the experiment in 20 to 30 minutes. 232 respondents did not start the

---

[11] The total number of consumers that ended the purchase simulations is equal to the number of respondents that fully passed through the complete experiment (1655) and those that completed the purchase simulations but did not complete the post-purchase questionnaire (i.e. those that dropped out during the post-purchase questionnaire: 111). After consultation of the staff of Hypervision, the majority of people that dropped out during the post-purchase questionnaire had problems with the pop-up appearing during the last questions (possibly because a pop-up blocker was activated) or with locking the account (technical difficulty where respondents did finish the questionnaire but were not registered doing so). Therefore, we decided to include these respondents when estimating the models as they fully completed the purchase simulations.

[12] Sum of all the respondents that ceased the experiment somewhere (pre-purchase questionnaire, demonstration, shopping session and post-purchase questionnaire).

purchase simulation because of low purchase frequencies for both products (2.23%). 775 respondents started the experiment but broke off somewhere during it (7.44%). The largest % of drop-outs occurred during the demonstration, the first shopping session and the post-purchase questionnaire, i.e. major transitions in the experiment. While some of the respondents dropped out because of technical problems (such as difficulties with the transition from the demonstration to the first shopping session or difficulties with the pop-up in the post-purchase questionnaire[13]), others ceased the experiment without being confronted with technical problems.

One possible reason that people dropped out during the (mainly first) shopping trips might be related to the (default) manipulations. To check whether consumers ceased the experiment because of the out-of-stock policy, the assortment or the default layout (mode and shelf organization) they were assigned to, we computed the number of respondents that dropped out during a shopping session across manipulations (see appendix 3.C, table 3.C.1). Comparing this figure with the prior (expected) distribution revealed no significant difference. We can therefore conclude that drop-outs occurred equally over the sample, irrespective of the manipulations.

In addition, we compared the profile of respondents that dropped out throughout the experiment with the profile of respondents that completed the purchase simulations (see appendix 3.C, table 3.C.2). Results indicate a self-controlling tendency: people less likely to be the main grocery shopper are more likely to drop out. Moreover, respondents that dropped out are also less likely to belong to an online grocery shopping population.

Hence, the major reason for respondents that drop out seems to be related to the moment in the experiment. More specifically, each time there was a transition to a new part of the experiment, a significant number of people decided to cease the experiment. Possible reasons might be partly related to technical problems but we can not exclude that consumers dropped out because they became tired or bored with the experiment.

---

[13] These problems came up when the first respondents were invited to participate in the experiment and were remedied by Hypervision in the course of the experiment.

It should be noted that the sample sizes reported in the next chapters are smaller than the global sizes reported in this section because we focus on sub-samples for each project/chapter[14]. Analyzing sub-samples not only avoids confounding/moderating effects but also keeps the models tractable. In chapter 4, we focus on the effect of the stock-out policy for only one assortment, namely the assortment extended by brands. We decided to focus on the assortment extended by brands as this resulted in the largest number of alternatives (for cereals). For this analysis, the sample size amounts to 584 respondents (more detailed information is given in section 4.4.1). In chapter 5, we focus on the effect of virtual shelf placement across different assortments for only one stock-out policy, namely the visible, no-replacement policy. We decided to focus on the visible, no-replacement policy because this is the policy that is most comparable to traditional (brick-and-mortar) grocery stores where stock-outs are typically visible (as empty spaces on the shelf) and no replacement items are suggested. So, for this project, all consumers clearly saw which of the products were unavailable. For this analysis, the sample size amounts to 387 respondents (more detailed information is given in section 5.2.1).

3.3.2 Sample characteristics

Table 3.8 reveals the socio-demographic characteristics of the final sample (i.e. respondents that did not drop out). The table indicates that our final sample has a large percentage of women and of young and better educated persons. In addition, the composition of the majority of the households in our sample includes children[15]. We can conclude that this is in line with the profile of the online grocery shopper that was discussed in chapter 1 (e.g. Degeratu et al., 2000; Morganosky and Cude 2002; Raijas and Tuunainen 2001). The figures in the table further indicate that the sample comprises a wide variety of respondents in terms of social class (occupation).

---

[14] Respondents who seemed not to take the task too seriously (indicated by consumers finishing the experimental task in a "suspiciously low" time or consumers with extremely large deviations between the indicated average consumption rate and the quantity purchased in the simulation module) were omitted from the model estimation (cf. Campo, 1997).

[15] The lack of single households in our sample profile can be attributed to the product category under consideration: cereals being a product that is typically consumed by children. This together with the fact that we explicitly asked for e-mail addresses where at least one of the members consumed cereal products, might explain why single households are missing in the sample used for our empirical study. However, as was indicated in chapter 1, the absence of single households is in line with the current online grocery shopper profile as recent studies indicate that average household size tends to be larger for online grocery shoppers than for brick-and-mortar consumers (Degeratu et al., 2000; Zhang, 2001).

Table 3.8: Socio-demographic characteristics of the sample

Socio-demographic characteristic		%
Gender	- Female	60%
	- Male	40%
Age	- < 25 years	13%
	- 26-35 years	37%
	- 36-45 years	26%
	- 46-55 years	18%
	- > 55 years	6%
Education	- High school or less	34%
	- College	30%
	- College graduate	25%
	- Post-graduate	11%
Occupation	Unemployed	15%
	Civil Servant	17%
	Other	7%
	Workman	7%
	Employee	46%
	Executive	5%
	Profession	1%
	Self-employed	3%
Family type	Single	8%
	Partner only	26%
	Partner & children	54%
	Children	5%
	Parents	6%
	Other	1%
Number of children	0	41%
	1	21%
	2	27%
	3	9%
	4	2%
	>5	1%

3.3.3 Product category characteristics

In our research, we included respondents as buyers of a product category when (1) they made at least 1 purchase during the experimental weeks (not including the purchases of the first week) and (2) they a priori indicated that they used the product category. For the complete sample, 1405 (1234) respondents completed the purchase simulation exercise for margarine (cereals). 1020 respondents participated in the research for both categories. In terms of purchase occasions, we have 5078 purchase occasions for margarine and 4890 for cereals (for the sub-samples used in the projects, we refer to the next chapters, section 4.4.1 for project 1 and section 5.2.1 for project 2, for more details).

In table 3.9, we split the number of purchases per week, per product category. Note that this table supports the necessity to consider the first week as an initialization week. Most respondents buy, on average, once every 2-3 weeks for margarine as well as for cereals (see figure 3.3). This is in line with realistic expectations and confirmed by prior research. Campo (1997), for instance, found that respondents, in a computer-simulated exercise, purchased on average during 8 of 12 shopping trips for margarine and 7 of 12 shopping trips for cereals.

Table 3.9: Number of purchase occasions, per week, per product category

	Week 1	Week 2	Week 3	Week 4	Week 5	Week 6
Margarine	1288	653	833	753	807	744
Cereals	1125	796	837	642	734	756

Figure 3.3: Purchase frequency during the purchase simulation, per product category

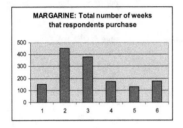 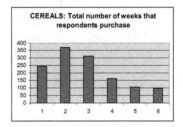

CHAPTER 4: OPPORTUNITIES FOR ACTIVE STOCK-OUT MANAGEMENT IN AN ONLINE STORE[1]

THE IMPACT OF THE STOCK-OUT POLICY ON ONLINE STOCK-OUT REACTIONS

INTRODUCTION

As outlined in chapter 2, stock-outs have a negative impact for retailers, both directly (on category sales and profit: Campo, Gijsbrechts and Nisol, 2003; Schary and Christoper, 1979) and indirectly (via store satisfaction, loyalty and image: Bell and Fitzsimons, 1999; Fitzsimons, 2000; McGoldrick, 2002; Zinn and Liu, 2001). Yet, as indicated previously, neither traditional stores, nor online stores will be able to completely avoid stock-out problems. Stock-outs may even be a larger problem for online merchants than for traditional ones due to forecasting problems and strongly fluctuating demand (e.g. Fitzsimons, 2000; Van Elburg – Emerce, 2001). What is more, stock-outs may be particularly detrimental to online retailers' long term success (Bhargava, Sun and Xu, 2005; Danaher, Wilson and Davis, 2003; McGree and Boyer, 2005). Indeed, a recent study indicates that product unavailability rates second in the top 3 of online shopping irritations (Marketing online, 9/11/2004).

Despite their importance, no research to date exists that has investigated stock-out reactions in an online grocery context. Yet, such research could be insightful for at least two reasons. First, as mentioned in chapter 2, online stock-out reactions might differ from those in brick-and-mortar settings because of, for example, the lack of sensory search attributes (Degeratu, Rangaswamy and Wu, 2000) or the convenience-driven motivation to use online grocery shopping services (e.g. Morganosky and Cude, 2002) (Alba et al., 1997; Danaher et al., 2003). More importantly, the online environment offers opportunities to mitigate the negative effects of stock-outs (which we will refer to as 'stock-out policies' hereafter) that are not or difficult to implement in a traditional grocery store. First, an online retailer has the possibility to make the service failure *less prominent*. Online retailers can, for instance, use pop-ups which allow them to announce stock-out problems only to those consumers interested in buying the product

---

[1] Part of this chapter appeared in Breugelmans, E., K. Campo, and E. Gijsbrechts (2006). Opportunities for active stock-out management in online stores: The impact of the stock-out policy on online stock-out reactions, *Journal of Retailing,* 82 (3), 215-228.

(i.e. after clicking). Second, the merchandising costs or the costs retailers incur when making physical changes to the shopping environment are lower for an online retailer than for a traditional one. Therefore, making adjustments to the online environment in an attempt to compensate for stock-out failures becomes easier. This enables online retailers to more efficiently implement a number of *compensation* stock-out policies. For instance, online retailers are in an ideal position to 'replenish the empty shelf space' (cf. the traditional practice; Borin and Farris, 1995; Campo and Gijsbrechts, 2005; Urban, 1998) through the suggestion of a replacement product (cf. online product recommendations: Bell and Fitzsimons, 1999; Fitzsimons and Lehmann, 2004; Senecal and Nantel, 2004). As soon as the online retailer has listed the replacement items (or specified a procedure to automate this), a technical process will make sure that suggestions are made immediately, each time an out-of-stock occurs (cf. Senecal and Nantel, 2004). In contrast, offline retailers have to physically reorganize the shelves when an out-of-stock is noticed, resulting in a more difficult and costly implementation of the replacement policy (Corsten and Gruen, 2003).

This research will contribute to the literature in two ways. First, it improves our understanding of online out-of-stock reactions. Our second, and main, contribution is to highlight the consequences for online retailers of actively pursuing alternative stock-out policies. In the next section, we give an overview of the opportunities that an online retailer has to deal with stock-out situations and point out the three different stock-out policies that we investigate. Afterwards, we derive hypotheses regarding the stock-out policy effects and describe the methodology and the data set used to test our hypotheses. Lastly, we discuss the results of our online shopping experiment (for two categories: margarine and cereals).

4.1 DIFFERENT STOCK-OUT POLICIES

Consumers typically consider stock-outs as a service failure. How they react to such a service failure depends on how retailers are perceived to deal with these stock-out occurrences. Based on service failure/recovery literature, we distinguish a number of options available for an online retailer to alleviate some of the negative consequences associated with stock-out situations: (1) apology, (2) prominence-reduction and (3) compensation (cf. Beuk, 2001; Smith, Bolton and Wagner, 1999). In the next paragraphs, we give an overview of the different options and indicate to what extent an online retailer, compared to a traditional retailer, has an advantageous position to implement some of these stock-out policies[2].

First, a retailer can simply offer his <u>apologies</u> to a consumer when s/he is confronted with a stock-out situation (Anderson, Fitzsimons and Simester, 2004; Beuk, 2001; Fitzsimons, 2000; Verhoef and Sloot, 2005). An apology from a retailer *"communicates politeness, courtesy, concern, effort and empathy to consumers who have experienced a service failure"* (Smith et al., 1999, p.359). The retailer can, together with an apology, also provide an explanation for the service failure. He can explicitly mention that the stock-out failure was due to, for instance, the popularity of the alternative, own faults in the ordering, replenishing or planning process or upstream causes (transporter/manufacturer) that have resulted in an incorrect or (too) late delivery. Providing extra information appears to work well for non-grocery catalog retailers (Anderson et al., 2004). Yet, (online) grocers are not very keen to provide such reasons as most consumers do not care how the stock-out situation arose and retailers themselves typically are unwilling to admit their own mistakes (e.g. Beuk, 2001; Verhoef and Sloot, 2005). In addition, the retailer can, next to the apology (possibly extended with an explanation), indicate the expected waiting time (i.e. the expected moment that the product will be available again in the store) (cf. Beuk, 2001; Verhoef and Sloot, 2005). Announcing the expected delivery time makes the retailer vulnerable, especially when inaccuracies and errors in delivery occur. Underestimating the time necessary to replenish might result in negative rather than positive reactions. In practice, therefore, most (online) retailers do not explicitly state a reason for the stock-out situation, neither do they often specify the expected recovery time (but they may promise to notify the buyer and reserve the product as soon as it becomes available again, see below).

Second, a retailer might strive to make out-of-stocks <u>less salient</u>. In contrast to a traditional grocer, an online grocer has the possibility to 'not mention' out-of-stock occurrences. First, an online retailer can decide to notify only buyers of the stock-out products with a pop-up emerging after clicking on such a product (this policy was

---

[2] Note that each of the undermentioned options/marketing strategies can be used in combination, thereby enriching the number of different stock-out policies that online retailers can adopt. For instance, an online retailer can decide to make stock-outs less salient by using a pop-up and at the same time compensate for the inconvenience by suggesting a replacement item.

adopted by the online grocery shopping service that was used in our experiment). Second, an online retailer can rearrange the products in such a way that out-of-stock alternatives 'disappear' (i.e. are no longer visible on the shelf). Both types of prominence-reduction policies can minimize or even completely eliminate the visibility of stock-out situations. We decided to focus on the first type because it clearly indicates temporary unavailability (although only to those interested in buying the product). Completely rearranging shelves to remove blank positions may well increase the consumers' variety perceptions. Yet, it also distorts the perceived assortment structure and increases search costs for all consumers – not just those looking for the stock-out product.

Third, a retailer might try to <u>compensate</u> for the inconvenience a stock-out causes. In this case, the retailer diverts attention away from the service failure by directing it to the suggested compensation (hence making the stock-out situation, to some extent, less salient). A number of compensation strategies are available. First, a retailer can use coupons and/or discounts and/or refunds to financially compensate for the stock-out failure (e.g. Anderson et al., 2004; Bhargava et al., 2005; Beuk, 2001; Verhoef and Sloot, 2005). Using coupons, for instance, allows consumers to return to the store and buy the preferred product – at a discount. Because the interaction between a consumer and a retailer in the 'real' world mainly occurs through face-to-face meetings, the coupon, discount or refund can be directly given to the persons that were confronted with the stock-out. In contrast, the interaction in cyberspace takes place through the retailer's web site. Online retailers, therefore, can decide to give a discount for the product on the next order, to give a (printable) coupon that can be used on the next order or to add the product to the next order without charging any money. Second, a retailer can use a reservation and/or delivery service to compensate for the stock-out failure. In this case, the retailer promises to notify the buyer and/or reserve and/or deliver the stock-out item as soon as it becomes available again. The high delivery costs compared to the relatively low margins of grocery products might make online grocery retailers reluctant to adopt such a recovery policy. Third, a retailer can try to compensate for the delivery failure by suggesting one (or several) replacement item(s) (cf. Beuk, 2001; Verhoef and Sloot, 2005). At this moment, suggesting one replacement product is the stock-out compensation strategy that is most often adopted by online grocery retailers (e.g. Netgrocer, Peapod, Tesco). Whereas the three types of compensation are possible for an online grocery retailer, we focus on the third type. While offering financial compensations and/or facilitating the backordering is widespread among catalog retailers, these practices are less appropriate and less commonly implemented in an online grocery context. Not only does their effectiveness appears to be limited, even for catalog selling (Anderson et al., 2004), online grocery shoppers typically are convenience-oriented and, therefore, want to receive their grocery products immediately and in one go.

In this research, we investigate the impact of the following three out-of-stock policies on online stock-out reactions (choice and incidence behavior):

(1) a 'visible, no-replacement' stock-out policy, i.e. a policy where stock-outs are visible for everyone and no replacement items are suggested (benchmark);

(2) a 'non-visible' stock-out policy, i.e. a policy where stock-outs are only visible for the buyers of the product (after clicking, a pop-up tells the buyer that the product is currently not available) ("prominence-reduction");

(3) a 'replacement' stock-out policy, i.e. a policy where a replacement product is suggested for each out-of-stock product ("compensation").

In traditional (brick-and-mortar) grocery stores, stock-outs are typically visible (as empty spaces on the shelf), and no replacement items are suggested. We use this approach as the benchmark case in our paper. The selection of the other policies was based on (1) the current usage of the policy in the actual online grocery shopping environment (both the benchmark policy as well as the other two policies are the ones that are most frequently adopted by existing online grocery stores) and (2) the noticeable advantages online retailers have when implementing the policy (hiding stock-out problems is not an option for traditional retailers, suggesting a replacement item for each out-of-stock product requires a very difficult and costly implementation for traditional retailers).

4.2 CONCEPTUAL FRAMEWORK & HYPOTHESES

In this section, we present a literature-based framework for consumers' response to alternative stock-out policies. To this end, we proceed in two steps. First, we briefly review decision process characteristics in 'regular' and 'disrupted' low-involvement choice settings (see chapter 2 for more details). Next, we describe how retailer actions aimed at recovering some of the stock-out losses, are evaluated by consumers and how they affect their ultimate purchase decisions. Based on these insights, we then formulate expectations on how a retailer's out-of-stock policy influences stock-out reactions.

4.2.1 Conceptual framework

4.2.1.1 Consumer reactions to online stock-outs

As mentioned in chapter 2, consumers typically engage in routinized response behavior (product concept utilization) when they have to make purchase decisions in a familiar, non-disrupted grocery context. Consumers have made these decisions a numerous times in the past and, therefore, tend to employ task-simplifying decision rules which allow them to reach a satisfactory, yet quick and effortless decision (Howard, 1989; Howard and Sheth, 1969; Hoyer, 1984; Leong, 1993). Stock-outs typically are unexpected, disturbing events that force consumers to react on the spot (Campo, Gijsbrechts and Nisol, 2004). To cope with such disruptions, consumers typically engage in a limited problem solving (product concept attainment) stage. In this case, they tend to adopt their previously-formed set of evaluative criteria and are, as a result, able to limit the necessary time and effort needed when making a purchase decision[3] (see figure 4.1).

Figure 4.1: Visual representation of conceptual framework (based on chapter 2)

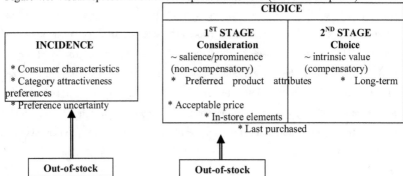

Stock-outs influence both the category purchase incidence and the choice decision. First, stock-outs have a negative impact on the category purchase incidence decision as

---

[3] As was noted in chapter 2, limited problem solving (or product concept attainment) is the stage that is *most typical* when consumers are confronted with a disruption in the choice environment. Yet, we can not exclude that consumers engage in an extensive problem solving stage, nor that they engage in routinized response behavior when the choice environment is interrupted by a 'disruption' (cf. Howard, 1989; van Waterschoot and Gijsbrechts, 2003).

they might increase consumers' preference uncertainty and reduce the attractiveness of buying in the category. The 'severeness' of these effects is largely governed by the consumers' preference for the missing items (e.g. Campo, Gijsbrechts and Nisol, 2000; Sloot, Verhoef and Franses, 2005) and the availability of suitable replacement items (e.g. Boatwright and Nunes, 2001; Broniarczyk, Hoyer and McAlister, 1998; Campo et al., 2000). In addition, purchase incidence effects will depend on the overall consequences of not making any purchase in the category (e.g. risk of running out of stock at home, see e.g. Campo et al., 2000; Sloot et al., 2005; Zinn and Liu, 2001).

Second, we expect stock-outs to influence the choice process via the first, consideration set formation stage, rather than by affecting the second, choice stage (cf. Mehta, Rajiv and Srinivasan, 2003). Evidently, items that are not available can not be taken into consideration (degree of consideration reduces to 0%). In addition, while out-of-stocks do not affect the intrinsic value of the remaining alternatives, they do enhance the degree of consideration of those alternatives, which can act as a replacement. The extent to which a stock-out increases another item's degree of consideration will depend on (1) shared attributes with the stock-out item (especially focal attributes, see e.g. Campo et al., 2003; Boatwright and Nunes, 2001), (2) the difference in price level, (3) in-store elements that highlight the item (see next section), and (4) whether the alternative item has been purchased before (for more details, see chapter 2).

4.2.1.2 Consumer reactions to service recovery policies

Consumers' response to disruptions in the choice environment (in casu: stock-outs) depends on how retailers are perceived to deal with these disruptions. Based on the service failure/recovery literature as well as equity literature (Clemmer and Schneider, 1993; Fitzsimons and Lehmann, 2004; Palmer, Beggs and Keown-McMullan, 2000; Smith et al., 1999), we expect consumers to judge such retailer policies on two criteria: outcome and procedure. First, the appreciation of the retailer's policy depends on the perceived fairness of the outcome, captured by the benefits (or lack thereof) consumers receive as a result of this policy. Second, the consumers' appreciation of the retailers' policy depends on the perceived fairness of the procedures or norms used. Prior research on attribution theory suggests that consumers make causal inferences about the behavior of others (in our case: the policy of retailers), which, in turn, affect their own subsequent behavior (in our case: choice and incidence) (Folkes, 1984; Mizerski, Golden and Kernan, 1979). Consumers can attribute the policy of the retailer either to customer-serving or to self-serving motives (Kelley, 1973; Ellen, Mohr and Webb, 2000). Whereas customer-serving motives *"refer to any motive that includes attention to the well-being of individuals outside the firm – but may also include firm interest as well"* (hence comprising an 'altruistic' as well as a 'win-win' policy), firm-serving motives *"refer to any motive that focuses solely on the needs of the firm itself"* (hence only comprising an 'egoistic' policy) (Ellen et al., 2000, p.2-3). The discounting principle of the attribution theory (Kelley, 1973) dictates that the consumer will believe in the retailers' genuine willingness to serve consumers, unless only policy benefits to the firm are salient (cf. Forehand and Grier, 2003). If the retailer's policy is thought to be guided by firm-serving (retailer-enriching) motives, consumers will produce backlash behavior (cf. Fitzsimons and Lehmann, 2004, Forehand and Grier, 2003).

4.2.2 Hypotheses

Based on the insights above, we now present hypotheses on how a retailer's out-of-stock policy influences stock-out reactions. We use the visible, no-replacement stock-out policy as the benchmark case in our paper. Below, we subsequently hypothesize how the introduction of a non-visible and a replacement stock-out policy affect consumer's category purchase incidence and choice. We hypothesize that the non-visible policy influences the incidence decision[4] while the replacement policy has an impact on both choice and incidence. For the latter policy, we also explore the moderating impact of higher-priced suggested replacement items (see figure 4.2).

Figure 4.2: Visual representation of the hypotheses

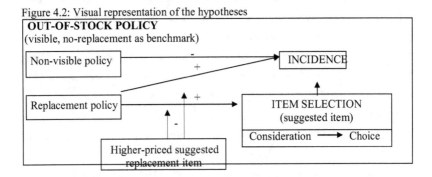

---

[4] As it is impossible to choose a product that is unavailable, we expect the non-visible policy to exert an effect on the incidence decision and not on the choice decision. Not showing products at first sight creates frustration that affects the buy/no buy decision. There is no indication on how it would affect the distribution of purchases over available items.

4.2.2.1 The impact of a non-visible out-of-stock policy

Instead of making all out-of-stock items visible on the screen, online retailers may opt for a non-visible policy. With such a policy, product unavailability is only announced to potential buyers of the stock-out product at the time they click on the item to activate their purchase.

This practice produces the following effects. On the positive side, as long as consumers do not hit a stock-out item, they perceive the assortment as complete. This may lead to a more positive evaluation (for instance, higher perceived freedom of choice, cf. Reibstein, Youngblood and Fromkin, 1975) compared to the visible policy, where the reduction in category attraction due to stock-outs is immediately observable. However, this positive effect should not be exaggerated. For one, even in a visible policy setting, consumers may fail to notice stock-outs (e.g. Beuk, 2001). Moreover, while the assortment in a non-visible policy setting is perceived more positively at the outset, this situation may rapidly change as the consumer – in an attempt to purchase from the category – clicks on a stock-out item and discovers that the product s/he is interested in is in fact a non-available, phantom product (Farquhar and Pratkanis, 1993). The more stock-out items the consumer clicks on in vain, the more likely it becomes that s/he will reach 'a point of frustration', i.e. a point where the category attractiveness in a non-visible policy becomes lower than the category attractiveness in a visible out-of-stock policy (see figure 4.3). At this point, s/he is less likely to make a purchase in the non-visible than in the visible policy.

Figure 4.3: The impact of the non-visible stock-out policy on the incidence decision

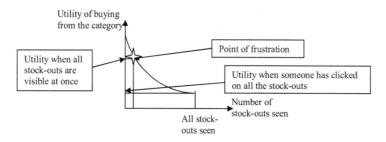

We conjecture that this point of frustration is reached very quickly (even after only one or a few clicks), each stock-out encounter in the non-visible policy producing

particularly strong backlash effects. For one, the *outcome* of the non-visible policy may quickly become unappealing to the consumer for at least three reasons. First, upon clicking, the consumer is confronted with unavailability of a preferred item. The disappointment and/or frustration arising from clicking on a stock-out item strengthens the loss experience resulting from the out-of-stock situation. Second, subsequent hits on unavailable items constitute segregated losses, which may quickly loom larger than the aggregated reduction in assortment attractiveness observed in the visible policy (Thaler, 1985). Third, not only does the consumer observe the stock-out in a stage where s/he is already set on buying the product, s/he also becomes aware of the uncertainty about the true availability of other alternatives. The anticipation of a complex 'trial and error' purchase sequence may make her/him refrain from purchasing (Dhar, 1997). Moreover, consumer reactions with respect to the non-visible stock-out policy are also influenced by the evaluation of the *procedures* that guide this policy. Consumers are likely to attribute the non-visible policy to 'self-serving' motives – retailers hiding their stock-out problems. This is likely to further reduce their willingness to purchase.

In brief, we expect the positive effects of a non-visible policy to be more than counterbalanced by the negative effects:

H_1: **When confronted with out-of-stocks, consumers are less likely to make a purchase in the category when the retailer follows a non-visible policy (where stock-outs are visible only after clicking) than when stock-outs are visible to all consumers.**

4.2.2.2 The impact of a replacement out-of-stock policy

With a replacement out-of-stock policy, the retailer accompanies notification of a stock-out by the suggestion of a replacement item (already present in the category). Such practice may limit the decrease in category attractiveness, as it diverts attention from the out-of-stock item – or the service failure – to the suggested item. At the same time, it may reduce preference uncertainty, the recommendation providing a simplifying choice heuristic that helps consumers in deciding which substitute item to buy (cf. Fitzsimons, 2000; Huffman and Kahn, 1998). For both reasons, suggesting a replacement item may decrease the consumers' tendency to drop a category purchase when they are confronted with a stock-out.

H₂: When confronted with out-of-stocks, consumers are less likely to refrain from a category purchase when the retailer suggests a substitute item than when no replacement item is suggested.

The replacement policy may also have a positive effect on the choice probability of the suggested alternative. Because suggested items 'stand out' on the shelf, their consideration and hence choice probability is likely to increase (cf. Bronnenberg and Vanhonacker, 1996; Fader and McAlister, 1990; Gupta, 1988; Siddarth, Bucklin and Morrison, 1995). As such, a replacement policy is bound to produce a choice shift towards the suggested items.

H₃: Suggesting an item as a potential substitute for an out-of-stock item increases the probability that the consumer will consider this item for selection.

It is important to note, however, that these effects only occur when consumers *accept* the suggestion as a simplifying choice heuristic. The size of the increase in incidence and choice probability depends on the perceived policy outcome and procedure. Specifically, to what extent highlighting a replacement item will actually produce choice shifts and enhance perceived category value/facilitate decision making, is shaped by the intrinsic utility of this item. Second, the appreciation also depends on the consumers' faith in the retailer's good intentions. When consumers trust the retailer's suggestion as being the best (closest) replacement item, they are more likely to consider it helpful, take the suggested alternative into consideration and make a purchase in the category. Conversely, when the retailer is suspected of 'bait and switch' practices (cf. Hess and Gerstner, 1998; Wilkie, Mela and Gundlach, 1998), opposite effects may occur. One of the core issues when adopting a replacement policy, therefore, is how to select an appropriate substitution product.

Price may play an important role in this decision. As indicated in chapter 2, consumers are more likely to consider items that have an acceptable or 'fair' price (Jedidi and Zhang, 2002; Xia, Monroe and Cox, 2004). Replacement items of a higher price, therefore, will have a lower intrinsic value (implying a lower expected *outcome* of the replacement policy). Moreover, when the suggestion is of a higher price, consumers may suspect the retailer of deliberately setting alternatives unavailable with the aim of selling more profitable items (a firm-serving *procedure*). In that case, consumers might show reactance-style responses (Brehm, 1966) and produce backlash behavior, i.e. switching away from the suggested item or not buying anything in the category (Fitzsimons and Lehmann, 2004; Simonson, Carmon and O'Curry, 1994). As a result, the price of the suggested replacement items moderates the main effect of the replacement out-of-stock policy[5]. Hence:

H₄: Suggesting a higher-priced replacement item negatively moderates the (positive) effect of the suggestion on choice and incidence probability.

4.3 MODEL DESCRIPTION

In this section, we present the model used to test our hypotheses. We subsequently discuss the choice and incidence models. We refer to appendix 4.A for an overview of the variables used in the final model estimation.

4.3.1 Two-stage choice model

To test the impact of stock-outs and stock-out policies on item selection, we use a two-stage choice model. Such a model allows us to distinguish the consideration set formation stage from the item selection stage. To select the two-stage choice model that was employed in our research, we used the review paper of Manrai and Andrews (1998). They evaluate the existing two-stage choice models that can be applied to scanner panel data by using five criteria (the most preferred outcome of each criterion is indicated in italics). Consideration set formation can be:

1. Memory-based (using only information from memory) versus stimulus-based (using only information from the external environment) versus *mixed* (using information from memory and the external environment);
2. Naïve (consumer and/or marketing characteristics do not have an effect) versus *based on consumer and/or marketing characteristics*;

---

[5] Note that the formulation of the higher-priced suggestion as a moderating effect might constitute a subject of discussion. Indeed, it is possible to formulate two different (although comparable) hypotheses: while the first one would be related to the effect of a suggestion of the same/lower price alternative (expected to be positive, significant), the second one would be related to the effect of a higher-priced suggestion (expected to be non-significant or negative, significant). Explicitly estimating this alternative formulation provided exactly the same results. We decided to use the former (moderating-effect) formulation because it allows to test the main effect of the suggestion while, at the same time, offering the flexibility to include (if desired) other potential moderating effects more easily.

3. *Attribute-based* (screen out alternatives that contain/do not contain specific attributes) versus alternative-based (evaluate alternatives holistically prior to inclusion in the consideration set);

4. Static (consideration set does not change over time) versus *dynamic* (consideration set varies over time);

5. Deterministic (or crisp consideration set where each alternative either belongs to the consideration set or not) versus probabilistic (where the composition of the consideration set is not known with certainty and non-zero occurrence probabilities are assigned to two or more different sets) versus grounded in the *fuzzy set* theory (where each alternative belongs to a greater or lesser extent than other alternatives to the consideration set)[6].

(see Manrai and Andrews, 1998 for a more elaborate review).

From a theoretical perspective, the model in our research is preferably a mixed, attribute-based, dynamic model centered around the fuzzy set theory and specified as a function of consumer and/or marketing characteristics. Based on the review of Manrai and Andrews (1998), we decided to use the model of Bronnenberg and Vanhonacker (1996) as a starting point[7]. This model meets our criteria on all points, except one: it is an alternative-based instead of an attribute-based model. However, existing attribute-based two-stage choice models all use a probabilistic consideration set formation process. Such models involve a higher degree of computational difficulty than fuzzy consideration set models due to the large number of possible consideration sets that must be estimated. As a result, probabilistic models are not very feasible for our research, especially because of the large number of alternatives (and thus the large number of possible consideration sets) in our research (e.g. Andrews and Srinivasan, 1995; Siddarth et al., 1995). Hence, we preferred an alternative-based, fuzzy two-stage consideration set model that – while parsimonious – allows us to distinguish the consideration from the choice stage as follows:

---

[6] Manrai and Andrews (1998) only make a distinction between a deterministic/crisp and a probabilistic consideration set formation. Yet, the emergence of the fuzzy set theory in the two-stage choice models prompts us to introduce this approach as well (see Bronnenberg and Vanhonacker, 1996; Fortheringham, 1988; Wu and Rangaswamy, 2003).

[7] Although the model of Wu and Rangaswamy (2003) has the same 'scores' on the criteria, we decided to use the less-complicated model of Bronnenberg and Vanhonacker (1996) due to the conditioning of the dataset.

$$p_{it}^h = \frac{\pi_{it}^h \exp(u_i^h)}{\sum_j \pi_{jt}^h \exp(u_j^h)} \quad \text{for } i = 1, \ldots, I \tag{4.1}$$

with

p_{it}^h = the choice probability of alternative i for consumer h at time t

u_i^h = the choice utility of consumer h for alternative i

π_{it}^h = degree of consideration (inclusion probability) of consumer h for item i at time t

In Bronnenberg and Vanhonacker (1996)'s model, consideration set formation (π_{it}^h) depends on differences in salience across alternatives. For a given consumer, the consideration utility for an alternative i must exceed a minimum threshold level to be included in the consideration set. From a modeler's perspective, the consideration utility (S_{it}^h) and the cut-off value (Θ) are observed indirectly with some error ξ_{it}^h. These errors are independent, identically distributed (iid) draws from the Type I extreme value distribution. Under these distributional assumptions, the probability that consumer h includes an alternative in the consideration set is given by:

$$\pi_{it}^h = \frac{1}{1 + \exp(\theta - s_{it}^h)} \quad \text{for } i = 1, \ldots, I \tag{4.2}$$

with

s_{it}^h = the consideration utility of alternative i for consumer h at time t

θ = the threshold level

Our first modification of Bronnenberg and Vanhonacker's model ensures that items not available in the virtual store can not be considered (or chosen). To this end, in line with Campo et al. (2003), we take an out-of-stock item out of the consideration set (equation 4.2) with an item stock-out dummy variable (OOS$_{it}$) that equals 1 when item i is not available at time t and 0 otherwise:

$$\pi_{it}^h = \frac{1}{1 + \exp(\theta - s_{it}^h)} * (1 - OOS_{it}) \tag{4.3}$$

Note that the structure of the choice probability (equation 4.1) guarantees that alternatives that are not on the shelves (i.e. have a degree of consideration equal to 0), can not be chosen (i.e. have choice probabilities equal to 0).

Second, the *consideration utility* s_{it}^h is based on differences in prominence across alternatives:

$$s_{it}^h = \omega_{lp}LP_{it}^h + \sum_A \omega_A OOS_{A,it} + \omega_{Sugg}SUGG_{it}^h + \omega_{Hpsugg}HPSUGG_{it}^h \qquad (4.4)$$

where

LP_{it}^h = last purchase dummy variable (equal to 1 when alternative i was last purchased by consumer h at the previous purchase occasion, 0 otherwise)

A = set of attributes relevant to the product category

$OOS_{A,it}$ = stock-out asymmetry variable for attribute A (equal to the number of items similar to i on attribute A that are out-of-stock in t)

$SUGG_{it}^h$ = suggestion dummy variable (equal to 1 when alternative i is suggested as a replacement item to consumer h at time t, 0 otherwise)

$HPSUGG_{it}^h$ = higher price suggestion dummy variable (interaction term, equal to 1 when alternative i is suggested as a replacement item to consumer h at time t and alternative i is of a higher package-equivalent price than the stock-out alternative, 0 otherwise)

ω_{lp}, ω_A, ω_{Sugg}, ω_{Hpsugg} = coefficients to be estimated

The salience or prominence of alternatives is not only influenced by the recency of purchase (Bronnenberg and Vanhonacker, 1996), it should also incorporate several out-of-stock-affected heuristics.

First, it was shown in chapter 2 (section 2.5.2) that the prominence of an available alternative is a function of how similar that item is to out-of-stock items (measured by the similarity on attributes such as brand, taste, type and/or package size). It has been shown by previous research that stock-outs might produce disproportionate shifts in attention to items that are similar on important attributes (Campo et al., 2003). Consumers might decide to focus on specific attributes in an attempt to facilitate the replacement decision while keeping substitution risks low (e.g. focus on brand as a risk-reducing tactic). For this reason – and because stock-outs may force consumers who do not normally switch items to select another product – the relative importance of product attributes may not be the same as in regular choice environments. To this end, we incorporate stock-out asymmetry variables per attribute, which are set equal to the number of items that are out-of-stock in t and similar to the considered item on attribute

A (Campo et al., 2003). A positive (negative) coefficient would point to an increase (decrease) in the degree of consideration of alternatives that have attribute levels similar to out-of-stock alternatives (cf. Campo et al., 2003). Using a count-based definition for the stock-out asymmetry variables captures the fact that multiple stock-outs 'aggravate' the consumers' feeling of disruption and enhance their recourse to heuristics. The count-based definition, therefore, takes into account that, when more items with the same focal attribute(s) are out-of-stock, consumers pay greater attention to remaining items with similar attributes. As a robustness check, we tested several alternative stock-out asymmetry definitions: (i) using weighted stock-outs instead of counts (taking into account that there might be a relation between the preference/loyalty of a consumer and the way they react) and/or (ii) 'normalizing' the asymmetry variables with respect to the number of stock-outs to values between zero and one. These alternative variable definitions did not change the substantive results and did not provide a significant increase in model fit[8].

Second, the increase in consideration probability for items that are suggested in the context of a replacement policy must be incorporated. The size of this increase is moderated by whether the replacement item has a higher price or not: recommending a higher-priced replacement item makes the retailer look suspicious and causes a reactance-style response (i.e. switching away from the recommendations). Hence, we expect a positive coefficient for the suggestion (hypothesis H_3) but a negative one when suggestions are higher-priced (hypothesis H_4).

Finally, the *choice utility* u_i^h is a function of long-term preference components that represent the base preference toward alternative i (Bucklin and Gupta, 1992; Bucklin, Gupta and Siddarth, 1998; Wu and Rangaswamy, 2003):

$$u_i^h = \sum_A \sum_{l \in L_A} \alpha_{A,l} * D_{A,l,i} + \alpha_{loy} Loy_i^h \qquad (4.5)$$

where

L_A = index set of levels relevant for attribute A

---

[8] It should be noted that adopting weights implies a marginal increase in overall goodness-of-fit. Yet, this comes at the cost of face validity – attribute constants in the choice model becoming highly unstable. A possible reason is the fact that – to some extent – the weights contain duplicate information. Indeed, even the simple count model already leads to large share increases for items more similar to higher-share stock-outs (i.e. stock-outs with more appealing attributes) due to the inherent structure of the choice model. Our data set does not seem able to disentangle more refined (weighted) effects from those already incorporated in the simple count model.

$D_{A,l,i}$ = attribute-level dummy variable (equal to 1 if alternative i is characterized by level l on attribute A, 0 otherwise)

Loy_i^h = loyalty (equal to the initial preference share of consumer h for item i)

$\alpha_{A,l}$, α_{loy} = parameters to be estimated

Rather than using product-specific intercept terms, we model consumer preferences over the attributes that represent the SKUs in a product category (and therefore only indirectly model preferences for SKUs themselves)[9] (cf. Fader and Hardie, 1996; Ho and Chong, 2003). We also include a loyalty variable defined as a consumer-specific (long-term) preference share measure. Hereto, we relied on question 5.e/f of the post-purchase questionnaire where consumers were asked to indicate the % that every product they bought during traditional shopping trips in the last 12 months takes in the total shopping basket (see appendix 3.A, post-purchase questionnaire). As such, the loyalty variable is more related to the concept of the initial preference share measure (cf. Ailawadi, Gedenk and Neslin, 1999; Wu and Rangaswamy, 2003) rather than the exponentially smoothed measure of Guadagni and Little (1983)[10].

4.3.2 Incidence model

Purchase incidence or the probability that consumer h will purchase in a category on a given purchase occasion t (PI_t^h) is modeled as a binary logit model (see e.g. Bucklin et al., 1998; Bucklin and Lattin, 1991):

$$PI_t^h = \frac{\exp(W_t^h)}{1 + \exp(W_t^h)} \tag{4.6}$$

The category purchase utility for consumer h at time t, W_t^h, is written as:

$$W_t^h = \gamma_0 + \gamma_{CR}CR^h + \gamma_{INV}INV_t^h + \gamma_{CV}CV_t^h + \gamma_{nv}NVPOL_{nv,t}^h \tag{4.7}$$

where

CR^h = rate of category consumption for household h

---

[9] Because price did not change in our experiment and is largely captured by the attributes that describe an SKU, we did not incorporate any price variable in the choice utility function. Estimation of a model incorporating both SKU attribute constants and price indeed led to serious estimation problems caused by extreme collinearity between both sets of variables.

[10] The lack of dynamics in our loyalty definition reduces the correlation with the last purchase variable, comprising only 0.610 for margarine and 0.435 for cereals.

INV_t^h = in-home inventory (mean-centered[11]) for household h at time t

$\rightarrow INV_t^h = INV_{t-1}^h + N_{t-1}^h - CR^h$

INV_0^h = in-home inventory level at the start of the purchase simulations

N_{t-1}^h = number of units bought by consumer h in t-1

CV_t^h = category value for household h at time t

$NVPOL_{nv,t}^h$ = non-visible out-of-stock policy dummy variable (equal to 1 when consumer h has been exposed to an out-of-stock policy where stock-outs are not visible at first sight and when there were stock-outs at time t, 0 otherwise)

γ_0, γ_{CR}, γ_{INV}, γ_{CV}, γ_{nv} = coefficients to be estimated

The purchase utility W_t^h is a function of traditional consumer characteristics affecting incidence. In our research, we include a consumer's category consumption rate and his/her in-home inventory level (based on data from the pre-purchase questionnaire). Next, we specify the purchase utility as a function of the attractiveness of the product category. In the literature, the category value is defined as the expected highest utility available to consumer h from buying a brand in the category at time t (e.g. Bucklin and Gupta, 1992). Mathematically, the category value is given by the log of the denominator of the choice probability (equation 4.1) (Ben-Akiva and Lerman, 1985; see for applications: Bucklin and Gupta, 1992; Bucklin et al., 1998):

$$CV_t^h = \ln\left(\sum_j \pi_{jt}^h \exp(u_j^h)\right) \qquad (4.8)$$

This category value concept integrates choice model information in the incidence model, making purchase incidence probabilities dependent on expected choice outcomes (cf. Bucklin et al., 1998). In our case, category value varies between purchase occasions (only) as a result of out-of-stock (policy) effects because other category characteristics like price and promotion are held constant throughout the experiment. As can be seen from equations 4.2-4.5 and 4.8, category value will be lower (i) when more products are unavailable and (ii) when more favorable/preferred products are

---

[11] Mean-centering indicates that the household's inventory level in the category at time t (INV_t^h) is subtracted by the mean of INV_t^h for household h ($INVM^h$). By mean-centering in-home inventory, we ensure that the values of the inventory level are closer to the centre. The rationale for mean-centering is two-fold. First, mean-centering helps to reduce scale differences between the inventory variable and the other variables. Second, mean-centering makes sure that the inventory variable captures changes in time for a specific consumer and not cross-sectional differences between consumers.

unavailable (see e.g. Broniarczyk et al., 1998; Campo et al., 2000). As a result, the purchase incidence decision will be more severely affected when *more* – or *more preferred* products – are unavailable (or otherwise said: when less acceptable replacement items are available) (cf. chapter 2, section 2.5.2). Conversely, proper suggestions for replacement items may limit this decrease in CV. A *positive* CV-coefficient in the incidence equation would thus imply that stock-outs – especially of preferred products – reduce the probability that a consumer purchases from the category[12]. Favorable effects of suggestions will carry through to the purchase incidence level via this positive CV-coefficient as well (hypothesis H_2: $\gamma_{CV} > 0$), while unfavorable effects are expected to negatively moderate this effect (hypothesis H_4).

Finally, in order to find out how the non-visible policy affects the incidence decision, we incorporate a non-visible stock-out policy dummy variable in the equation. The coefficient of this dummy variable is expected to be negative, pointing to a reduced likelihood of a category purchase when customers are confronted with a non-visible stock-out policy (hypothesis H_1)[13].

4.3.3 Estimation approach

We use the maximum likelihood procedure to jointly estimate the model parameters of the incidence and two-stage choice models. In order to incorporate heterogeneity in out-of-stock (policy) and other reactions, we use a latent class approach (cf. Bronnenberg and Vanhonacker, 1996; Campo et al., 2003; Wu and Rangaswamy, 2003). We specify the parameters of the incidence model (γ's in (4.7)) and of the two-stage choice model (θ in (4.2), ω's in (4.4) and α's in (4.5)) at the segment level. Let $\psi(s)$ denote the relative size of segment s and W(s) the purchase utility (see equation 4.7), $\pi(s)$ the degree of consideration (see equation 4.3) and u(s) the choice utility (see equation 4.5) of segment s. Segment-level parameters of the incidence and two-stage choice model can be estimated using the following likelihood function:

---

[12] To check whether the CV variable can fully capture the negative effects of stock-outs on purchase incidence, we also estimated a model with a CV ánd an aggregated stock-out variable. The latter could capture additional psychological effects of the service failure, over and above the decrease in category attractiveness. Yet, inclusion of the aggregate stock-out variable did not significantly improve model fit.

[13] As a robustness check, we also considered testing whether the inclusion of the number of clicks had a significant moderating impact on the non-visible policy. However, such a test did not reveal very meaningful because most consumers typically clicked on at most one stock-out item per week. Only a minority of consumers had to click on more than two items to find a suitable and available alternative.

$$LL = \sum_h \ln \sum_s \Psi(s) \prod_t \left\{ (PI_{t|s}^h)^{y_t^h} * (1 - PI_{t|s}^h)^{(1-y_t^h)} * \prod_i \left[p_{t|s}^h (i|incidence) \right]^{y_{it}^h} \right\} \quad (4.9)$$

where $PI_{t|s}^h$ is given by equation 4.6, $p_{t|s}^h (i|incidence)$ is given by equation 4.1, y_t^h is equal to 1 if consumer h has made a purchase in the category at time t and 0 otherwise and y_{it}^h is equal to 1 if consumer h chooses alternative i at time t and 0 otherwise.

4.4 EMPIRICAL STUDY

In this section, we briefly look at the parts of the experimental design that are relevant for this research. Next, we discuss the overall estimation results. We end by specifically testing and interpreting the stock-out policy effects.

4.4.1 Experimental data

Subjects were randomly assigned to one of the three different out-of-stock policies: (1) *no-replacement* with out-of-stocks *visible* on the screen, (2) no-replacement with out-of-stocks *not visible* on the screen (only after clicking), (3) *replacement* with variations of the suggested substitution products according to different attributes (see for more information, chapter 3, section 3.2.3.2)[14]. The dataset contained 17 SKUs for margarine and 46 SKUs for cereals. For these analyses, the net sample is equal to 584 respondents. 473 (414) respondents completed the purchase simulations for margarine (cereals), leading to 2493 (2443) purchase occasions for margarine (cereals). The first week is used as an initialization week. Therefore, model estimation is based on weeks 2 to 6.

As a manipulation check, we look, per stock-out policy, at the number of respondents that have noticed that some of the products were temporary unavailable (see table 4.1). For both categories, the number of people that have noticed stock-outs is significantly smaller for a non-visible policy compared to a policy where stock-outs are immediately visible. Second, compared to a (visible) no-replacement stock-out policy, consumers exposed to a replacement policy (where a substitution product is put in place for each stock-out product) are less likely to see stock-outs. This is in line with our expectations.

---

[14] In this research, we focused on the assortment extended by brands and limited our analyses to this subset. We further pooled the data for the verbal and pictorial mode as well as for the brand and flavor organization. As a robustness check, we tested for differences between the verbal and pictorial mode and the brand and flavor organization. These more refined analyses did not reveal any significant differences. Therefore, we decided to proceed with the complete, pooled, dataset. In addition, we pooled the brand- and flavor-focused replacement policy as we did not find any significant differences between them.

Table 4.1: Number of respondents that noticed temporary unavailability

	Visible, no-replacement	Non-visible	Replacement
Margarine	69.70%	27.35%	47.60%
Cereals	68.60%	28.57%	49.31%

4.4.2 Estimation results

Models are estimated for a varying number of classes and re-estimated using different sets of starting values[15]. Both the BIC and CAIC measures (Leeflang et al., 2000) indicate that a two-segment model better fits the data than a single-segment and a three-segment model, for margarine as well as cereals (see table 4.2). The criteria also reveal that the two-stage model outperforms a simple (one-stage) MNL model (that includes the same variables as the two-stage model) in both categories. Separating out the consideration decision (affected by stock-outs and stock-out policy) from the final choice decision improves the models' descriptive validity[16]. We therefore retain the two-segment, (simultaneous incidence and) two-stage choice models for both categories.

Table 4.2: Goodness-of-fit (BIC, CAIC-statistics) for simultaneous incidence and choice models (margarine and cereals)

	Margarine				Cereals			
	Simultaneous with two-stage choice			Simult. with 1-stage choice	Simultaneous with two-stage choice			Simult. with 1-stage choice
Seg	1	2	3	2	1	2	3	2
LL	-0.0816	**-0.0759**	-0.07358	-0.07961	-0.04625	**-0.0454**	-0.04467	-0.0462
BIC	7174	**6960**	7025	7296	11011	**10857**	10971	10988
CAIC	7198	**7009**	7099	7249	11064	**10912**	11051	10941

Table 4.3 presents the parameter estimates for the two-segment models, for margarine as well as for cereals.

---

[15] Due to the conditioning of the dataset and the large number of SKUs in the cereals category, we used a two-step approach for this category. In a first step, we estimate the model with a given threshold (the value of the threshold was determined on the basis of prior research (Bronnenberg and Vanhonacker, 1996) and the results of margarine). In a second step, we re-estimate the value of the threshold, given the parameter estimates. We repeated this procedure using the parameters of the previous iteration as starting values until the change in log-likelihood value was smaller than 0.01%.

[16] As an additional check, we also re-estimated the one-stage (simple MNL) and the two-stage (consideration and choice) models on a smaller estimation sample comprising (1) only the first five weeks of the data set (except the first, initialization, week) and (2) a subset (approximately 85%) of (randomly selected) households. We then compared the models' performance on a holdout sample containing respectively (1) observations from week six and (2) the subset (approximately 15%) of the remaining households. For both checks, the two-stage model is found to substantially outperform the one-stage model in terms of predictive validity, for cereals as well as margarine.

Table 4.3: Estimation results for the simultaneous incidence and two-stage choice model

Variable	Margarine segment 1	Margarine Segment 2	Variable	Cereals segment 1	Cereals segment 2
CONSIDERATION SET FORMATION MODEL					
Stage 1: Consideration set formation			**Stage 1: Consideration set formation**		
Brand asymmetry	1.0982***	0.4657*	Brand asymmetry	-0.1449	0.5742***
Size asymmetry	-0.0819	0.0536	Taste asymmetry	0.0297	0.2029***
Suggestion	1.3789***	-0.0864	Type asymmetry	0.0987	0.0871
Suggestion (higher price)	-1.0449 (1)	0.2404 (1)	Suggestion	0.5663**	0.4169
Last purchase	2.9992***	1.4677**	Suggestion (higher price)	-0.3645 (1)	-0.0200 (1)
Threshold	6.5874	4.3681	Last purchase	-0.7793***	5.0513***
			Threshold	3.9994***	3.1230***
Stage 2: Item selection			**Stage 2: Item selection**		
Brand			**Brand:**		
Alpro	0.0401	0.1059	Nestlé	-0.5482*	-0.0350
Belolive	-0.4608*	0.0502	Others†	-1.4213***	-0.1869
Benecol	-1.0809***	-0.2695*	Private label	-0.7564***	-1.3670***
Bertolli	0.1344	0.1585	**Taste:**		
Delhaize	0.3347	-0.5428*	Nature	0.3004	-0.1821
Derby	0.2182	-0.0193	Honey	0.4555*	0.3816**
Effi	-0.2363	-0.2499	Fruit	0.1924	0.4692***
Planta	-0.2634	-0.1657	Mixed	0.3117	-0.1041
Roda	-0.8718*	-1.1981**	**Type:**		
Solo	-0.7633**	-0.3191*	Corn	0.6428**	0.7944***
Vitelma	0.2149	0.0493	Wheat	0.4643*	-0.4210**
Size:			Filled	-0.0499	-2.2536***
Large size	-0.6637**	-0.5334***	Muesli	0.7959**	0.4631***
Loyalty	2.6845***	3.2386***	Crunchy	0.6679***	-0.4613***
			Mixed	0.2945	-0.2826
			Variety	-0.0073	-0.2033
			Loyalty	9.1276***	1.8783***
PURCHASE INCIDENCE MODEL					
Constant	-0.6695	0.7010	Constant	-1.2369***	-0.2465
Category consumption	0.6273***	0.9740***	Category consumption	1.6876***	0.3324***
Inventory	-2.2610***	-0.0979**	Inventory	-1.0835***	-0.1415***
Non-visible policy	-0.2540**	-0.1798	Non-visible policy	0.1320	-0.1972**
CV	0.1254**	0.0808	CV	-0.0501	0.0592
Heterogeneity, relative size	67.35%	32.65%	Heterogeneity, relative size	42.04%	57.95%

† We decided to collapse some low-share cereal items (e.g. Breakfast Club, Jordans, Weetabix) because of estimation reasons. Yet, they are uniquely defined through the use of the other (taste/type) attributes.

(1) Because this is a moderating effect, the approach of Jaccard, Turrisi and Wan (1990) must be adopted. Applying their rule indicates that higher-priced suggestion items have a significant moderating effect in the first segment of margarine and in the first segment of cereals. In both segments, the (main, positive) suggestion effect is no longer significant when higher-priced replacement items are suggested.

*** = sign. at 1% level; ** = sign. at 5% level; * = sign. at 10% level (1-tailed significance test)

At the consideration set level, we expect a positive effect of the last purchase variable on consideration utility when behavior is of the reinforcing type (cf. enduring set; Roberts and Lattin, 1991) and a negative one when behavior is of the variety-seeking type (cf. McAlister, 1982) (Bronnenberg and Vanhonacker, 1996). Whereas the margarine category is typically characterized as a category where consumers tend to repurchase the same product, the cereals category is more likely to be characterized as a category with variety-seeking respondents (Campo et al., 2003; Roberts and Lattin, 1991). Our results reflect these category differences: we found 2 segments with a positive last purchase coefficient in the category of margarine and 1 segment with a negative (i.e. variety-seeking behavior) and 1 segment with a positive (i.e. reinforcing behavior) last purchase coefficient in the category of cereals. The results of table 4.3 also show that short-term preferences in the consideration stage are different from long-term preferences in the choice stage. Although respondents of the first segment of cereals tend to switch away from the previously purchased item (negative effect of last purchase), they have stable (long-term) preferences within a set of alternatives (positive effect of loyalty) (Bronnenberg and Vanhonacker, 1996). The constants for each attribute (brand, taste, type and/or size) reflect the difference in attractiveness (on the item selection level) with respect to a reference item.

At the incidence level, the coefficients of the category consumption rate and the in-home inventory level are both strongly significant and in the expected directions. The consumption rate has a positive significant effect, while the inventory level has a negative significant effect for both categories in all segments. For example, consuming one extra unit of margarine in the first segment positively influences incidence utility in the category: +0.6273 (statistically significant at the 1% level), while the inventory level has a negative impact on incidence utility: -2.2610 (statistically significant at the 1% level).

Concentrating on stock-out effects, we find that, for the two categories under consideration, switching to one of the remaining alternatives is the predominant reaction. This result is in line with observed stock-out responses in offline stores (see chapter 2, section 2.2.1). Moreover, we find significant out-of-stock asymmetry effects in one of the two segments for both categories. For margarine, consumers of segment 1 are more likely to consider alternatives of the same brand (positive, 1%-significant

ω_{brand} coefficient of 1.0982). For cereals, consumers of segment 2 are more likely to consider alternatives of the same brand and/or taste (positive, 1%-significant ω_{brand} and ω_{taste} coefficients of 0.5742 and 0.2029 respectively). These results are comparable to findings for the same categories in a traditional store setting (Campo et al., 2003).

The reduction in category attractiveness caused by out-of-stocks – and reflected by a decrease in category value – has a significant negative effect on purchase incidence decisions only for the first segment of margarine (captured by the 5%-significant effect of the category value parameter, 0.1254). For the other segment and the cereals category, changes in category value have no significant effect on purchase incidence probabilities. Research in a brick-and-mortar setting has shown similar findings: the number of consumers that canceled or switched stores in these categories being rather low (Campo et al., 2000). Besides, as indicated in chapter 2, a number of online grocery characteristics further intensify the probability to select another alternative instead of deciding not to make a purchase in the category.

In the next paragraphs, we first discuss the formal hypotheses test of the stock-out policy effects and then look at the consequences of actively pursuing a stock-out policy.

4.4.3 Test of the stock-out policy hypotheses

Impact of the non-visible policy. In support of H_1, we find that not showing stock-outs has a significant and negative impact on purchase incidence probability for the majority of margarine buyers (γ_{NV} = -0.2540, p<0.05 in segment 1 representing 67% of the sample) and more than half of the cereal buyers (γ_{NV} = -0.1972, p<0.05 in segment 2 representing 58% of the households). Households in the remaining segments do not react negatively to the non-visible policy. One possible reason is that these households, despite the random assignment of stock-outs and households, simply faced fewer stock-out encounters. To check this, we computed the average number of stock-outs seen by households in the non-visible policy condition that had an intention to buy from the category (clicked on at least one item), before they either successfully purchased or decided to cancel planned purchases. This number is not significantly different between segments that do and do not buy less under the non-visible policy, indicating that the difference in response is not an 'artifact' of the experimental set-up. What we *do* find is that the negative policy reaction occurs among consumers that tend to repurchase the same item (segments with a strong positive impact of the last purchase variable). For these habitual buyers, the false expectations of being able to buy their favorite products – created by the non-visible policy – may reinforce the loss they experience when they find out that their preferred item is unavailable after clicking.

Impact of the replacement policy: main effect. To assess the significance of the main and moderating effect of the replacement policy on choice, we use the approach outlined in Jaccard, Turrisi and Wan (1990). Starting with the main effect of the replacement stock-out policy, we find that the suggestion of a replacement item has a significant and positive impact on the consideration utility of that alternative, for one of the two segments in both categories. Table 4.3 reveals a positive effect of 1.3789 (significant at 1%) for the first segment of margarine (67%) and a positive effect of 0.5663 (significant at 1%) for the first segment of cereals (42%). As hypothesized in H_3, consumers in these segments are significantly more likely to consider (and hence select) an alternative when it was suggested than when it was not. Especially consumers who find the product category less important (lower ratings on importance scales, $p<0.05$, lower consumption rates, $p<0.05$) appear to appreciate the retailer's guidance[16]. For these segments, suggesting a substitute item also tempers the decrease in category attractiveness (CV) caused by out-of-stocks. Yet, as indicated in the previous section, changes in category value only carry through to incidence probabilities for the first segment of margarine. It follows that the replacement policy only has a limited effect on purchase incidence decisions, providing partial support for hypothesis H_2. A possible explanation is that equation (4.7) only allows for indirect effects of suggestions on category purchase, through the CV variable. As a robustness check, we therefore ran a model where a replacement policy dummy was added to equation (4.7) to capture influences of the replacement policy on incidence directly. However, in neither

---

[16] The segment analysis revealed a significant difference on the variety seeking tendency with respect to segment-differences for the non-visible policy and on the product usage rates (pre-purchase questionnaire, question 4) and product importance (post-purchase questionnaire, question 2) with respect to segment-differences for the replacement policy. Other factors characterizing consumers' behavior (the selected package size, the tendency to select private labels and the presence of favorite items in the assortment) or other questions of the pre- (question 3: time pressure and shopping frequency) and post-purchase questionnaires (question 2: item loyalty and acceptable alternatives available, question 3: perceived assortment variety and ease of processing and question 4: satisfaction with purchase decisions) did not significantly explain segment differences for the two stock-out policy reactions.

category/segment did the replacement policy dummy reveal significant, leaving conclusions unchanged.

Impact of the replacement policy: moderating effect of a higher-priced suggestion. Based on the results in table 4.3 and using the approach of Jaccard et al. (1990), we find that the positive impact of the replacement policy on consideration is no longer significant when the suggestion is a higher-priced item[17]. Hence, in both categories, the positive consideration (and choice) effect of the suggestion is neutralized when a replacement item with a higher price is suggested. It follows that, in the margarine category where the replacement policy has a significant main effect on incidence, this positive effect is nullified when higher-priced replacement items are suggested (support of hypothesis H_4).

4.4.4 Consequences of the stock-out policy

In order to assess the overall consequences of the adopted stock-out policy, we use the actual purchase data as a simulation basis. We start by calculating the choice and incidence probabilities for a base scenario, i.e. a scenario where all the stock-out products are visible and no suggestions are made. Next, we change the setting by introducing (1) a non-visible dummy variable (non-visible stock-out policy) and (2) suggestion dummy variables for (non-suspicious) replacement items (replacement stock-out policy) and recalculate the incidence and choice probabilities in these new settings. Table 4.4 reports the average changes[18] in incidence and choice probability in the new settings compared to the base setting, for margarine as well as for cereals.

---

[17] In the model presented here, the suggestion is considered as 'higher priced' as soon as its price per volume-unit (say, ounce) exceeds that of the stock-out item. We also considered alternative operationalizations, where (i) the price difference was required to exceed a (10% and 15%) threshold, or where (ii) the comparison was between package (instead of volume-unit) prices. The substantive results remained unaltered: significant and negative moderating effects nullifying the positive impact of the suggestion.

[18] Note that we portray relative instead of absolute changes. Relative changes are percentage changes between two settings of interest and are calculated by dividing the absolute change or difference with the value of the base setting. In contrast, we could also portray absolute changes which are simply defined as the value of the initial (base) setting minus the value of the other (focal) setting. Both approaches are correct (as they compare the same numbers). We decided to focus on the relative measures as they control for the scale dimension, making comparisons between the two product categories easier.

Table 4.4: Average changes in incidence and choice probabilities (relative to the base setting) from changes in the stock-out policy (actual data set)

	Margarine			Cereals		
	Seg 1	Seg 2	Total	Seg 1	Seg 2	Total
Non-visible policy						
- change in incidence probability	-10.48%	n.s.	-5.04%	n.s.	-8.21%	-4.74%
(Non-suspicious) replacement policy						
- change in choice probability of the <u>suggested</u> item	64.03%	n.s.	45.59%	42.93%	n.s.	15.83%
- change in incidence probability	0.79%	n.s.	0.38%	n.s.	n.s.	n.s.

n.s. = not significant

In addition, to obtain better insights into the mechanisms underlying the changes in category and item purchase decisions, we derive analytical expressions for the stock-out effects under different policies.

Impact of the non-visible policy. Compared to the visible/no-replacement policy, a non-visible stock-out policy was expected and found to reduce the consumers' tendency to buy in the category (see H_1 and section 4.4.3). The results reported in table 4.4 indicate that the non-visible policy leads to a non-negligible decrease in category purchase incidence in both categories. The purchase probability drops by 10.48% and 8.21% for margarine and cereals, respectively, in the segments where a significant response is noted. These figures represent a 5.04% and 4.74% decrease for the market as a whole.

As can be seen from equation 4.10 (see appendix 4.B for more details on the derivation of this expression), the decrease in incidence probability (ΔPI) strongly depends on the parameter γ_{NV} :

$$\Delta PI = \frac{PI|0 - PI|\Delta pol}{PI|0} = 1 - \frac{1}{e^{-(\gamma_{NV})} * (1 - PI|0) + PI|0} \tag{4.10}$$

where $PI|0$ is the purchase incidence probability when consumers are exposed to the benchmark policy (visible, no-replacement) and $PI|\Delta pol$ is the purchase incidence probability when the policy changes to a non-visible policy. Larger values of γ_{NV} (in absolute terms) will lead to stronger reductions in purchase rates, and hence to larger retailer losses. In other words, the more clicking on phantom items in vain frustrates consumers, the larger the reduction in category purchases will be, compared to the visible stock-out policy. From the estimation results reported above, we know that this will especially be the case when consumers are strongly attached to their favorite item. At the same time, equation (4.10) indicates that the effect will be smaller for consumers with strong initial purchase intentions (high $PI|0$). This makes intuitive sense: consumers with high purchase needs (high usage rates, low inventories) are less likely to be put off by the non-visible policy.

Impact of the replacement policy. Based on the estimation results, suggesting a replacement item may affect incidence as well as choice decisions. The simulation results reported in table 4.4 show that, on average, the choice probability of the suggested alternative, within the segments where the replacement policy is significant, increases dramatically. The likelihood that a suggested item is chosen, increases on average with 64.03% (margarine, segment 1) and 42.93% (cereals, segment 1) as compared to the visible/no-replacement policy. Looking at the implications at the market level (both segments), the average increase in choice probability of the suggested item still amounts to 45.59% (margarine) and 15.83% (cereals). Despite the large effects on the choice probability, the incidence probability is only marginally affected in the margarine category (increase of 0.7% for segment 1; increase of 0.38% for the whole market) and not affected at all in the cereals category.

Equation 4.11 provides more detailed insights into the underlying mechanisms (see appendix 4.B for derivations). The change in **choice probability** when item i is suggested ($p_i|S$) compared to when it is not suggested ($p_i|NS$) is equal to:

$$\frac{p_i|S - p_i|NS}{p_i|NS} = \frac{1}{\left[\pi_i|S + (1 - \pi_i|S) * \exp(\omega_{Sugg})\right]^{-1} * (1 - p_i|NS) + p_i|NS} - 1$$

(4.11)

A first important conclusion that can be derived from equation 4.11 is that the increase in choice probability for suggested items will be smaller for items that already received a high degree of consideration. Second, the increased attention for suggested items will only translate into substantial increases in choice probability when the items' intrinsic value is sufficiently high. Note that these insights would not be revealed if a one-stage choice model would be used, which could lead to an over- or underestimation of the suggestion effect, depending on the estimated coefficients of the suggestion effect for the one-stage compared to the two-stage model (as explained in appendix 4.B). To illustrate these implications, we use a hypothetical example described in table 4.5.

Table 4.5: Changes in incidence and choice probabilities when a replacement item is suggested (hypothetical example)[19]

	Item selection				Category
	A	B	C	D	purchase
Panel (a) Regular choice environment					
Degree of consideration	0.69	0.4	0.69	0.85	
Choice utility	0.18	0.74	0.74	0.6	
Choice probability	18%	18%	31%	33%	
Incidence probability					57%
Panel (b) Disrupted choice environment (stock-out of D)					
Choice probability	27%	27%	47%	0%	
Incidence probability					55%
Panel (c) Suggesting replacement items for the out-of-stock item					
Degree of consideration if item is suggested	0.90	0.72	0.90	0	
Choice utility	0.18	0.74	0.74	0.6	
Choice probability if item is suggested (others not)	32%	40%	53%	0%	
Incidence probability if item A is suggested					56%
Panel (d) Effect of replacement policy					
Δ in consideration probability if item is suggested (others not)	30.2%	81.7%	30.2%		
Δ in choice probability if item is suggested (others not)	20.5%	49.0%	14.2%		
Δ in incidence probability if item A is suggested (others not)					0.4%

Consider an assortment of 4 items (A, B, C and D) with 'regular' choice probabilities (no disruptions) as defined in panel a. Note that alternatives A and B have the same choice probability but differ in their degree of consideration and choice utility. In comparison with B, A has a high degree of consideration and a low choice utility. Alternatives B and C, in contrast, have the same choice utility, but different degrees of consideration (C has a higher degree of consideration than B). To isolate the effects of the out-of-stock policy, we assume that there are no differences between the items in asymmetric switching effects.

---

[19] Based on expressions (4.11) and (4.12). In this example, we do not take the effects of asymmetric switching into account. As an example, we take the coefficient of the suggestion/category value variable of segment 1, margarine (see table 4.3): 1.3789 and 0.1254, respectively.

Suppose alternative D is out-of-stock. Panel b of table 4.5 shows the change in choice probabilities for the remaining alternatives if no suggestions are made. Items with the same prior choice probability (A and B) lever up to the same point. Yet, this is no longer true with a replacement policy. Panel c reports the choice probability for each item when it is the suggested alternative for item D. Comparing the change in choice probability for items B and C indicates that the suggestion works better for alternatives with a low degree of consideration (item B). In line with this, among items with the same prior propensity of being chosen (A and B), the effect of the suggestion is far more pronounced for the low consideration, high utility item (B)[20]. Although consideration and choice utility of alternatives will often be closely and positively related, low consideration items may have high choice utilities in some cases. For instance, in case of cereals, consumers are not very likely to take private label products into consideration because of the dominance of strong market leaders. Yet, these low-consideration items are often a very close copy of the market leaders' product variants and, therefore, typically have a high intrinsic utility[21].

Purchase incidence effects of the replacement policy ($PI|\Delta pol$) – compared to the benchmark (visible, no-replacement) policy ($PI|0$) – are given by the following expression (see appendix 4.B for derivations):

$$\Delta PI = \frac{PI|0 - PI|\Delta pol}{PI|0} = 1 - \frac{1}{e^{-(\gamma_{CV}\Delta CV)} * (1 - PI|0) + PI|0} \qquad (4.12)$$

Equation 4.12 demonstrates that a replacement policy will reduce the negative effect of stock-outs on purchase incidence decisions when (i) suggesting a substitute leads to a lower decrease in category attractiveness (ΔCV; see appendix 4.B), and (ii) decisions to make a purchase in the category more strongly depend on category attractiveness (γ_{CV}). The estimation results discussed in section 4.4.2 indicate that the second condition is not satisfied for the categories under study. Only for one segment of the margarine category, a significant yet small effect of CV on incidence probabilities is observed.

---

[20] Note that, compared to a two-stage model, a one-stage model can lead to serious biases of the suggestion effect. Indeed, in the one-stage model, items with the same prior choice probability (A and B) would obtain the same gain from being suggested irrespective of the underlying consideration and intrinsic choice utility (see appendix 4.B for example).
[21] Incorporating the moderating effect of private-label suggestions in our model, confirmed this. Suggesting a private label item resulted in an increase in the degree of consideration and, therefore, in choice probability of the suggested, private label item.

This explains why the replacement policy has no (cereals) or only a very limited (margarine) effect on purchase incidence decisions.

4.5 DISCUSSION AND LIMITATIONS

In this research, we investigated how online purchase incidence and choice decisions are affected by the retailer's stock-out policy. The results of the incidence and two-stage choice models indicate that the adopted stock-out policy has a significant impact on whether consumers make a purchase in the category or not, and if so, what they buy. Our findings have important policy implications for retailers.

First, we find that a non-visible policy, where consumers only become aware of a stock-out when they click on the product to purchase it, reduces the probability of purchasing in the category for the majority of consumers. Furthermore, our results point out that consumers reach their point-of-frustration very quickly, even after one or a few clicks – a remarkable finding as groceries typically are a category where many alternatives are offered. Consumers clearly prefer to know the real assortment they can choose from upfront. A retailer who masks his stock-out problems evokes negative consumer reactions, resulting in reduced purchase rates. An interesting observation is that, in both product categories, especially consumers who tend to repurchase the same item react negatively to the non-visible policy. These consumers, in fact, face a 'double-jeopardy' effect. First, given their stronger preference to stay with the same item, unavailability of this favorite item creates confusion and intensifies the reduction of the assortment's appeal. Second, because they typically repurchase the same product and hence, have little experience with other alternatives, identifying a suitable replacement item is a more difficult and risky task for these consumers. Our results suggest that online retailers that use a typical online environment characteristic such as the pop-up to reduce the prominence of stock-outs make consumers refrain from purchasing, and maybe even renege from buying in the online store altogether.

Second, we find that suggesting a replacement item, in general, dramatically increases the consideration and choice probability of the suggested item for a large number of consumers. These consumers are more likely to consider – and hence select – the suggested item (cf. Senecal and Nantel, 2004). In contrast to findings of Beuk (2001) who was not able to find a significant effect of the suggestion in a traditional, brick-and-mortar store (cf. Verhoef and Sloot, 2005), we do find that online retailers (or manufacturers in their role of online category captains) have opportunities to re-direct choices in case of a stock-out situation, by suggesting appropriate replacement items. The fact that we do find significant effects can be partly explained by differences between the online and offline environment, such as the increased presence of a suggestion on a (small) computer screen (more eye-catching) or the convenience-driven motivation to shop online (more likely to adopt task-simplifying decision rules). What is more, in contrast with Beuk (2001), we also explicitly test the boundary conditions (limits) of the suggestion effect. For one, our results indicate that consumers can not be lured into purchasing more expensive items. When consumers become suspicious of the retailer's fairness, the positive effects of the suggestion cancel out. Second, suggesting a replacement item affects its choice probability through an increase in consideration utility rather than a change in intrinsic utility. It follows that suggesting an item as replacement will have little effect if that item does not really appeal to consumers. Third, the change in choice probability also depends on the item's initial consideration utility. More specifically, items that would otherwise have a low probability of being considered as a substitute have more to gain from being suggested than items that are already highly salient without the suggestion. The appropriateness of a replacement item should be evaluated with a link to the objectives of the retailer (e.g. improving the relationship with specific manufacturers, focusing on margin/profit, raising the share of the private label, …). For cereals, for instance, the private label item often constitutes a valuable substitute. For one, while the consideration utility of a private label item may remain low until 'forced' into the consumers' consideration set, its choice utility is typically high as retailers practically duplicate the national brands' cereals assortment. As such, consumers tend to appreciate a private label suggestion. In addition, suggesting private label items is also for (online) retailers useful as these items often have a higher margin.

A somewhat surprising finding is that stock-out-related changes in the assortment's appeal, as captured in the 'category value' variable, have only a limited to no effect on the consumers' propensity to buy from the category. No effects are found for cereals and only small effects are found for margarine. This also implies that the replacement policy does not significantly improve purchase incidence. This might be linked to the categories under consideration. Previous research has shown that the number of consumers that cancel or switch stores is rather low in these categories (Campo et al., 2000). What is more, finding no results for the category of cereals might be caused by the large assortment and the variety-seeking tendency in this category. Consumers are more likely to find and select an acceptable available alternative in the category, thereby limiting the impact of stock-outs and the stock-out policy on the incidence decision. Besides, being confronted with an online stock-out strengthens the propensity to choose another alternative instead of deciding not to buy in the category as the online environment substantially decreases the costs of searching a substitute (see chapter 2, section 2.3 for more details). Yet, finding small or no effects on incidence might also be partially explained by the experimental design that was used in our research. Although we explicitly and repeatedly stressed that respondents were not obliged to purchase during a specific week and could, in such a situation, leave the store without any problems, we can not completely exclude that the lack of impact on category purchase incidence is also partly a result of the artificial setting.

In sum, our results demonstrate that online retailers can guide a consumer's choice in a stock-out situation by adopting a replacement policy but that they should be careful in the selection of the suggested replacement item. Second, the results indicate that the stock-out reaction may be more negative when customers become skeptical about the retailer's stock-out policy (hiding stock-outs or suggesting higher-priced options as a retailer-enriching strategy). Taken together, the findings clearly reveal that consumers value and reward an open and honest retailer, i.e. a retailer who puts all his cards on the table and truly helps the consumer in making an easy and effortless decision. These observations are consistent with other research findings. Fitzsimons and Lehmann (2004), for instance, found that recommendations aimed at facilitating the online search process are generally highly appreciated, except when dubious recommendations are made. In line with customer relationship marketing principles, this confirms that a customer-oriented stock-out approach will benefit both the retailer and consumer.

Obviously, our research has several limitations and provides guidelines for future research. First, as mentioned in chapter 3, using an artificial setting (e.g. no real budget or time constraint, lack of competitive context and clutter/other disruptions, no real consumption, fixed shopping frequency, lack of personalized shopping list) might result in biases (Campo et al., 1999; Swait and Andrews, 2003). Therefore, doing the research in a virtual store 'in real time' would be a valuable extension. Moreover, because of the experimental design, we only had a small number of observations per respondent and were not able to take dynamic effects into account. Yet, recent literature has shown that stock-outs might have an impact on the purchase incidence and choice decision in post-out-of-stock periods (cf. Campo et al., 2003).

Second, we only focused on a limited set of the various stock-out policies that online retailers can adopt. Investigating and comparing other stock-out policies (such as shelf rearrangements, suggesting several replacement items or combining the non-visible and replacement policy) might be an interesting topic for future research. What is more, our results reveal that an online retailer might have other possibilities to introduce a particular product in a consumer's consideration set during a stock-out as well as during a non-stock-out situation. For instance, attaching a promotional tag or using a striking color might bring specific products to the attention of consumers and might increase their choice probability. Investigating if and how such other 'merchandising variables' or alternative 'marketing strategies' work, might be a topic worth investigating in future research.

Third, we did not explicitly test whether fairness procedures are really underlying the suggestion of higher-priced replacement items. Although there are a number of (theoretical) indications that seem to suggest that the principle of justice is closely related to the suggestion of higher-priced replacement items, the lack of a manipulation check is an important limitation of this research. Future research could explicitly test which mechanisms are underlying revealed purchase behavior.

Fourth, our results apply to grocery e-tailers and not necessarily to all online e-tailers. Investigating the impact of a replacement policy in another (non-frequently purchased goods) environment might be a useful extension. For instance, whereas we found negative moderating effects of higher-priced items, up-selling might pay off in a non-frequently purchased goods setting. In such a setting, consumers might consider the high-price justified for more valuable substitute products.

Fifth, in this research, we used the generally accepted 8% as the baseline stock-out level. Although this figure appears to be representative for most grocery stores, it could be interesting to examine whether and how stock-out policy reactions change with higher stock-out rates (especially for the non-visible policy).

Sixth, it should be noted that this research, at the moment, is not normative and allows to investigate different scenarios at most. Given a specific assortment/segment, we can estimate the impact of the non-visible or replacement policy on incidence and choice probability. Future studies could, for instance, investigate the appropriateness of a replacement item with an explicit link towards possible retailer objectives.

Finally, broadening the scope by incorporating more (grocery) categories or investigating the effect of stock-out policies for the (online) store as a whole might be a valuable extension for future research.

CHAPTER 5: THE VISUAL SALIENCE OF A PRODUCT IN AN ONLINE STORE[1]

THE IMPACT OF THE VIRTUAL SHELF PLACEMENT ON ONLINE CHOICE DECISIONS

INTRODUCTION

According to the Point of Purchase Advertising Institute, almost 80% of the consumers tend to choose an alternative at the point of purchase (POPAI, 2001). Although the figures reported by POPAI tend to be rather high because of the methodology[2] they use, there is a general belief that the in-store environment does have an important influence on actual shopping behavior for a significant number of consumers (cf. Chandon, Hutchinson and Young, 2001; Chandon, Hutchinson and Young, 2002; Sloot, 2001). The in-store environment becomes especially important when consumers show a low level of involvement with the decisions and have to make numerous decisions on a single shopping trip (cf. Drèze, Hoch and Purk, 1994; Hoyer, 1984). In a world where supermarket shelves are cluttered with hundreds of alternatives, all begging for attention, retailers and manufacturers spend increasing amounts of money and effort to gain consumers' interest in front of the shelf (e.g. through package design, point-of-purchase displays, shelf placement,...) (Chandon, et al., 2001; Chandon, et al., 2002; Pieters and Warlop, 1999; van der Lans, 2002). Retail practices as well as academic research illustrate that traditional retailers (sometimes driven by manufacturer's requests) try to manage their shelves as efficiently as possible in order to increase sales and profit (e.g. planograms[3] such as Apollo (IRI) and Spaceman (Nielsen); Campo and Gijsbrechts, 2005; Corstjens and Corstjens, 1995; Desmet and Renaudin, 1998; Drèze et al., 1994; Simonson and Winer, 1992).

---

[1] Part of this chapter appeared in Breugelmans, E., K. Campo, and E. Gijsbrechts (2007). Shelf sequence and proximity effects on online grocery choices, *Marketing Letters,* 18 (1-2), 117-133.
[2] POPAI asks shoppers, during an entry interview, what they are planning to buy on the next shopping trip (explicit shopping list). After the shopping trip, POPAI conducts an exit interview where the real purchases of the shoppers are noted. Using such an explicit shopping list might result in biases as some consumers tend to use the shelf to remember their needs (i.e. using the store and shelves as a mental shopping list). Biases might further result because many people know which item they want to purchase but not necessarily mention it on their shopping list (mentioning the product category, e.g. coffee, on the shopping list instead of the brand, e.g. Douwe Egberts, one wants to select) (Sloot, 2001).
[3] A planogram is a diagram generated by photographs, computer output, or artists' renderings that illustrates exactly where the retailer should place every SKU (Levy and Weitz, 1995).

With the start of the Internet-hype, it was suggested that shelf management in a virtual store was no longer an issue. Indeed, the shelf space was no longer a constraint for online stores (cf. Alba et al., 1997; Häubl and Trifts, 2000) and the convenient arrangement of the products on a small computer screen reduced the shelf placement problem (cf. Bakos, 1997; Menon and Kahn, 2002). This seems to suggest that there exists no such thing as a battle for virtual shelf space, making slotting fees and the role of category captains in an online supermarket unimportant. Yet, after the Internet-bubble more realistic sounds indicated that online stores do face (their own) shelf management problems. Although online stores are not restricted by the limitations of physical store space, they do have 'screen space' constraints. In addition, information acquisition patterns (captured, for instance, by eye-movements) have shown that the position/placement of stimuli in a medium (e.g. on a website) might have a significant effect on consumer's attention and, resultantly, on choice behavior (e.g. Ansari and Mela, 2003; Gallagher, Foster and Parsons, 2001; Lohse and Wu, 2001).

Our research taps into the issue of virtual shelf management by investigating the impact of (1) the location of the products within a display (visibility, placement as such) and (2) product adjacencies (proximity, placement relative to other items) on online choice decisions. Whereas the visibility-effect might be present in every choice occasion, the proximity-effect is particularly important in an out-of-stock situation. Being confronted with a stock-out, consumers tend to be fixated on a particular section of the shelf. When deciding which of the remaining alternatives they want to purchase – if any (cf. Campo, Gijsbrechts and Nisol, 2000; Sloot, Verhoef and Franses, 2005), they are more likely to focus on that part of the shelf. Up till now, little research has investigated how virtual shelf placement affects routinized choice decisions in an online grocery context and how disrupting events, like stock-outs, can strengthen the impact of virtual shelf placement as a simplifying decision rule. An exception is the study of Kucuk (2004) who investigates the effect of shelf placement on stock-out reactions in a traditional supermarket. In this study, shelf placement did not have any significant effect. Yet, consumers were *asked* whether they would switch to an alternative that had a prominent place on the traditional shelf or that they saw first (proximate to the out-of-stock item). Research to date, however, has shown that most people claim not to be affected by contextual factors but – in practice – do become prey to the steering power of these variables (cf. impact of the background of an online store on purchase behavior: Mandel and Johnson, 2002; cf. impact of (web)atmospherics on purchase behavior: Baker et. al. 2002; Bellizzi, Crowley and Hasty 1983; Spangenberg, Crowley and Henderson, 1996; Yalch and Spangenberg 1990).

Next to studying the effects of virtual shelf placement on online choice decisions, we also investigate if and to what extent these virtual shelf placement effects are strengthened in larger compared to smaller assortments. Traditional literature has suggested that consumers are more responsive to the in-store environment in case of large assortments. Offering a large number of items hinders consumers to obtain a clear and complete overview as the entire assortment is no longer within the limits of the 'eye-field' and increases the search time, costs and effort needed to select and find a suitable (replacement) item. Consumers are therefore more likely to adopt simplifying heuristics, such as in-store related tactics, in large assortments (Campo and Gijsbrechts, 2005; Hoyer and Cobb-Walgren, 1988; van der Lans, 2002).

Our research generates insights into the question whether (and how) virtual shelf placement is (unconsciously) used by consumers as a task-simplifying heuristic, in regular as well as disrupted (by stock-outs) online choice environments. These results help online retailers to better manage existing virtual shelves and, thereby, help them to improve their performance (e.g. by shifting consumers to higher margin items such as private labels). They also allow category managers to identify the 'promising areas' of the virtual shelf. This helps them to better allocate the allowances/fees they pay to a retailer and, thereby, ultimately helps them to improve their brand's sales potential.

In the next section, we indicate why the placement of products on the shelf/screen is also important in a virtual store and derive hypotheses regarding virtual shelf placement effects (visibility and proximity). To test our hypotheses, we use data coming from a tightly controlled yet realistic online grocery shopping experiment. The experimental design and the methodology used to test our hypotheses are described in section 5.2. In section 5.3, we discuss the results of our online shopping experiment for two categories: margarine and cereals. We end by summarizing the major findings of our research.

5.1 HYPOTHESES

In this paragraph, we investigate how virtual shelf placement influences choice decisions in an online grocery store. In contrast with the previous chapter (out-of-stock policy effects), we focus on the choice (item selection) decision only, for two reasons. First, shelf placement is typically considered as an in-store tactic that might be used by a retailer to guide (choice) decisions from consumers once they are in the store (e.g. Drèze et al., 1994). Second, the results of the previous chapter have shown that there is no or only a small effect of stock-outs on the category purchase incidence decision.

In the first section, we briefly review the shelf management decisions for traditional supermarkets and counter the claims/expectations that virtual shelf management is not or of minor importance in e-grocery stores. Next, we formulate hypotheses regarding the impact of virtual shelf placement (absolute and relative to others) on online choice decisions. In the third section, we hypothesize and discuss how these effects might be moderated by assortment size.

5.1.1 Why should shelf management matter in an online store?

One of the aspects that shelf management encompasses is the space allocation problem, i.e. the optimization of the retailer's allocation of scarce shelf space among a set of alternative products. Both the space allocated to the product category and the number of facings assigned to a specific alternative need to be determined (Buttle, 1984; Corstjens and Doyle, 1981). A second decision for shelf managers is related to the shelf organization problem. This involves decisions such as placing products on eye-level, top or bottom shelf, left or right side, next to a familiar or unfamiliar brand, next to a high-market or low-market share brand (Buttle, 1984; Kahn and McAlister, 1997).

Research in traditional grocery supermarkets has shown that both space and placement have a significant impact on attracting consumers' attention and, thereby, affect their choices. First, it is generally agreed that more space (hence more facings) increases the visibility of an alternative and its purchase probability (cf. positive own space elasticity effects; Bultez and Naert, 1988; Campo and Gijsbrechts, 2005; Corstjens and Corstjens, 1995; Desmet and Renaudin, 1998; Drèze et al., 1994). Second, it has been shown that the way products are positioned on a shelf has an important impact on the necessary effort to search for an item and, therefore, influences the final choice of a consumer. In the literature, there is a general consensus that products which are positioned at eye- (or hand-) level are more visible and generate the best results (e.g. Buttle, 1984; Campo and Gijsbrechts, 2005; Chandon et al., 2001; Corstjens and Corstjens, 1995; Drèze et al., 1994).

In contrast, new Internet-based consumer business models have suggested that shelf management is no or a negligible problem in an online shopping environment. First, the Internet alleviates the space constraint. While floor/shelf space is often the scarcest resource for offline retailers (e.g. Corstjens and Doyle, 1981; Drèze et al., 1994), the Internet proposes new opportunities for online retailers as the shelf space in a virtual store is in principle unlimited/endless[4] (cf. Alba et al., 1997; Häubl and Trifts, 2000). *"Brick-and-mortar stores must carefully determine which products from which brands to give precious shelf space, but online sellers can carry a practically unlimited collection of products"* (Center for Competitive Analysis, 2000). Second, an online store typically uses only one reference per product, making the 'number of facings-problem' a non-issue. Third, studies investigating the online environment have shown that electronic shopping lowers search costs. Search costs decrease as a result of the convenient arrangement of the products on a small computer screen, eliminating the need to physically move when comparing products (e.g. Bakos, 1997; Childers, et al., 2001; Lynch and Ariely, 2000; Menon and Kahn, 2002; see also studies using/investigating computer-simulated shopping experiments: Burke et al., 1992; Campo, Gijsbrechts and Guerra, 1999). Also the flow/pleasure resulting from surfing on the Internet tends to lower perceived search costs (e.g. Hoffman and Novak, 1996; Smith and Sivakumar, 2004). As a result, consumers would be able to consider/compare more alternatives and identify/purchase alternatives that better match their needs (Bakos, 2001). In sum, these online expectations seem to point out that shelf management decisions – as known in the traditional supermarket – are less valid for online stores. *"The new supply chain can be rebuilt to bypass parts of the current structure such as the shelves of the supermarket"* (Department of Commerce, 1998 cited in Yrjölä, 2001).

---

[4] As indicated previously, the availability of an unlimited virtual shelf space is only valid with respect to the communication function of the e-channel. From a stock-management/distribution point of view, the e-channel does impose limits with respect to the availability of alternatives (physically stocking products).

Recently, however, more realistic arguments point out that a virtual store does face its own shelf management problems. First, although the whole virtual shelf space is in principle endless, the 'screen space' is not. Because the amount of information that can be presented on a single screen is limited, virtual stores often are forced to use several screens to present their products. As a result, online consumers only see a fraction of all the alternatives at once and have to make an effort to see the other products. Second, the communication literature has shown that the position/placement of, for instance, advertisements in newspapers, magazines, yellow pages or store flyers and on a web page (e.g. banner ads) might have a significant effect on consumer's attention and, resultantly, on choice behavior (e.g. Fangfang and Shyam, 2004; Gallagher et al., 2001; Gijsbrechts, Campo and Goossens, 2003; Lohse, 1997; Lohse and Wu, 2001; Rossiter and Percy, 1997; Wedel and Pieters, 2000). Similar positioning effects might be at stake in an online store. Some products might be more visible than others, depending on their position/placement on the virtual shelf. Third, traditional shelf literature has recently shown that it is not the total organization of the shelf but proximity that matters (cf. Hoch, Bradlow and Wansink, 1999), a notion also relevant in a virtual supermarket. These arguments indicate that the sequence/position of the products on a computer screen (the virtual shelf placement) is a valid and important problem for online retailers.

Two online grocery shopping characteristics might further intensify the use of virtual shelf placement as a task-simplifying heuristic. First, as was shown in chapter 1, shoppers using online grocery shopping services typically are more convenience-oriented (e.g. Andrews and Currim, 2004; Keh and Shieh, 2001; Morganosky and Cude, 2002) and are, therefore, more likely to adopt simple tactics (McGree and Boyer, 2005). Second, while search costs 'as such' might be lower in online than in traditional stores, online assortments are often larger in size because of the unlimited/endless shelf space (e.g. Anckar, Walden and Jelassi, 2002; Verhoef and Langerak, 2001). As shown in chapter 2, consumers typically face information acquisition and processing limitations (see e.g. Manrai and Andrews, 1998; Mehta, Rajiv and Srinivasan, 2003; Roberts and Lattin, 1991; Siddarth, Bucklin and Morrison, 1995; Wu and Rangaswamy, 2003). When consumers expect large search costs, they are more likely to turn to task-simplifying heuristics from the start. Therefore, it is highly unlikely that consumers look through the complete assortment when selecting a (replacement) product in an online virtual store (Shankar, Smith and Rangaswamy, 2003; Wu and Rangaswamy, 2003).

So, despite previous claims indicating that shelf management might not be of great importance in online stores, we argue that online retailers face opportunities to influence consumer's choices by better managing their shelves. What is more, shelf might be even a more active marketing mix instrument for online retailers than for traditional ones as they can far more easily change it[5]. Despite the potential importance and possibilities of online shelf management, up till now, influences of virtual shelf placement on online choice decisions have not been investigated systematically in an online (grocery) context.

5.1.2 The impact of the virtual shelf placement on online choice decisions
In this section, we discuss how the placement of products on a virtual shelf might affect customer's attention and, hence, choice. We focus on virtual shelf placement as such (captured by the visibility-effect) and virtual shelf placement relative to other alternatives (captured by the proximity-effect). We first formulate hypotheses regarding the visibility-effect and then turn to the proximity-effect.

5.1.2.1 Visibility-effect
The visibility-effect stems from the fact that online retailers are often forced to use more than one screen to present their products. This is a direct shelf effect that might occur at each choice occasion as long as more than one screen is needed to present the products. In analyzing the impact of the first-screen on item selection, we draw on two streams of literature: the traditional shelf placement literature and the communication literature that focuses on the position of a stimulus in the medium. In both streams of literature, the prominence as well as the primacy of the stimuli in the medium are specified as important characteristics that influence consumer's attention and – therefore – choice.

---

[5] On many e-commerce sites, also consumers have the possibility to sort the alternatives according to specific attributes – thereby changing the placement of the products on the shelf (see e.g. Netgrocer, Peapod). Yet, the issue of shelf placement remains important because (1) the position of products within each sorting option remains a relevant question. Indeed, a retailer faces multiple possibilities to position products on a screen, despite the chosen attribute along which the shelf is sorted. For instance, in a shelf sorted by brand, a retailer can decide to start with listing/grouping their own (private label) products before alternatives of competitors or doing the reverse. In addition, (2) as sorting tends to be limited (see e.g. Wu and Rangaswamy, 2003), the default/start option (i.e. the option that is selected by the retailer when a consumer logs in), and hence the placement of products within this option, is of high importance.

First, it has been shown that stimuli placed at more prominent (eye-catching) positions are more likely to attract a consumer's attention and trigger (re)actions. Traditional shelf literature has shown that items that 'stand-out' on the (physical) shelf are more likely to be chosen. For instance, a product that is positioned at a highly-visible shelf place (such as eye-/hand-level) will experience an increase in salience and – as a result – in choice probability (Chandon et al., 2001; Corstjens and Corstjens, 1995; Drèze et al., 1994; Nedungadi, 1990; Simonson, 1993). Also communication literature has shown that the prominence of advertisements and featured promotions in a medium (e.g. magazines, newspapers or store flyers) has a significant impact on subsequent (choice) behavior (e.g. Gijsbrechts et al., 2003; Lohse, 1997; Lohse and Wu, 2001; Rossiter and Percy, 1997). Advertisements that are shown on prominent places, such as the first (cover) or last (back) page of a newspaper, magazine or store flyer are more likely to attract consumer's attention and have a positive effect on the choice probability of the featured product (Gijsbrechts et al., 2003; Griffith, 1990; Rossiter and Percy, 1997).

Second, it has been shown that stimuli that are seen earlier (primacy-effect) have a greater probability to be chosen. Traditional shelf research has shown that choices are influenced by the point of shelf entrance (i.e. the starting point from which the shelf is approached). Consumers walk through a store and approach most shelves either from the left or the right side. Broere, Van Gensink and Van Oostrom (1999) found that alternatives at the beginning of the shelf (seen from the entrance point of the shopper) have a 15% greater chance to be chosen than alternatives at the end of the shelf (Sloot, 2001). The importance of the serial position on the attention-catching and action-triggering ability is also recognized in the communication literature (e.g. Finn, 1988; Hanssens and Weitz, 1980; Holbrook and Lehmann, 1980; Hoque and Lohse, 1999; Lohse, 1997; Lohse and Wu, 2001; Pieters and Bijmolt, 1997). In an advertising context, there is strong support for a primacy as well as for a recency effect on consumer's *memory* for brands. Advertisements that are in earlier and later positions of a sequence are generally remembered better than advertisements in the middle position (print media: Wedel and Pieters, 2000; TV advertisements: Pieters and Bijmolt, 1997; Floor and van Raaij, 1998). Yet, when consumers have to make a (low-involvement) choice decision, they tend to stop searching as soon as they find a satisfactory product. Findings in the communication literature confirm that the primacy effect prevails in a situation where consumers have to select one of the stimuli. Hoque and Lohse (1999) found that consumers exposed to an electronic yellow directory are more likely to select a firm cited on the first screen. Also evidence from search engines indicates that firms pay large up-front payments to procure top placement in the results of search engine queries (e.g. Lohse and Wu, 2001). Most users typically limit their attention to the top 10 websites in the list (i.e. those presented on the first page) and only 1% goes beyond the third page of the search engine list (Zhang and Dimitroff, 2005).

Both arguments are at play for items that are shown on the first screen in an online grocery shopping service. First, first-screen products are more prominent for the consumer and, therefore, are more likely to be noticed and selected. Second, consumers start to acquire and process information from the first screen and tend to stop as soon as they find a satisfactory product. Both arguments indicate that consumers are unlikely to exhaustively scan the complete product offer. Hence, we expect that alternatives that are offered on the first screen will receive greater attention and are more likely to be chosen than alternatives that are not offered on the first screen.

H_1: Consumers are more likely to select an alternative that is more visible (i.e. offered on the first screen).

5.1.2.2 Proximity-effect

The proximity-effect focuses on the 'nearness' of other products within a small section of the screen and therefore might be at play even if all products are offered on a single screen. Simonson and Winer (1992), for instance, provided evidence of a proximity effect on the tendency to seek variety. They found that consumers who were asked to make a number of purchases at one time (simultaneous decisions) were more likely to select a variety of flavors from the favorite brand on a shelf where alternatives of the same brand were located next to each other compared to a shelf where alternatives of the same flavor were located next to each other. This shows that consumers in a by-brand organization tend to fix their eyes on the shelf section of their favorite brand and are more likely to stay within that part of the shelf. The effort that is required to identify and compare flavors of other brands is much higher, making consumers less likely to seek variety in the brands selected.

In this research, we focus on consumers that were planning to buy a stock-out product. Once consumers have spotted their favorite item and noticed that it is unavailable, they tend to become fixated on that part of the shelf (e.g. Morales et al., 2005; Russo and Leclerc, 1994; Simonson and Winer, 1992; van der Lans, 2002). As consumers are more influenced by local than by non-local information, we expect that consumers confronted with an out-of-stock situation for their favorite item are more likely to direct their attention to (and, hence, select) products close to this item rather than distant ones (cf. Hoch et al., 1999; Pieters and Warlop, 1999; Simonson and Winer, 1992).

H$_2$: When confronted with an out-of-stock situation, consumers are more likely to select items that are proximate (i.e. located next) to the out-of-stock item.

5.1.3 The moderating impact of assortment size
As mentioned in chapter 1, online retailers have the possibility to offer a larger product assortment. We expect that consumers are more likely to turn to task-simplifying tactics, such as the visibility and proximity heuristic, in a large than in a small assortment. Searching for a (replacement) product in a large assortment is more complex (information overload) and requires more time and effort (increase in search cost) than searching for a (replacement) product in a small assortment (De Clerck et al., 2001; Huffman and Kahn, 1998; Hoch et al., 1999; van Ketel, van Bruggen and Smidts, 2003).

First, compared to the first-screen alternatives, search costs tend to be larger for alternatives that are presented on (one of) the following screens (cf. Hoque and Lohse, 1999; Lohse, 1997; Lohse and Wu, 2001). As a result, the first-screen effect (given that more than one screen is needed to present the products) is more important for a large compared to a small assortment. Consumers that anticipate assortments covering many screens, are more likely to renounce from a full search and settle for a first screen alternative right away. Second, the proximity-effect might come into play even when only one screen is needed to present the products. Yet, we expect that consumers are more susceptible to the proximity heuristic when they expect a large assortment as the effort that is required to identify and compare other (distant) replacement products is higher in a large than in a small assortment. In sum, when consumers know (from earlier purchase occasions where they were confronted with the offered assortment) or suspect (from past category experiences) a large assortment, they are more likely to select a 'satisfying' product on the first screen and, in case of a stock-out, tend to switch to proximate items rather than to distant ones.

H$_3$: The visibility (first screen) effect is stronger for a large than for a small assortment.
H$_4$: The proximity (located next to out-of-stock items) effect is stronger for a large than for a small assortment.

5.2 METHODOLOGY

In this section, we first (briefly) discuss the experimental design. Next, we indicate how shelf placement effects, the effects of assortment size and household heterogeneity can be incorporated. We end by discussing the estimation procedure.

5.2.1 Experimental data

We manipulated shelf placement (visibility and proximity) through changes in the shelf organization. We used two different shelf organizations (either by brand or by flavor) at the start instead of randomizing the products. Depending on the organization of the shelf, other alternatives were presented on the first screen and adjacent products differed. The shelf organization was made as realistic as possible and the assignment of products on the virtual shelf was irrespective of the product's success (e.g. market share). Therefore, there was no systematic link between a specific product and its place/position on the virtual shelf (see chapter 3, section 3.2.3.3 and appendix 3.B). In order to make the online shopping task as realistic as possible, we did not force the shelf organization upon consumers. Instead, consumers were offered the ability to change the shelf organization (although few did). To control for allocation biases, we controlled the default presentation layout, i.e. the layout that consumers saw first and that was set by the online retailer/researcher (see chapter 3, section 3.2.4).

With respect to the manipulation of assortment size, we explicitly took into account that retailers can enlarge their assortment along different attributes. For instance, retailers can decide to add new flavors of existing brands or new brands of existing flavors. In this research, subjects were randomly assigned to one of three different assortments: (1) a limited assortment, (2) an assortment extended with flavors and (3) an assortment extended with brands[6] (see for more information, chapter 3, section 3.2.3.4). We focused on the brand and flavor attributes as previous research has indicated them as the two most important attributes for consumers when evaluating the assortment (Boatwright and Nunes, 2001). Table 5.1 summarizes the attribute levels for each assortment for the 2 categories under consideration and indicates, per assortment, the number of alternatives, respondents and purchase occasions. We also indicate whether or not more than one screen was needed to present all the products. When consumers wanted to examine alternatives that were not shown on the first screen, they could scroll to the next screen (thus having a 'smooth' transition between the different screens). Because the first week is used as an initialization week, consumers could have expectations about assortment size (and the number of screens) in advance. Model estimation is based on weeks 2 to 6.

Table 5.1: Attributes levels for each assortment (margarine and cereals)

	MARGARINE		
Attribute	**Assortment 1 (limited)**	**Assortment 2 (add new flavors of existing brands)**	**Assortment 3 (add new brands of existing flavors)**
Brand	Becel control	Becel control	Becel control
	Benecol	Benecol	Benecol
	Delhaize margarine	Delhaize margarine	Delhaize margarine
	Derby	Derby	Derby
	Effi	Effi	Effi
	Roda	Roda	Roda
	Solo	Solo	Solo
	Vitelma	Vitelma	Vitelma
			Add new brands: * Alpro * Belolive * Bertolli * Planta
Flavor		Add minarine: * Becel, essential * Becel, pro-active * Benecol, light * Delhaize, minarine * Vitelma, minelma	
# alternatives	11	19	17
# respondents	113	120	100
# purchase occasions	296	289	279
# screens needed	< 1	> 1	> 1

---

[6] In this research, we focused only on those respondents that were exposed to a visible, no-replacement stock-out policy and limited our analyses to this subset. Within this stock-out policy, each stock-out item was accompanied with an indication that it was currently unavailable. Consumers could thus clearly see which of the products were unavailable.

	CEREALS		
Attribute	**Assortment 1 (limited)**	**Assortment 2 (add new flavors of existing brands)**	**Assortment 3 (add new brands of existing flavors)**
Brand	Kellogg's Others[†]	Kellogg's Others[†]	Kellogg's Others[†]
			Add new brands: Private label Nestlé
Flavor	Nature Choco Honey	Nature Choco Honey	Nature Choco Honey
		Add new flavors: Sugar Health	
# alternatives	21	32	46
# respondents	93	100	89
# purchase occasions	334	268	287
# screens needed	> 1	> 1	> 1

[†] We decided to collapse some low-share cereal items, such as Breakfast Club, Jordans and Weetabix, into one category because of estimation reasons. Yet, they are uniquely defined through the use of the other (taste/type) attribute variables.

5.2.2 Model formulation

To test the impact of shelf placement on item selection, we use the traditional multinomial logit (MNL) model. Due to the conditioning of the dataset and because of the complexity of the model (e.g. simultaneous estimation of three assortments), we decided to use the one-stage MNL model. While the key variables' impact remained very consistent, estimating the two-stage choice model did not improve the results (fit, face validity) and resulted in unstable estimates for other variables[7].

In this section, we initially make abstraction of assortment differences, discussing a 'general' choice model, valid for each of the three assortments separately. Next, we discuss pooling issues and indicate how we take household heterogeneity into account. We refer to appendix 5.A for an overview of the variables used in the final model estimation.

5.2.2.1 Choice model structure

---

[7] Estimation problems especially arose for the parameter estimates of the threshold and the last purchase variable.

For this project, we use the approach of Campo, Gijsbrechts and Nisol (2003). They adjust the traditional MNL-model such that items that are not available in the virtual store can not be chosen:

$$p_{it}^h = \frac{\exp\left[\mu(u_{it}^h)\right]*(1-OOS_{it})}{\sum_{j \in C}\exp\left[\mu(u_{jt}^h)\right]*(1-OOS_{jt})} \quad \text{for } i \in C \tag{5.1}$$

with

p_{it}^h = the choice probability of alternative i for consumer h at time t

u_{it}^h = the choice utility of alternative i for consumer h at time t

OOS_{it} = stock-out dummy variable (equal to 1 if item i is out-of-stock, 0 otherwise)

C = set of alternatives among which choice is exercised

μ = Gumbel scale factor

We define the choice utility u_{it}^h of consumer h for alternative i at time t as follows:

$$u_{it}^h = \sum_A \sum_{l \in L_A}\beta_{A,l}*D_{A,l,i} + \beta_{loy}Loy_i^h + \beta_{lp}LP_{it}^h + \sum_A \beta_{A,oos}OOS_{A,it} + \beta_{Vis}Vis_{it}^h + \beta_{Prox}\text{Pr}ox_{it}^h \tag{5.2}$$

with

A = set of attributes relevant to the product category

L_A = index set of levels relevant for attribute A

$D_{A,l,i}$ = attribute-level dummy variable (equal to 1 if alternative i is characterized by level l on attribute A, 0 otherwise)

Loy_i^h = loyalty variable (equal to the initial preference share of consumer h for alternative i)

LP_{it}^h = last purchase dummy variable (equal to 1 when alternative i was last purchased by consumer h at the previous purchase occasion, 0 otherwise)

$OOS_{A,it}$ = stock-out asymmetry variable for attribute A (equal to the number of items similar to i on attribute A that are out-of-stock in t)

Vis_{it}^h = visibility variable (equal to 1 if alternative i for consumer h is shown on the first screen at time t, 0 otherwise)

$\text{Pr}ox_{it}^h$ = proximity variable (equal to the weighted sum of the number of out-of-stock items (i_{oos}) that are positioned next to alternative i at time t for consumer h, with weights equal to the preference of consumer h for the stock-out item ($Loy_{i_{oos}}^h$))

$$\rightarrow \Pr ox_{it}^{h} = \sum_{i_{oos}} Loy_{i_{oos}}^{h} * Adj_{i-i_{oos},t}^{h} \qquad (5.3)$$

with $Adj_{i-i_{oos},t}^{h}$ = adjacent dummy variable (equal to 1 if alternative i is adjacent to

stock-out item i_{oos} for consumer h at time t, 0 otherwise)

$\beta_{A,l}, \beta_{loy}, \beta_{lp}, \beta_{A,oos}, \beta_{Vis}, \beta_{Prox}$ = parameters to be estimated

Like before, we model consumer preferences over the attributes that represent the SKUs in a product category (and therefore only indirectly model preferences for SKUs themselves)[8] (cf. Fader and Hardie, 1996; Ho and Chong, 2003). We also include a consumer-specific (long-term) preference measure (captured by loyalty), as well as a (short-term) purchase event feedback measure (captured by last purchase). It has been shown that incorporating the three phenomena is justified: leaving one out would lead to over-estimation of the other[9] (e.g. Ailawadi, Gedenk and Neslin, 1999).

Next, we take into account that previous research has shown that stock-outs produce disproportionate shifts in attention to items that are similar on important attributes (Campo et al., 2003). Using attributes as cues facilitates the replacement decision while keeping substitution risks low. For instance, consumers may focus on items of the same brand because they expect them to be of the same quality level or buy a product of the same flavor expecting that it will provide similar consumption experiences (see also previous chapter and chapter 2, section 2.5.2). In line with Campo et al. (2003), we incorporate asymmetric switching variables per attribute, which are set equal to the number of items that are out-of-stock in t and similar to the considered item on attribute A[10]. A positive (negative) coefficient would point to asymmetric switching towards

---

[8] As argued in the previous chapter, we did not incorporate any price variable in the choice utility function because price did not change in our experiment and is largely captured by the attributes that describe an SKU.

[9] As in the previous chapter, we used question 5.e/f of the post-purchase questionnaire to construct the loyalty variable (see appendix 3.A, post-purchase questionnaire). As such, loyalty is a consumer-specific (time-invariant) measure that captures the share a product takes in the total shopping basket (i.e. an initial preference share measure). Using a loyalty measure that is constant over time reduces its correlation with the last purchase variable. For this research, the correlation amounts to 0.492 (assortment 1), 0.585 (assortment 2) and 0.560 (assortment 3) for margarine and 0.453 (assortment 1), 0.539 (assortment 2) and 0.431 (assortment 3) for cereals.

[10] The validity of using a count-based definition for the stock-out asymmetry variables was confirmed by the robustness checks in the previous chapter.

(away from) alternatives that have attribute levels similar to out-of-stock alternatives (cf. Campo et al., 2003).

In order to test whether shelf placement (visibility and proximity) are additional, valid heuristics consumers use to simplify their choice decision, we explicitly add shelf placement effects in the choice utility.

To capture absolute shelf placement effects, we include a visibility variable. This variable indicates whether an alternative is offered on the first screen or not. We expect a positive coefficient for the visibility-effect (hypothesis H_1) as first-screen alternatives are more eye-catching and more likely to be selected than alternatives that are not visible at first sight (on one of the following screens). In addition to the first-screen definition that captures the placement of products *across* different screens, we also tested a number of alternative 'on-screen' definitions, capturing the placement of products *on* the virtual shelf/screen. Appendix 5.B describes the different 'on-screen' operationalizations that we tested. Comparing the model fit and face validity for the alternative model estimations revealed that the model where only the first-screen definition was included, outperformed these alternative, more detailed, models.

Next, to capture relative shelf placement effects, we include a proximity variable. This variable determines whether alternative i is positioned next to (one or more) out-of-stock items. In order to take into account that not all stock-out items are noticed by respondents (see e.g. previous chapter and Beuk, 2001), we use the attractiveness (preference) for a stock-out item as weights. More specifically, our weights are based on the loyalty (initial preference share) variables. Because consumers in a stock-out situation are fixated on a small part of the shelf, they are more likely to select one of the adjacent items than to select a distant one. Hence, we expect a positive coefficient for the proximity-effect (hypothesis H_2).

5.2.2.2 Pooling models across assortments

As argued before, consumers are more likely to turn to task-simplifying tactics when they have to search for a (replacement) product in a large compared to a small assortment. We expect differences with respect to the visibility, proximity and asymmetric switching variables[11] between assortments: the effects being (more)

---

[11] Although we did not explicitly include hypotheses with respect to the moderating effect of assortment size on the tendency to asymmetrically switch towards items with specific attributes, it is not

significant in a large than in a small assortment (cf. hypotheses H_3 and H_4). For the remaining model parameters, we use an approach similar to Swait and Andrews (2003) and Andrews and Currim (2002). We estimate unique brand-, size-, taste- and/or type-specific constants (not restricted to be equal across assortments) and a pooled last purchase and loyalty variable (constrained to be identical across assortments, up to a scale factor). The validity of these choices was confirmed by robustness checks that explicitly tested whether variables should be pooled or not. More specifically, the choice probability of alternative i (ignoring household and time indications), per assortment (c = 1, 2 or 3) ($p_i|a_c$) reads as follows:

$$ (p_i|a_1) = \frac{\exp\left[\mu^{a_1}\left(\beta^{a_1}X_i^{a_1} + \gamma V_i\right)\right]*(1 - OOS_i)}{\sum_{j \in C^{a_1}} \exp\left[\mu^{a_1}\left(\beta^{a_1}X_j^{a_1} + \gamma V_j\right)\right]*(1 - OOS_j)} \quad \text{with } i \in C^{a_1} \tag{5.4} $$

$$ (p_i|a_2) = \frac{\exp\left[\mu^{a_2}\left(\beta^{a_2}X_i^{a_2} + \lambda W_i\right)\right]*(1 - OOS_i)}{\sum_{j \in C^{a_2}} \exp\left[\mu^{a_2}\left(\beta^{a_2}X_j^{a_2} + \lambda W_j\right)\right]*(1 - OOS_j)} \quad \text{with } i \in C^{a_2} \tag{5.5} $$

$$ (p_i|a_3) = \frac{\exp\left[\mu^{a_3}\left(\beta^{a_3}X_i^{a_3} + \omega Z_i\right)\right]*(1 - OOS_i)}{\sum_{j \in C^{a_3}} \exp\left[\mu^{a_3}\left(\beta^{a_3}X_j^{a_3} + \omega Z_j\right)\right]*(1 - OOS_j)} \quad \text{with } i \in C^{a_3} \tag{5.6} $$

The three assortments have a common vector $X_i^{a_c}$ (containing last purchase and loyalty), for which the parameter vector is the same across assortments ($\beta^{a_1} \equiv \beta^{a_2} \equiv \beta^{a_3} \equiv \beta$), up to a scale factor. In contrast, the assortments differ in the set of alternatives among which choice is exercised (C's) and the vectors (V, W, Z) containing attribute level, asymmetry, visibility and proximity variables (cf. Andrews and Currim, 2002; Swait and Andrews, 2003; Swait and Louvière, 1993). When estimating the assortments separately, these equations reduce to a traditional multinomial logit model. In this case, the scale parameter (μ^{a_c}) is not identifiable and often implicitly assumed to have a value of 1 (Swait and Andrews, 2003). Yet, when estimating the three assortments simultaneously, the scale parameter becomes

---

inconceivable that a similar logic holds for these asymmetry variables. The probability that consumers will focus on key product attributes as a heuristic to make easy and effortless decisions is more likely in a large than in a small assortment. Not only the size of the assortment, also the composition of the assortment might affect the tendency to turn to specific asymmetric switching heuristics. For these reasons, we decided not to constrain asymmetric switching variables to be equal across assortments. In contrast, the tendency to exhibit loyalty or to repurchase the same item is a personality trait that is expected to be prevalent across assortments (cf. Andrews and Currim, 2002).

important. The scale parameter is known to be inversely related to the variance (Ben-Akiva and Lerman, 1985; Swait and Louvière, 1993). It allows error variances (caused by unobservable/situational factors) to vary across datasets (in our case: assortments) while underlying choice behavior remains identical (Andrews and Currim, 2002; Swait and Andrews, 2003). Hence, differences between scale factors (or precision measures) point to differences in 'fuzziness' (noise) in the decision of a consumer as a result of the data source (in our case: the assortment they were exposed to) (Louvière, Hensher and Swait, 2003). Because it is not possible to identify the scale factor for each assortment separately, we estimate a *relative* scale factor between assortments. In this respect, we normalize the scale factor of the first assortment to one ($\mu^{a_1} = 1$) and empirically estimate the scale factors for the other assortments[12] (cf. Andrews and Currim, 2002; Swait and Andrews, 2003; Swait and Louvière, 1993).

5.2.2.3 Incorporating household heterogeneity

While we are not interested in household-specific coefficients as such, we need to model household heterogeneity in order to avoid parameter biases. To this end, we could use either continuous distributions of heterogeneity (e.g. a random coefficient/mixed MNL model with a normal mixture) or discrete distributions of heterogeneity (e.g. a latent class approach) (Andrews, Ainslie and Currim, 2002). Because we used the latent class approach in the previous chapter, we initially selected the same approach for this chapter as well. Yet, the results of the latent class approach were very unstable because of both the nature of our dataset (multiple assortments with a large numbers of SKUs) and the complexity of our model (simultaneous estimation with a large number of parameters). Therefore, we opted in this chapter for a continuous mixture approach with normally distributed parameter coefficients across households (McFadden and Train, 2000; Train, 2003). Although two different approaches in each of the chapters were used, it has been shown by previous research that both are equally good a recovering heterogeneity (Andrews et al., 2002).

---

[12] For variables that are constrained to be identical across assortments, we have only one (mean) coefficient and do not have independent coefficients per assortment. In order to find the assortment-specific coefficients, we multiply the respective values of the normalized assortment (assortment 1) by the relative scale factor of the other assortments (cf. Andrews and Currim, 2002). For example, let β_{loy} be the coefficient of loyalty for the first assortment, then is $\mu^{a_2}\beta_{loy}$ ($\mu^{a_3}\beta_{loy}$) the coefficient of loyalty for the second (third) assortment.

As suggested by Train (2001), we do not introduce random effects for attribute-specific constants[13] or for parameters that already capture preference heterogeneity in itself such as loyalty (and proximity – because it is weighted with loyalty for stock-out items) (Ailawadi et al., 1999). In our research, we associate independent normal distributions with the last purchase[14], the asymmetry and the visibility variables. For these variables, the parameters estimated in a mixed (random coefficient) logit model are φ, the vector of fixed coefficients, and θ, the vector with parameters that describe the normal distribution (mean, b, and variance, σ^2). Robustness checks explicitly testing whether variables should be fixed or not, confirmed the validity of these choices.

5.2.3 Estimation procedure

We estimate the mixed MNL (MMNL) model through simulated maximum likelihood using the quasi-random Monte Carlo (or Halton) method (Bhat, 2001; Train, 2003). Choice probabilities in mixed logit models take the form of a multidimensional integral and, therefore, do not have a closed form, making it impossible to give an analytical solution. To overcome this, we use the simulated maximum likelihood approach and approximate the integral by using draws from the mixing distribution. Simulation encompasses a number of steps: taking a draw from a density, calculating a statistic for each draw and averaging the results (Train, 2003). Numerous procedures have been proposed in the numerical analysis literature for taking 'intelligent' draws from a distribution rather than random ones (e.g. Bhat, 2001; Train, 1999). One of the procedures that have been shown to take more 'intelligent' draws is the quasi-random (Halton) procedure. Compared to random sequences, Halton sequences reduce the number of draws needed and lower run time and/or simulation error (Bhat, 2001; Train, 2003). We use Halton sequences to draw (independently) values for the normally

---

[13] There are various reasons why we decided to keep the attribute-specific coefficients constant. First, it has been shown that mixed logit models have a tendency to be unstable when all coefficients are allowed to vary (Ruud, 1996; Train, 1999; Train, 2001). Models where all the coefficients varied, did indeed not converge in any reasonable number of iterations. Fixing the attribute-specific coefficients resolved this instability. Second, Train (2001) has indicated that the mixture might be unidentifiable empirically in a model where, next to the final idd extreme value terms, the coefficients of alternative-specific dummies are assumed to be random. Including similar distribution (which is the case for the normal and extreme value distribution) results in unstable estimations because the final idd extreme-value terms in a model with alternative-specific constants already constitutes the random portion of these constants.

[14] For variables that are pooled and normally distributed (in our case the last purchase variable), we only constrain the mean to be equal across assortments. Swait and Andrews (2003) argue that there are no reasons to constrain the dispersion (variance) of normally-distributed variables to be equal across different data sources/assortments.

distributed coefficients (ρ) from the normal distribution $f(\rho|b,\sigma^2)$ for each individual. These values allow us to calculate $p_{it}^h(\varphi,\rho^r)$, the choice probability (equation 5.1), evaluated at φ and ρ^r (the value of ρ at the rth draw). The simulated probability is then the average of these calculated logits of R draws. In this research, we used 100 repetitions[15] (cf. Bhat, 2001; Swait and Andrews, 2003; Train, 2003).

$$\hat{p}_{it}^h = \frac{1}{R}\sum_{r=1}^{R}\prod_{t=1}^{T}\prod_{i=1}^{I}\left[p_{it}^h(\varphi,\rho^r)\right]^{y_{it}^h} \tag{5.7}$$

where

$\hat{p}_{it}^h$ = the simulated choice probability of consumer h choosing alternative i at time t, given φ and θ (the unbiased estimator of the actual choice probability p_{it}^h)

$p_{it}^h(\varphi,\rho^r)$ = probability that consumer h chooses alternative i at time t, conditional on φ and ρ^r, i.e. the value of ρ at the rth draw

y_{it}^h = 1 if consumer h chooses alternative i at time t and 0 otherwise.

R = number of draws

T = number of purchase occasions for that household

I = number of alternatives in choice set

The simulated probabilities are inserted in the log-likelihood function to create the simulated log likelihood:

$$SLL = \sum_{h=1}^{H}\ln(\hat{p}_{it}^h) \tag{5.8}$$

where   H = number of households

The log-likelihood of the joint model (i.e. the model that is simultaneously estimated over assortments) is simply the sum of the mixed multinomial log-likelihoods of each assortment separately because the assortments are independent:

$$SLL = SLL(a_1) + SLL(a_2) + SLL(a_3) \tag{5.9}$$

5.3 RESULTS

---

[15] As a robustness check, we ran a model with 300 draws: results were very similar to results of a model with 100 draws (cf. Bhat, 2001; Swait and Andrews, 2003; Train, 1999).

In this section, we first present some overall estimation results. In a next step, we specifically test and interpret the shelf placement effects and indicate to what extent assortment size moderates these effects. We end by discussing the results of the hypotheses tests.

5.3.1 Estimation results

For each product category, we estimated a standard MNL model as well as a Mixed MNL model. Both the BIC and CAIC measures (Leeflang et al., 2000) indicate that allowing for heterogeneity leads to an improvement in fit, for margarine as well as cereals (see table 5.2). We therefore retain and discuss the mixed multinomial logit model for both categories.

Table 5.2: Goodness-of-fit (BIC, CAIC-statistics) for standard multinomial logit model (MNL) and mixed/random coefficient multinomial logit model (MMNL)

	Margarine		Cereals	
	MNL	MMNL	MNL	MMNL
LL	-0.0469	-0.04547	-0.0415	-0.0401
BIC	3081	**2929**	4989	**4763**
CAIC	3035	**2871**	4940	**4699**

Table 5.3 presents the parameter estimates for the MMNL models, for margarine as well as for cereals. The constants for each attribute (brand, taste, type and/or size) reflect the difference in attractiveness with respect to a reference item (which is the same across assortments in a category). For the variables that are pooled across assortments, the coefficients of assortment 2 and 3 are the same as those presented for assortment 1, up to the scale factor. We can derive these coefficients by multiplying the respective values of assortment 1 with the relative scale factors[16] (cf. Andrews and Currim, 2002). The normally distributed coefficients allow to check whether there is heterogeneity in reaction between households. Three outcomes are possible for normally-distributed variables: (1) the variable does not have a significant effect (no significant mean and standard deviation), (2) the variable has a significant effect but there is no heterogeneity (significant mean, no significant standard deviation) and (3) there is heterogeneity across households (significant standard deviation). In the last case, the estimated mean and standard deviation give information about the share of the households that places a

---

[16] Note that the scale factors in our empirical estimation are relatively close to one. As such, it is not surprising that the results hardly change when they are left out. Yet, a robustness check explicitly testing whether scale parameters should be included or not, confirmed the validity of retaining the scale factors.

positive versus negative value on a coefficient (Train, 2003). Table 5.4 gives an interpretation of the parameter estimates of table 5.3 and indicates for the shelf placement effects (visibility and proximity) the average changes in choice probability that result when shelf placement effects are taken into account compared to a situation where this is not the case.

Table 5.3: Model estimation results [*** = sign. at 1% level; ** = sign. at 5% level; * = sign. at 10% level (1-tailed significance test)]

Margarine

Variable / Scale factor	Assortment 1 (11) [1.00](2)	Assortment 2 (19)	Assortment 3 (17)
Scale factor	[1.00](2)	1.2550***	1.3045***
Mean			
Last purchase	2.0406***	[2.5610***](3)	[2.6620**](3)
Loyalty	2.7312***	[3.4277***](3)	[3.5629***](3)
Brand asymmetry	0.2885	0.3401*	0.5137
Size asymmetry	-0.1112	-0.1036	0.0175
Visibility	(1)	0.3962**	-0.1101
Proximity to oos	0.9980	0.9279**	0.6057
Brand			
Becel, control	0.000 (2)	0.000 (2)	0.000 (2)
Benecol	-0.1549	-0.7576***	-1.1862**
Delhaize, margarine	-0.0370	0.9624***	-0.3222
Derby	-0.6741**	-0.3190	-0.2644
Effi	-0.3352*	0.4312	-0.0276
Roda	-0.4246	0.0751	-1.3863*
Solo	0.2897	0.0098	-0.9399***
Vitelma	0.5099	0.0869	-0.3168
Becel, essential	-	-0.0865	-
Becel, pro-activ	-	-0.0648	-
Delhaize, minarine	-	-0.4502*	-
Alpro			-0.0409
Belolive			-0.4499*
Bertolli			0.0480
Planta			-0.3300
Size			
Small size	0.000 (2)	0.000 (2)	0.000 (2)
Large size	-0.3962	-0.9966***	-0.4227**
Variances			
Last purchase	1.8681***	1.9556***	2.1925***
Brand asymmetry	0.0228	0.0402	0.0773
Size asymmetry	0.0028	0.0143	0.0211
Visibility	(1)	0.1662	0.0215

Cereals

Variable / Scale factor	Assortment 1 (21) [1.00](2)	Assortment 2 (32)	Assortment 3 (46)
Scale factor	[1.00](2)	1.0717***	0.7573***
Mean			
Last purchase	0.6455***	[0.6918***](3)	[0.4888***](3)
Loyalty	5.1643***	[5.5346***](3)	[3.9109***](3)
Brand asymmetry	0.1055	0.6385	0.0969
Taste asymmetry	0.0510	0.2740**	-0.1596
Type asymmetry	0.2887	-0.0552	0.3816**
Visibility	-0.1429	-0.0416	0.6190**
Proximity to oos	1.6748**	0.7445	4.1140***
Brand			
Kellogg's	0.000 (2)	0.000 (2)	0.000 (2)
Others[†]	-0.9314**	-0.1235	-1.2232***
Private label	-	-	-1.7760***
Nestlé	-	-	-1.1367***
Taste			
Choco	0.000 (2)	0.000 (2)	0.000 (2)
Nature	-0.2280	-0.2543	-0.0597
Honey	-0.0404	0.4094*	-0.4073
Sugar	-	0.1515	-
Health	-	0.3499*	-
Fruit			0.3226
Type			
Rice	0.000 (2)	0.000 (2)	0.000 (2)
Corn	0.2059	0.3377	0.9734***
Wheat	-0.7356**	0.3729	0.3231
Muesli	-0.3729	-0.1898	0.6461
Crunchy	-0.4009	-0.1136	-0.5938
Mixed	-		0.6281
Variety	-0.5526*	-0.3201	0.0495
Variances			
Last purchase	3.1542***	0.9718***	2.6386***
Brand asymmetry	0.4950**	0.6364**	0.5193
Taste asymmetry	0.1512	0.1364	0.7050***
Type asymmetry	0.0374	0.4710***	0.4332
Visibility	0.5212	0.1868	0.8247**

† We decided to collapse some low-share cereal items (e.g. Breakfast Club, Jordans, Weetabix) because of estimation reasons. Yet, they are uniquely defined through the use of the other (taste/type) attributes.
(1) In assortment 1 (margarine), all alternatives are shown on the first page. We were therefore not able to estimate the visibility-effect for this assortment.
(2) This constant is used as the reference.
(3) These coefficients are derived parameter estimates (found by multiplying the values for these variables by the relative scale parameter).

Table 5.4: Interpretation of model estimation results (table 5.3)

Variable	Expected sign	Margarine		
		Assortment 1 (11)	Assortment 2 (19)	Assortment 3 (17)
Last purchase	+/-	+ (86.27%)	+ (90.48%)	+ (88.77%)
Loyalty	+	+ (100%)	+ (100%)	+ (100%)
Brand asymmetry	+/-	n.s.	+ (100%)	n.s.
Size asymmetry	+/-	n.s.	n.s.	n.s.
Visibility	+	n.r.	+ (100%)	n.s.
Average Δ in choice probability when item i is presented on first screen			8.54%	
Proximity to oos	+	n.s.	+ (100%)	n.s.
Average Δ in choice probability when item i is located next to a (preferred) oos item			6.32%	

Variable	Expected sign	Cereals		
		Assortment 1 (21)	Assortment 2 (32)	Assortment 3 (46)
Last purchase	+/-	+ (58.11%)	+ (76.18%)	+ (57.35%)
Loyalty	+	+ (100%)	+ (100%)	+ (100%)
Brand asymmetry	+/-	+ (58.44%)	+ (84.21%)	n.s.
Taste asymmetry	+/-	n.s.	+ (100%)	- (58.95%)
Type asymmetry	+/-	n.s.	- (87.94%)	+ (100%)
Visibility	+	n.s.	n.s.	+ (77.35%)
Average Δ in choice probability when item i is presented on first screen				24.12%
Proximity to oos	+	+ (100%)	n.s.	+ (100%)
Average Δ in choice probability when item i is located next to a (preferred) oos item		12.72%		41.42%

Numbers between brackets indicate the share of households for which the coefficient is in the reported direction

n.s. = not significant

n.r. = not relevant

For both categories, the coefficients of last purchase and loyalty are strongly significant and in the expected directions (see table 5.3). Comparing the two categories, we find that last purchase has a positive impact on subsequent choice behavior for a larger share of households in the category of margarine than in the category of cereals (table 5.4). This is in line with category characteristics: margarine is a category where consumers tend to repurchase the same product while cereals is more likely to be characterized as a variety-seeking category (cf. previous chapter; Campo et al., 2003; Roberts and Lattin, 1991). Concentrating on stock-out effects, we find significant out-of-stock asymmetry effects, for the two categories under consideration. The results in table 5.4 demonstrate that (some) consumers adopt simplifying asymmetric switching cues when they are confronted with an out-of-stock situation (cf. previous chapter and Campo et al., 2003). In addition, the results reveal that the tendency to focus on specific attributes is a function of the assortment offered.

5.3.2 Test of the hypotheses

Impact of visibility: main effect. With respect to the visibility-effect, we find that, for the two categories (and given that more than one screen is needed to present the product offer), alternatives that are shown on the first screen are more likely to be selected (table 5.3: positive, 5%-significant β_{Vis} coefficient for assortment 2 (margarine) and for assortment 3 (cereals)). While the visibility-effect is present for all households in the margarine category (no significant standard deviation for assortment 2), the effect differs across households for cereals (significant standard deviation for assortment 3). All or the vast majority of consumers (100% and 77.35%, respectively for margarine and for cereals, see table 5.4) have a higher probability of choosing first-screen alternatives (support hypothesis H_1). Within the assortments where visibility is significant, first-screen alternatives experience an important increase in choice probability of 8.54% (margarine, assortment 2) and 24.12% (cereals, assortment 3) (see table 5.4). In order to better understand consumer differences, we calculated the mean visibility-coefficient per individual and correlated this consumer-specific mean with a number of household-specific characteristics[16] (coming from the pre- and post-purchase

---

[16] We did not find any significant correlation between the (mean) consumer-specific visibility coefficient and other factors characterizing consumers' behavior (the variety seeking tendency – approximated by calculating an entropy measure over the shopping period) or other questions of the pre- (question 3: store loyalty, time pressure and shopping attitude) and post-purchase questionnaires (question 2: item loyalty and acceptable alternatives available and question 4: satisfaction with purchase decisions).

questionnaire). This analysis did not reveal any significant findings for the margarine category, which is in line with our empirical results as the standard deviation of visibility was never significant for this category. Yet, the analysis did show, for cereals buyers that were exposed to assortment 3, a significant, negative, correlation between the tendency to rely on the first screen and the importance attached to the category. This indicates that especially consumers who find the product category less important appear to make use of the visibility heuristic. This finding is in line with the previous chapter where it was shown that consumers that attach less importance to the category were more likely to appreciate the suggestion effect.

Impact of visibility: moderating effect. The visibility variable is only significant in the two 'largest' assortments (assortment 2, margarine and assortment 3, cereals). The positive effect of visibility on item selection is thus only at play when assortment size reaches a critical point (support of hypothesis H_3). When consumers anticipate a large assortment (from earlier views of the assortment and/or from past category experiences), they are more likely to select a 'satisfying' product on the first screen. Nevertheless, although assortment size explains a part of the picture, other elements seem to be at play. Indeed, despite the fact that assortment 2 and 3 of margarine have a similar number of alternatives (19 and 17, respectively), the visibility effect works only for assortment 2 and not for assortment 3. We elaborate further on this issue in section 5.3.3.

Impact of proximity: main effect. With regard to the proximity-effect, we find that consumers, when confronted with an out-of-stock situation, are more likely to select an alternative that is positioned next to an out-of-stock item than a distant one (table 5.3: positive β_{Prox} coefficient for assortment 2 (margarine, significant at 5%) and for assortment 1 and 3 (cereals, significant at 5% and 1% respectively)). As hypothesized in H_2, consumers tend to direct their attention to items adjacent to a (preferred) out-of-stock product, increasing the probability of selecting one of these items as a replacement item. The simulation results reported in table 5.4 show that when consumers bump into an out-of-stock, the probability of selecting an item close to the out-of-stock item increases substantially with 6.32% (margarine, assortment 2), 12.72% (cereals, assortment 1) and 41.43% (cereals, assortment 3).

Impact of proximity: moderating effect. As hypothesized in hypothesis H_4, we find that proximity is (more) influential in larger than in smaller assortments. Note that in contrast to the visibility-effect, the proximity-effect can be at play even if all products are presented on a single screen. Consumers use proximity as a heuristic to simplify their choice decisions in the first and third assortment for cereals and in the second assortment for margarine (see table 5.3). Proximity does not have an effect in the first assortment of margarine – thereby indicating that the assortment size still has to be large enough for proximity to be at play. Yet, once again, assortment size does not explain all the results. For cereals, proximity is a valid heuristic in the first (21 items) and third (46 items) assortment but is not significant in the second (32 items) assortment. Similarly, for margarine, proximity does not have a significant effect for assortment 3 (17 items) while it has a significant effect for assortment 2 (19 items). In the next section, we elaborate further on these results.

Robustness check. As a robustness check, we estimated a model with the inclusion of an interaction term between asymmetry, visibility or proximity and shelf arrangement (by brand or by flavor) or shelf mode (verbal or pictorial). Including these interaction terms allows us to check whether previously-found results were driven by the organization or mode of the shelf. The addition of the interaction terms did not improve the results. There was no improvement in the fit of the model and interaction terms were practically never significant.

5.3.3 Discussion of the results

To better understand how the mechanisms underlying our model influence the average changes in choice probability, we derive analytical expressions for the virtual shelf placement effects. In addition, the hypotheses tests of the moderating effects of assortment size revealed that the visibility- and proximity-heuristics are more likely to be used in large compared to small assortments. Yet, this relationship is not perfect and elements other than assortment size seem to be at play. In order to better understand what is driving our results, we used additional information from the post-purchase questionnaire. After completing the six purchase occasions, consumers were asked to report the amount of variety and the ease of processing they perceived in the two categories (see appendix 3.A, question 3 of post-purchase questionnaire).

5.3.3.1 The virtual shelf placement effects

Equation 5.10 indicates how the choice probability changes (Δp_i) when the visibility effect is taken into account ($p_i|Vis$) compared to a situation where this is not the case ($p_i|NVis$) (see appendix 5.C for derivations).

$$\Delta p_i = \frac{p_i|Vis - p_i|NVis}{p_i|NVis} = \frac{\exp(\beta_{Vis}Vis_{it}^h) * \sum_j \exp(u_{j|NVis})}{\sum_j \exp(\beta_{Vis}Vis_{jt}^h) * \exp(u_{j|NVis})} - 1 \qquad (5.10)$$

As can be seen from this equation, the effect of visibility on the choice probability of an alternative will be stronger when there is more to gain from being suggested on the first screen. This is the case when (i) more alternatives are battling for a prominent shelf position and (ii) less alternatives can be shown on the first screen. To illustrate this, we use a hypothetical example described in table 5.5. By way of illustration, we have assumed that each alternative has the same a priori choice utility – resulting in the same $p_i|NVis$ for each of the alternatives.

Table 5.5: Changes[17] in choice probability for an item that is offered on the first screen (hypothetical example)[18]

# of items in assortment	# of items on first screen: 8 items can be offered on first screen	16 items can be offered on first screen
21 alternatives in the assortment	+ 25.39%	+ 8.45%
46 alternatives in the assortment	+ 37.03%	+ 27.12%

Table 5.5 demonstrates that the choice probability of alternatives on the first screen more strongly increases when more alternatives are battling for precious 'screen space'. The choice probability of first-screen alternatives increases with 37.03% (27.12%) when the assortment consists of 46 alternatives while it only increases with 25.39% (8.45%) when the assortment consists of 21 alternatives in the case that 8 (16) items can be offered on the first screen. Second, the increase in choice probability for an alternative that is offered on the first screen is larger when the screen space becomes more 'precious', i.e. when less alternatives can be offered on the first screen. The probability

---

[17] For the same reason as in the previous chapter, we portray relative changes instead of absolute ones as relative changes take the initial amount into account, making comparisons between the 2 product categories more clear-cut.
[18] Based on expression (5.10). As an example, we take the coefficient of the mean of the visibility variable of assortment 2, margarine (see table 5.3): 0.3962.

of a first-screen alternative increases with 25.39% (37.03%) when 8 items can be offered on the first screen while there is only an increase of 8.45% (27.12%) when 16 items can be offered on the first screen in the case that the assortment consists of 21 (46) alternatives.

Second, results in table 5.3 and 5.4 indicate that the proximity heuristic can co-occur with other task-simplifying heuristics (such as asymmetric switching variables) when consumers are confronted with an out-of-stock situation. For instance, for the second assortment of margarine, we found a significant brand asymmetry variable as well as a significant proximity variable for all consumers. Proximity and asymmetry heuristics are thus not necessarily in 'competition' with each other but can be used in combination.

Equation 5.11 shows how the choice probability of alternative i is affected (Δp_i) when out-of-stocks for other alternatives occur ($p_i|OOS$) compared to a situation where all alternatives are available ($p_i|AV$) (see appendix 5.C for derivations):

$$\Delta p_i = \frac{p_i|OOS - p_i|AV}{p_i|AV} = \frac{\exp(\sum_A \beta_{A,oos} OOS_{A,it} + \beta_{\text{Prox}} \text{Pr}\,ox_{it}^h) * \sum_j \exp(u_{j|AV})}{\sum_j \exp(\sum_A \beta_{A,oos} OOS_{A,jt} + \beta_{\text{Prox}} \text{Pr}\,ox_{jt}^h) * \exp(u_{j|AV})} - 1$$

(5.11)

Following the model, the choice probability of alternative i will more strongly increase when (i) next to alternative i more (highly preferred) products are out-of-stock, (ii) alternative i shares important attributes with stock-out items that produce positive asymmetric choice shifts (cf. Campo et al., 2003) and (iii) less other, available, attractive alternatives (i.e. alternatives that share important attributes with stock-out items) are adjacent to stock-out alternatives. To illustrate this, we use a hypothetical example described in table 5.6. Once again, for illustration purposes, we assume that the choice utility (and therefore choice probability) when all alternatives are available is the same for each of the alternatives. In addition, we assume that only one product is unavailable, that the preference of consumer h for the stock-out item ($Loy_{i_{oos}}^h$) is high (0.6) or low (0.1), that the alternative shares important (brand) attributes with the stock-out item or not and that none or two other attractive alternatives are located next to the stock-out item.

Table 5.6: Changes[19] in choice probability for an item that is located next to an out-of-stock item (hypothetical example)[20]

Case	Preference out-of-stock item	Share important attributes with out-of-stock item	Other attractive alternatives next to out-of-stock items	Δp_i
1	Low	No	No	18.80%
2	High	No	No	39.88%
3	Low	Yes	No	57.45%
4	High	Yes	No	83.54%
5	High	Yes	Yes	62.10%

The results of table 5.6 indicate that, for mean parameters, the increase in choice probability is larger for an item that is located next to a high-preferred stock-out item than for an item that is located next to a less-preferred stock-out item (increase of 39.88% versus 18.80%, respectively). The increase in choice probability is further intensified when the alternative shares attributes with the stock-out item that produce significant positive asymmetric choice shifts. There is an increase of 83.54% (57.45%) versus 39.88% (18.80%) for an alternative that shares important attributes versus an alternative that does not share important attributes when it is located next to a high-preferred (less-preferred) stock-out item. Finally, the results indicate that the increase in choice probability is diminished when other attractive alternatives (i.e. other alternatives that share important attributes with stock-out items) are adjacent to the stock-out alternative (83.54% when no other attractive items are adjacent versus 62.10% when other attractive alternatives are adjacent).

5.3.3.2 Moderating effects of assortment

In the post-purchase questionnaire (see appendix 3.A, module 3, question 3), consumers were asked to evaluate the assortment on two criteria: the perceived variety of the product category (the number of different products offered and the diversity of these products; Kahn and McAlister, 1997) on the one hand and the perceived ease of processing in the category (the difficulty of finding and choosing an alternative in the

---

[19] See footnote 18
[20] Based on expression (5.11). As an example, we take the significant (mean) coefficients of the proximity variable and asymmetric switching variables of assortment 2, margarine (see table 5.3): 0.9279 for proximity and 0.3401 for brand asymmetry.

product offer; van Ketel et al., 2003) on the other hand. Whereas the perceived variety relates more to the benefits, the perceived ease of processing relates more to the costs associated with buying in the category. We focus on perceptions, investigating how consumers *perceive* the variety of and the effort required with purchasing from the product category, instead of using actual (objective) measures. ANOVA-analyses revealed significant differences between assortments with respect to perceived variety and ease of processing, for margarine as well as for cereals[21] (see table 5.7).

Table 5.7: ANOVA-results for the impact of assortment (margarine and cereals)

Variable	Margarine			Cereals		
	Ass 1 Limited	**Ass 2** Ext flavors	**Ass 3** Ext brands	**Ass 1** Limited	**Ass 2** Ext flavors	**Ass 3** Ext brands
# of items	11	19	17	21	32	46
Perceived variety	4.89	5.32	**5.63**	5.07	**5.62**	5.37
	Significant difference: 1 & 2, 1 & 3, 2 &3			Significant difference: 1 & 2, 1 & 3, 2 & 3		
Ease of processing	5.59	5.67	**5.89**	5.48	**5.85**	5.28
	Significant difference: 1 & 3, 2 & 3			Significant difference: 1 & 2, 2 & 3		

In both categories, consumers perceive significantly more variety in a larger (2/3) than in a smaller assortment (1). Not only assortment size but also assortment composition has an effect on perceived variety in both categories. Consumers exposed to an assortment that was extended with 'popular' attributes (new brands for margarine – assortment 3 and new flavors for cereals – assortment 2) perceive significantly more variety than those exposed to an assortment that was extended with 'unpopular' attributes (new flavors for margarine – assortment 2 and new brands for cereals – assortment 3). With respect to ease of processing, we find, for both categories, that the assortment should contain enough alternatives in order to simplify the decision. For both categories, consumers perceive significantly more difficulty in making a decision in a (small) assortment that misses 'popular' attributes (assortment 1) compared to an assortment that was extended with these 'popular' attributes (margarine, assortment 3 and cereals, assortment 2). Including too many alternatives with 'redundant' attributes also causes a negative effect on ease of processing. In both categories, consumers perceive significantly less difficulty with finding and choosing an alternative in an assortment that was extended with 'popular' attributes (margarine, assortment 3 and

---

[21] The underlying structure was confirmed by a principal components analysis. The two factors had a cronbach alpha of 0.847 (0.891) for perceived variety and 0.814 (0.875) for ease of processing for margarine (cereals).

cereals, assortment 2) compared to an assortment that was extended with 'unpopular' attributes (margarine, assortment 2 and cereals, assortment 3).

Our classification of 'popular'/'unpopular' attributes is in line with category characteristics. Previous research has shown that consumers attach more importance to the brand attribute in the category of margarine (cf. brand asymmetric switching when confronted with out-of-stocks) and to the flavor attribute in the category of cereals (cf. taste asymmetric switching when confronted with out-of-stocks) (see chapter 4 and Campo et al., 2003). Also the outcomes of our post-purchase questionnaire confirm this (see appendix 3.A, module 3, question 2.b/d): in the cereals category 70% of our respondents would focus on flavor when their preferred item would be unavailable, whereas only 44% would do so in the margarine category.

The previous findings help us to better understand the moderating effects of assortment on shelf placement (visibility and proximity). First, as discussed in the previous section, visibility has a positive, significant effect for assortment 2 (margarine) and assortment 3 (cereals) (see also table 5.3). Comparing, per category, the assortments for which the visibility-effect is relevant (i.e. assortments where more than one screen is needed to present the products), we find that visibility is significant in those assortments where the ease of processing is the lowest (see table 5.7). Similarly, the proximity-effect is especially important in assortments where consumers have a lower perceived ease of processing, i.e. assortment 2 for margarine and assortment 1 and 3 for cereals (see table 5.3 and 5.7).

Consumers are thus more likely to adopt simplifying heuristics, such as in-store related tactics, when they perceive more difficulty with finding and choosing an alternative in the assortment. This ease of processing in a category is not only a function of the number of alternatives offered (size) but depends also on the number of alternatives with 'popular' attributes (composition). Our results are in line with previous research where it has been confirmed that not only size but also composition of the assortment has an important impact on consumer reactions (Boatwright and Nunes, 2001; Broniarczyk, Hoyer and McAlister, 1998). For instance, in the study of Boatwright and Nunes (2001), it was shown that retailers could reduce assortment without negatively affecting sales by eliminating 'redundant' (i.e. 'unpopular') attributes (cf. attribute-based approach, van Herpen and Pieters, 2002).

5.4 SUMMARY AND IMPLICATIONS

In this research, we have investigated the impact of the virtual shelf placement on online choice decisions. Despite debates about the ease of searching on the Internet, the flow/pleasure resulting from surfing and the endless Internet space that seem to suggest that virtual shelf management is not or of minor importance, our results show that virtual shelf management is an important issue for online stores. Both the location of products across screens (placement as such) as well as the adjacencies of products (placement relative to other items) have a significant impact on online choice decisions. Our findings further reveal that consumers are more likely to turn to these shelf-based heuristics in large than in small assortments. Yet, not only assortment size but also assortment composition is found to have an important impact on the use of visibility and proximity as task-simplifying heuristics.

First, we find that the way in which products are presented in an online store (i.e. absolute shelf placement effects) strongly affects the choice of a consumer. Alternatives that are shown on the first screen are not only more salient than alternatives that are located on (one of) the following screens (prominence-effect), consumers also start to acquire and process information from the first screen (primacy-effect). Our findings indicate that these first-screen alternatives are more likely to be selected during the choice process, especially by consumers who attach less importance to the product category. A possible caveat is that, on many e-grocery sites, consumers have the possibility to change the layout of the shelf themselves. Yet, consumers do see the default/start option (i.e. the shelf layout that is selected by the retailer when a consumer logs in) first. Moreover, previous research (Wu and Rangaswmay, 2003) as well as the current study reveal that consumers tend to stay with this option. As a result, online retailers (or category managers) have opportunities to improve their performance by using the first screen (especially of the default option) as an in-store stimulus to highlight specific alternatives (e.g. higher-margin and/or private label items). In addition, explicitly including, next to an *across*-screen variable, different 'on screen' variables that capture the effect of product placement *on* a screen did not significantly improve the results. This might indicate that, in contrast to the traditional world where placement of products on the shelf is shown to have a strong effect (such as the vertical position, hand/eye-level, on the shelf), there is no such clear-cut effect of placement of products on a computer screen in a virtual store. This finding is confirmed by recent research of van der Lans (2002). His research reveals that consumers use different strategies to locate a target product on a computer-simulated supermarket shelf: horizontal zigzag, vertical zigzag, inward and upward spirals or even a random search strategy.

Second, we also find that the placement of products relative to the other items in the category has a significant impact on what consumers choose in a stock-out situation. Indeed, once consumers become fixated on a particular section of the shelf (i.e. once they have spotted their preferred item and noticed that it is not available), they are more likely to stay within that section. As a result, they pay more attention to items close to the out-of-stock item, dramatically increasing the chances of selecting one of these adjacent items. Especially alternatives that are attractive but that otherwise would not be taken into consideration when a high-preferred alternative is unavailable gain from being (implicitly) suggested (e.g. a private label that is highly similar to a market leaders' product) (cf. suggestion-effect of previous chapter). In contrast to Kucuk (2004) who was not able to find a significant proximity effect when consumers are confronted with a stock-out in a traditional (brick-and-mortar) store, we do find that online retailers can 're-direct' consumers to items in the neighborhood of a stock-out item. That we do find such a proximity effect can be partly explained by the research design: whereas Kucuk used a questionnaire (asking respondents how they would react), we used an online computer experiment (registering how consumers actually reacted). In addition, typical online environment characteristics such as the small computer screen or the convenience-driven motivation to shop online might make online consumers more prone to the proximity heuristic.

Our analyses further indicate that the extent to which visibility (focusing on alternatives that are offered on the first screen) and proximity (focusing on alternatives in the neighborhood of a stock-out item) are adopted as heuristics depends on the assortment offered. Both heuristics become especially important when consumers perceive more difficulty with finding and choosing an alternative in the assortment. This ease of processing in a category is not only a function of the number of alternatives in the assortment (size) but depends also on the number of alternatives with 'popular' attributes (composition). Because the first screen-effect can only be at play when more than one screen is needed to present the products while the proximity-effect might be at play even if all products are offered on a single screen, different 'thresholds' are causing both effects. First, consumers are more likely to select a 'satisfying' product on the first screen when assortment size (for a given category) reaches a critical point after which it becomes difficult to make an easy decision. The proximity heuristic, in contrast, seems to be at play from the moment that assortment can not be evaluated at a single glance and consumers perceive difficulty with finding and choosing an alternative within the assortment.

Our research has several limitations and indicates a number of interesting venues for future research. Like in the previous chapter, this research is limited by the use of an artificial setting and by the focus on only two product categories within a single, online supermarket.

Second, we only focused on 'general' shelf placement effects. Using eye-tracking techniques would allow to more exactly measure the eye movements of consumers. Eye-tracking data would, therefore, give additional (more detailed) insights into how consumer's attention (and resulting choice behavior) is affected by the placement of products on the virtual shelf. Our results already reveal that some of the 'general' traditional shelf placement effects (e.g. eye/hand-level position) could not be confirmed in the virtual store, while other effects seem to be similar on a virtual and traditional shelf (e.g. proximity). This implies that one should be very careful when using the virtual store (or related to this, a computer-simulated shopping experiment) as a laboratory to make predictions for traditional shelf placement effects. Explicitly investigating if and to what extent the virtual store (or the related computer-simulated shopping experiment) gives valid predictions for the impact of marketing stimuli (such as the shelf placement) in a traditional store would be an interesting theme for future research.

Third, we only briefly looked into the classification of 'popular'/'unpopular' attributes. Based on our results, this definition seems to be a function of the category under consideration. Yet, future research should go more deeply into the question of how 'popular' attributes can be defined.

Fourth, in this research, we only manipulated two possible assortment extensions (by brand or by flavor). More thoroughly investigating assortment differences (e.g. more variations in size as well as composition) might add to the understanding of what factors are important for consumers to perceive less difficulty with finding and choosing an alternative. Investigating how results change when other meaningful (category-specific) attributes are taken into account might also be a very interesting topic for future research (cf. Boatwright and Nunes, 2001).

Fifth, results point out that online grocery shoppers might be prone to influences of online retailers that facilitate the online search process (cf. previous chapter). As such, investigating other ways to highlight specific products (such as the use of a promotional tag or a striking color) constitutes a very interesting item on the research agenda.

Finally, in this chapter, we used the sub-sample of respondents that were exposed to the benchmark (visible, no replacement) out-of-stock policy. In future research, it could be interesting to investigate if and to what extent there exists a moderating effect between the adopted out-of-stock policy and consumers' tendency to employ shelf-related task-simplifying decision rules (e.g. effect between offering a replacement item and the use of the proximity heuristic).

CONCLUSION

This dissertation aims to investigate how consumers make purchase decisions in an online grocery context (both in a regular and especially in a disrupted – by stock-outs – choice environment). A second objective is to investigate if and to what extent these decisions are influenced by online retailer's merchandising actions. Doing the research in the context of an online grocery shopping service is especially valuable for at least two reasons. First, differences between the traditional and virtual supermarket environment might cause differences between online and offline shopping behavior. Also reactions towards a stock-out might be different as a result of these environmental differences. At this moment, online stock-outs are a major problem in the e-grocery business and are unlikely to disappear with a strong-growing e-grocery market. Second, the online environment offers e-tailers the flexibility to implement a number of merchandising actions that are not or difficult to implement in a traditional supermarket. More specifically, in this dissertation, the following two merchandising actions that were expected to influence online purchase decisions were identified: retailer actions aimed at recovering some of the stock-out losses (project 1, stock-out policy) and the placement of products in the virtual store (project 2, virtual shelf placement).

Whereas the first project provides guidelines for active online stock-out management, the second project identifies the 'promising areas' of the virtual shelf. Based on our results, online retailers can improve their performance by adopting the most appropriate stock-out policy and/or by better managing existing virtual shelves. Similarly, our results help manufacturers – in their role of category captains – to better allocate the allowances/fees they pay to a retailer and, thereby, ultimately help them to improve their brand's sales potential. After summarizing findings with respect to the global research question of this dissertation, the key findings and main contributions per project are highlighted. We end by formulating some general conclusions and pointing out the general limitations and avenues for future research.

How do consumers make purchase behavior decisions in a regular online choice environment and in an online choice environment disrupted by stock-outs?

Throughout the dissertation, it was pointed out that consumers use task-simplifying heuristics when making a purchase decision for grocery products, in a regular as well as in a disrupted online grocery shopping environment. Using simple tactics allows consumers to reach a satisfactory, yet quick and effortless decision. This finding is grounded in the level of elaboration with grocery products in general (more likely to engage in peripheral-route processing) and in the stage of the buying process associated with buying grocery products (typically – although not exclusively – routinized response behavior in case of a 'regular' choice environment and a limited problem solving process in case of a 'disrupted' choice environment). Also the motivations underlying the use of electronic grocery shopping (convenience being the most important motivator to order grocery products via the web) stimulate the use of task-simplifying heuristics. Empirical results of both projects underscore these premises. In the first project, it was shown that consumers are more likely to select suggested alternatives (suggestion effect, chapter 4). In the second project, it was shown that consumers are more likely to focus on more salient items (visibility as well as proximity effect, chapter 5). These results indicate that consumers tend to turn to simple choice heuristics when choosing a product in an online grocery shopping environment.

In addition, both from a conceptual point of view (theoretical framework, chapter 2, section 2.3) as well as from an empirical point of view (out-of-stock policy, chapter 4, section 4.4), it is shown that consumers confronted with a stock-out situation in an online shopping environment tend to stay in the online store and select another alternative within the category. The tendency to switch to another (substitution) product instead of deciding not to make a purchase in the category can be explained by a number of online grocery characteristics (such as the convenience-driven motivation to shop online and the decrease in online search costs). This premise is empirically confirmed in our results by the small/lack of effects of stock-outs on purchase incidence (although it should be admitted that it can not be completely excluded that the small/lack of impact on purchase incidence is partly a result of the product categories under consideration and/or the artificial setting used in our research).

What is the effect of actively pursuing alternative stock-out policies on category purchase incidence and choice?

This project investigates the impact of an online retailer's stock-out policy on purchase incidence and choice. Three stock-out policies were distinguished: (1) stock-outs are immediately *visible* and there are *no suggestions* for replacement items, (2) stock-outs are only *visible after purchase attempts* (after clicking on the product) and (3) a *replacement item is suggested* for each stock-out product. The results of the incidence and two-stage choice models indicate that the adopted stock-out policy has a significant impact on whether consumers – confronted with a stock-out situation – make a purchase in the category or not, and if so, what they buy.

First, the results indicate that using a typical online environment feature – the pop-up – to hide stock-outs reduces the probability of purchasing in a category, especially for consumers who tend to repurchase the same item. For these habitual buyers, the false expectations of being able to buy their favorite products – created by the non-visible policy – intensifies the loss they experience when they find out that their preferred item is unavailable after clicking. Our results further point out that consumers reach their point-of-frustration very quickly, even after one or a few clicks. Finding this in an (online) grocery context is all the more surprising as groceries typically are a category consisting of many alternatives. So, although it looks a priori valuable to use a pop-up to mask stock-out problems, our results demonstrate that consumers react negatively and prefer to know the real assortment they can choose from at the start.

Second, the results reveal that, in general, suggesting a replacement item substantially increases the consideration and choice probability of the suggested item, especially for consumers that attach less importance to the category. Our results show that, in contrast with Beuk (2001) who did not find an effect of the replacement policy in a traditional brick-and-mortar store, suggesting a replacement item is a valuable policy for online retailers. Yet, the results show, at the same time, that suggesting a replacement item has only a strong positive effect under certain conditions. For one, the results point out that the positive suggestion effects are canceled out when higher-priced – suspicious – items are suggested. The results further demonstrate that suggestions are especially valued by consumers when the suggested items have a low consideration (i.e. are not already salient) yet high utility (i.e. appeal to the consumer). This implies that online retailers can guide choices in case of stock-outs by suggesting *appropriate* replacement items.

Third, while the replacement policy does guide the choice decision of an important segment of consumers, its impact on category purchase incidence remains small to non-existent. Therefore, the replacement policy's potential to reduce the probability that consumers decide not to make a purchase in the category when confronted with an out-of-stock situation, is only of minor importance. The absence of strong incidence effects can be explained by online grocery characteristics (in any case being more likely to select another product because of convenience-oriented motivations). Yet, we can not exclude that the absence of or small effect on purchase probability is partly driven by the categories under consideration (the large assortment and the variety-seeking tendency for cereals) and/or the artificial research environment.

Overall, our results reveal that online retailers (or manufacturers, in their role of category captains) can re-direct a consumer's choice in a stock-out situation towards the suggested replacement item. At the same time, however, it is also demonstrated that e-tailers should be careful in the selection of the suggested replacement item as consumers can not be lured into purchasing more expensive items. The results are especially valuable for an online retailer as it is much easier to successfully implement a replacement policy in an online supermarket than in an offline one. The results further indicate that consumers react even more negative when they become skeptical about the perceived fairness of the procedures underlying the retailer's stock-out policy (e.g. hiding stock-outs or suggesting higher-priced options as a retailer-enriching strategy). On the whole, results of this project indicate that consumers value and reward an open and honest retailer, i.e. a retailer who puts all his cards on the table and truly helps the consumer in making an easy and effortless decision. In line with customer relationship marketing principles, this confirms that retailers have an interest in pursuing open and customer-oriented stock-out policies.

Research questions of the second project

What is the effect of virtual shelf placement on online choice decisions?

This project investigates the impact of the virtual shelf placement on online choice decisions. Counter to previous claims/expectations that virtual shelf management was no longer an issue for online supermarkets, our results indicate that online stores do have to cope with (their own) shelf management problems. In this project, the stock-out situation is used as a case in point to investigate whether consumers tend to stay with items close to the favorite out-of-stock item when choosing a replacement item. Next to the impact of product adjacencies in a stock-out situation, this project also focuses on virtual shelf placement as such. Although the virtual shelf space might appear unlimited, the screen space is not. As such, the location of products across screens or on a screen might have a significant effect on resulting choices. Results indeed point out that both the location of products on the virtual shelf (virtual shelf placement as such) as well as the adjacencies of products (virtual shelf placement relative to other items) have a significant impact on online choice decisions.

First, results indicate a significant effect of the placement of products *across* different screens as products that are offered on the first screen are more likely to be selected during the choice process (visibility-effect), especially for consumers that attach less importance to the category. First-screen alternatives are not only more prominent for the consumer and, therefore, more likely to be noticed and selected, consumers also start to acquire and process information from the first screen and tend to choose the first, satisfactory product they run across. As it is highly unlikely that consumers exhaustively scan the complete product offer, this offers online retailers the possibility to use the first screen (especially of the default option) as an in-store stimulus to highlight specific alternatives. It is not only the screen that all consumers see first, many consumers tend to stay with the start/default option, despite the fact that they have the possibility to change the layout of the shelf themselves. In contrast to this *across-screen* effect, we were not able to find an effect of the placement of products *on* a computer screen. This is in contrast with traditional shelf placement literature where the placement of products on the shelf is shown to have a strong effect (such as the vertical position, hand/eye-level, on the shelf).

Second, once consumers become fixated on a particular section of the shelf (e.g. once they have spotted their preferred item and noticed that it is not available), they are more likely to stay within that section. Results demonstrate that consumers confronted with a stock-out for a preferred product are more likely to pick one of the items located next to this stock-out item (proximity effect). Online retailers can thus improve their performance by 're-directing' consumers towards items in the neighborhood of a stock-out item. In line with the suggestion effect, especially low-consideration, high-utility alternatives tend to gain from being (implicitly) suggested.

Lastly, our findings demonstrate that the tendency to turn to the visibility as well as the proximity heuristic depends on the assortment offered. Both heuristics become especially important when consumers perceive more difficulty with finding and choosing an alternative in the assortment. This ease of processing in a category is not only a function of assortment size but depends also on the composition of the assortment, i.e. the number of alternatives with 'popular' attributes.

Overall, this project indicates that consumers tend to simplify their online choice decisions by (unconsciously) using shelf-related tactics – especially when they know (from earlier purchase occasions where they were confronted with the offered assortment) or suspect (from past category experiences) 'difficult-to-process' assortments. Online retailers (or manufacturers, in their role of category captains) therefore have opportunities to influence consumer's choice decisions by efficiently managing their shelves.

Final conclusions and directions for future research
In the realm of the convenience-oriented motivation to use online grocery shopping services, online consumers in general are likely to value and/or (unconsciously) make use of choice heuristics that help them to make easy and effortless decisions. Our results further reveal that especially consumers that find the product category less important are more likely to (unconsciously) adopt such task-simplifying decision rules. This implies that especially these consumers are prone to influences of online retailers that simplify the online search process. The increase in flexibility offered in the online shopping environment gives online retailers (or manufacturers in their role as category captains) more opportunities to either directly (active stock-out management: e.g. suggesting

replacement items) or indirectly (virtual shelf management: e.g. making particular items more salient) stimulate or affect the use of these heuristics. Overall, our results will help online retailers (or category captains) to improve their performance. Continuing this line of thinking, it would be very interesting to investigate in future research other ways of bringing specific alternatives to the attention of consumers in an online store (e.g. using customized suggestions/interfaces, using promotional tags, using a striking color, ...).

Obviously, our research has several limitations. First, the use of an experimental design – though necessary for our purposes – may have entailed some biases because an experiment is always associated with a number of artificial features (e.g. no real budget or time constraint, lack of competitive context and clutter/other disruptions, no real consumption, fixed shopping frequency, lack of personalized shopping list). Although we can not rule out that our results are partly affected by some of these artificial aspects, there are reasons to believe that these biases are limited. For instance, even without an explicit time pressure, our results reveal that consumers tend to rely on task-simplifying decision rules. As such, our experiment constitutes a conservative test and it can be expected that the tendency to use heuristics might even increase when consumers are actually pressed for time.

Second, the narrow scope of this research (investigating effects for two product categories in one online supermarket) is a limitation. Broadening the scope by investigating stock-out, stock-out policy and virtual shelf placement effects for other grocery categories or other (less frequently purchased) product categories might be a very interesting topic for future research. What is more, future studies could investigate other stock-out policies or other, more refined, shelf placement effects or even stock-out policy and shelf-related effects in combination.

Finally, an online store differs on a number of important aspects from the traditional store. Empirically comparing to what extent these typical online environment characteristics cause differences between online and traditional shopping behavior might be a useful extension. Related to this, it would be interesting to investigate if and to what extent the virtual store (or the related computer-simulated shopping experiment) gives valid predictions for the impact of marketing stimuli (such as shelf placement) in a traditional store.

Module 1: Pre-purchase questionnaire

1. Socio-demographic characteristics

Screen 1

---

a. Gender:
       ☐ female
       ☐ male

b. Age [   ]

c. Postal code [   ]

d. Who belongs – except yourself – to the household?
(several answers are possible)
       ☐ partner   ☐ other family members or friends
       ☐ children   ☐ none
       ☐ parents

[If 'children' is checked in question d, go to question e. Else, go directly to question f]
[Question f/g/h: answer for oneself and partner if 'partner' is checked in question d. Else, only for oneself]

Screen 2

---

e. How many children (living at home) are there in your household, divided by age:

[0] less than 3 years old   [0] 13 to 18 years old

[0] 3 to 6 years old   [0] older than 18 years

[0] 7 to 12 years old

f. Which work situation fits best?

	I	Partner
Unemployed (work-seeking, outworker, student, retired)	☐	☐
Less than part-time (less than 20 hours per week)	☐	☐
Part-time (between 20 and 30 hours per week)	☐	☐
Full-time (more than 30 hours per week)	☐	☐

[If one is unemployed: go to question h. Else, go to question g]

Screen 3

g. What is your (and your partner's) occupation?

	I	Partner
Official	☐	☐
Workman	☐	☐
Employee	☐	☐
Executive	☐	☐
Profession	☐	☐
Self-employed	☐	☐
Other	☐	☐

h. What is the highest diploma that you (and your partner) possess at this moment?

	I	Partner
Elementary school	☐	☐
Lower secondary school	☐	☐
Higher secondary school	☐	☐
College, short type (3 years)	☐	☐
College, long type (4 years)	☐	☐
University	☐	☐
Post-university	☐	☐

2. Internet experience

Screen 4

a. How often do you use Internet?	
□ daily	□ weekly
□ 5 à 6 days per week	□ monthly
□ 3 à 4 days per week	□ never
□ 2 days per week	
b. Have you ever bought something via Internet?	
□ never	□ several times
□ only once	□ often

[If 'never' is checked in question b, go to question c. Else, go directly to question e]

Screen 5

c. Can you indicate your most important reason of not buying on the Internet?
(several answers are possible)
   □ I want to feel, see and/or touch the products I buy
   □ I want to receive my products immediately
   □ I don't want to miss the social contacts of traditional stores
   □ I am not familiar enough with Internet
   □ I do not trust the delivery of the products
   □ I do not trust the financial aspects (payment) on the Internet
   □ I do not like to give my purchase or other information via the Internet
   □ I think it is too expensive
   □ Other: _____

d. What is the chance that you will use the Internet to purchase something in the
next 12 months? (choose a figure between 0 and 100, with 0% = very unlikely, 50% = equal chance of using the Internet or not using it, 100% = very likely)

[Go to question g]

Screen 6

e. Which products have you already bought via the Internet? (several answers are possible)
   □ books
   □ CDs/DVDs/Videos
   □ computer products (software, hardware)
   □ clothing
   □ travel products (airline ticket, hotel reservations, ….)
   □ tickets for events (concerts, theater, cinema,…)
   □ grocery products
   □ Other: _____

f. What is the chance that you will use the Internet again to purchase something in
the next 12 months? (choose a figure between 0 and 100, with 0% = very unlikely, 50% = equal chance of using the Internet or not using it, 100% = very likely)

[If 'grocery products' are not checked in question e, go to question g. Else, go directly to question h]

Screen 7

g. What is the chance that you will use the Internet to purchase grocery products the next 12 months? (choose a figure between 0 and 100, with 0% = very unlikely, 50% = equal chance of using the Internet or not using it, 100% = very likely)

[Go to question 3.a]

Screen 8

h. What is the chance that you will use the Internet again to purchase grocery products the next 12 months? (choose a figure between 0 and 100, with 0% = very unlikely, 50% = equal chance of using the Internet or not using it, 100% = very likely)

i. How often did you use Caddyhome (the online site of Delhaize) to purchase grocery products?

□ never   □ regularly
□ 1 or a few times   □ often

3. Grocery shopping information

Screen 9

a. How often do you go to the supermarket?
    □ less than once per week
    □ once per week
    □ more than once per week
 	
b. How often do you yourself purchase grocery products?
    □ never   □ often
    □ sometimes   □ almost always

[If 'never' is checked in question b, STOP (respondent is thanked for cooperation)]

Screen 10

c. Where do you purchase most of your grocery products?
(several answers are possible)

□ Aldi	□ GB
□ Carrefour	□ Lidl
□ Cash Fresh	□ Makro
□ 't Centrum	□ Match
□ Colruyt	□ Prima
□ Delhaize	□ Spar
□ Local shop	□ Other

d. Indicate how much you agree with each of the following statements. All statements concern grocery shopping.
(1 = totally disagree, 4 = neutral, 7 = totally agree)

1) I think of myself as a loyal customer of my supermarket. [Store loyalty]

Totally	1	2	3	4	5	6	7	Totally
disagree	□	□	□	□	□	□	□	agree

2) When I go to a supermarket, I am often in a hurry. [Time pressure]

Totally	1	2	3	4	5	6	7	Totally
disagree	□	□	□	□	□	□	□	agree

3) Shopping is truly a joy. [Shopping attitude]

Totally	1	2	3	4	5	6	7	Totally
disagree	□	□	□	□	□	□	□	agree

4) A good store visit is one that is over quickly. [Shopping attitude]

Totally	1	2	3	4	5	6	7	Totally
disagree	□	□	□	□	□	□	□	agree

4. Product information

Screen 11

---

1. The next questions concern the consumption of margarine/minarine to spread (thus no margarine to bake and roast)

a. Which package size do you use at home?
(several answers are possible)

□ we never use this product
□ 250 g (normal package size)
□ 500 g (large package size)

[If 'never' is checked in question a, go to 4.2.a (cereals category) – no questions asked for this category]
[If '250 g' is checked in question a, use this package size in question b/c/d]
[If '500 g' is checked in question a, use this package size in question b/c/d]

---

b. Indicate whether your household consumes more or less than one package per week

	More than 1 package per week	Less than 1 package per week
250 g (normal package size)	□	□
500 g (large package size)	□	□

[If 'more than 1 package per week' is checked in question b, go to question c]
[If 'less than 1 package per week' is checked in question b, go to question d]

---

c. How many packages do you usually consume per week (on average)?

250 g (normal package size) [0]

500 g (large package size) [0]

---

d. How many weeks can you do with one package (on average)?

250 g (normal package size) [0]

500 g (large package size) [0]

[Treat respondents with an interval > 5 weeks, as the same as those that clicked 'never']

---

e. How much margarine/minarine do you have at your home pantry at this moment

	Opened package	Unopened package
250 g (normal package size)	[0]	[0]
500 g (large package size)	[0]	[0]

Screen 12

---

2. The next questions concern the consumption of cereals, i.e. cornflakes and similar products like choco, muesli,...

a. Which package size do you use at home?

(several answers are possible)

☐ we never use this product
☐ variety/multi-pack (8 mini-packs of +/- 20 g)
☐ normal package (350 – 500 g)
☐ large package (750 g)

Attention! Packages of muesli/crunchy look small but contain 750 g

---

[If 'never' is checked in question a, no questions asked for this category]
[If 'never' is checked in question 4.1.a (margarine) and 4.2.a (cereals), STOP (respondent is thanked for cooperation)]
[If 'variety/multi-pack' is checked in question a, use this package size in question b/c/d]
[If 'normal package' is checked in question a, use this package size in question b/c/d]
[If 'large package' is checked in question a, use this package size in question b/c/d]

b. Indicate whether your household consumes more or less than one package per week	More than 1 package per week	Less than 1 package per week
variety/multi-pack (8 mini-packs of +/- 20 g)	☐	☐
normal package (350 – 500 g)	☐	☐
large package (750 g)	☐	☐

[If 'more than 1 package per week' is checked in question b, go to question c]
[If 'less than 1 package per week' is checked in question b, go to question d]

c. How many packages do you usually consume per week (on average)?	
variety/multi-pack (8 mini-packs of +/- 20 g)	⬦ 0
normal package (350 – 500 g)	⬦ 0
large package (750 g)	⬦ 0

d. How many weeks can you do with one package (on average)?	
variety/multi-pack (8 mini-packs of +/- 20 g)	⬦ 0
normal package (350 – 500 g)	⬦ 0
large package (750 g)	⬦ 0

[Treat respondents with an interval > 5 weeks, as the same as those that clicked 'never']

e. How much cereals do you have at your home pantry at this moment?	Opened package	Unopened package
variety/multi-pack	⬦ 0	⬦ 0
normal package	⬦ 0	⬦ 0
large package	⬦ 0	⬦ 0

Module 2: Purchase simulation

1. Instructions
Hereafter, we will ask you to do **six** successive, fictitious purchases. Each new purchase occasion starts with a small animation and represents a **WEEKLY** shopping trip. During a shopping trip, you can make purchases for two product categories (margarine/minarine to spread and cereals) for a *complete week*.

You are **not obliged** to purchase every 'week'. If your product is not available (because it is not offered in the assortment or because it is *temporary* unavailable), you can decide to buy nothing. Temporary unavailability in the online store is clearly indicated.

Off course, you may also purchase **more products** during one week. **Try to imitate you real purchase behavior as good as possible, taking into account the purchases made during the previous weeks.** To help, your inventory (the number of products you have at home), is indicated in the left, at the top of the screen. After this, we will give a short demonstration showing the possibilities of the Internet store.

2. Demonstration
In this demonstration we will show respondents how they can use the online shop:
- inventory
- the product categories
- the possibility to change the shelf layout (mode & organization)
- the possibility to request more information (i.e. (larger) picture, product and price)
- placing products in the shopping cart
- going to the check-out (with the possibility to change the basket)

3. Simulation exercise (repeated 6 times)
a) animation (intro-flash: picture of an entering shopper)

b) purchase simulation
- Shelf layout (verbal versus pictorial; organized by brand or by flavor)
- Inventory level
- Following possibilities: * Zoom in (i.e. (larger) picture)
                                         * Retrieve product & price information
                                         * Purchase one or more packages of product

Example of a pictorial screen, organized by brand

Example of a verbal screen, organized by type

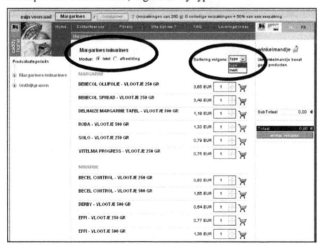

Repeat purchase simulation for cereals.

- Shopping basket
      * purchase nothing → leave store
      * purchase something → order products (if desired: change shopping basket)

c) animation (outro-flash: picture of a leaving shopper)

d) delivery-page
Overview of delivered product

e) going to another store
Screen 1
[Only ask if (1) there was no purchase in the product category of margarine and (2) the inventory is insufficient for the consumption of the next week]

a. You did not purchase in the product category of margarine. Does this mean that you would purchase your product in another store?
    □ yes
    □ no

[If 'yes' is checked in question a, go to question b]

b. Indicate how many packages you would buy there 250 g (normal package size)   0 500 g (large package size)   0

Screen 2
[Only ask if (1) there was no purchase in the product category of cereals and (2) the inventory is insufficient for the consumption of the next week]

c. You did not purchase in the product category of cereals. Does this mean that you would purchase your product in another store?
    □ yes
    □ no

[If 'yes' is checked in question c, go to question d]

d. Indicate how many packages you would buy there variety/multi-pack (8 mini-packs of +/- 20 g)   0 normal package (350 – 500 g)   0 large package (750 g)   0

Repeat steps a-e during weeks 2-6

Module 3: Post-purchase questionnaire

[If a respondent indicated in the pre-purchase questionnaire (4.1/2.a) that s/he *never* uses the product or *uses 1 package of the product more than 5 weeks*, no questions regarding this product category are asked]

1. Revisit/repurchase intention
Screen 1

a. What is the chance that you will use this site to purchase grocery products in the next 12 months? (choose a figure between 0 and 100, with 0% = very unlikely, 50% = equal chance of using the Internet or not using it, 100% = very likely).

b. What is the chance that you will use this site to purchase margarine in the next 12 months? (choose a figure between 0 and 100, with 0% = very unlikely, 50% = equal chance of using the Internet or not using it, 100% = very likely).

c. What is the chance that you will use this site to purchase cereals in the next 12 months? (choose a figure between 0 and 100, with 0% = very unlikely, 50% = equal chance of using the Internet or not using it, 100% = very likely).

2. Product perception and normal buying behavior information
Screen 2

a. Indicate how much you agree with each of the following statements. All statements concern the purchase of margarine/minarine to spread (thus no margarine to bake or roast).
(1 = totally disagree, 4 = neutral, 7 = totally agree)

1) I like to switch between margarine and minarine. [Type Loyalty]

Totally disagree	1 ▢	2 ▢	3 ▢	4 ▢	5 ▢	6 ▢	7 ▢ Totally agree

2) I like to switch between different brands of margarine/minarine. [Brand loyalty]

Totally disagree	1 ▢	2 ▢	3 ▢	4 ▢	5 ▢	6 ▢	7 ▢ Totally agree

3) There are few differences among different types of margarine/minarine. [Acceptable alternative types available]

Totally disagree	1 ▢	2 ▢	3 ▢	4 ▢	5 ▢	6 ▢	7 ▢ Totally agree

4) There are few differences among different brands of margarine/minarine. [Acceptable alternative brands available]

Totally disagree	1 ▢	2 ▢	3 ▢	4 ▢	5 ▢	6 ▢	7 ▢ Totally agree

5) Compared to other grocery products, I find margarine/minarine an important product. [Product importance]

Totally disagree	1 ▢	2 ▢	3 ▢	4 ▢	5 ▢	6 ▢	7 ▢ Totally agree

6) I think of myself as a loyal buyer of margarine/minarine. [Item loyalty]

Totally disagree	1 ▢	2 ▢	3 ▢	4 ▢	5 ▢	6 ▢	7 ▢ Totally agree

7) When choosing a product in the category of margarine/minarine, there is little to loose by choosing poorly. [Acceptable alternatives available]

Totally disagree	1 ▢	2 ▢	3 ▢	4 ▢	5 ▢	6 ▢	7 ▢ Totally agree

b. Suppose that you have to select another product than your preferred one, which of the following characteristics is the most important for your choice?
  □ brand
  □ type
  □ I always purchase the same product and would not buy any other product

[If answer c is checked, go directly to question d. Else go to question c]

c. How big is the difference in importance that you attach to brand or type?
(1 = very small difference – brand and type are almost equally important, 7 = very large difference – brand or type is much more important)

Difference in importance between brand or type

Small difference	1	2	3	4	5	6	7	Large difference
□	□	□	□	□	□	□	

Screen 3

d. Indicate how much you agree with each of the following statements. All statements concern the purchase of cereals, i.e. cornflakes and similar products like muesli, choco pops,...
(1 = totally disagree, 4 = neutral, 7 = totally agree)

1) I like to switch between different tastes and types of cereals. [Type Loyalty]

Totally disagree	1	2	3	4	5	6	7	Totally agree
□	□	□	□	□	□	□	

2) I like to switch between different brands of cereals. [Brand loyalty]

Totally disagree	1	2	3	4	5	6	7	Totally agree
□	□	□	□	□	□	□	

3) There are few differences among different types (tastes) of cereals. [Acceptable alternative tastes available]

Totally disagree	1	2	3	4	5	6	7	Totally agree
□	□	□	□	□	□	□	

4) There are few differences among different brands of cereals. [Acceptable alternative brands available]

Totally disagree	1	2	3	4	5	6	7	Totally agree
□	□	□	□	□	□	□	

5) Compared to other grocery products, I find cereals an important product. [Product importance]

Totally disagree	1	2	3	4	5	6	7	Totally agree
□	□	□	□	□	□	□	

6) I think of myself as a loyal buyer of cereals. [Item loyalty]

Totally disagree	1	2	3	4	5	6	7	Totally agree
□	□	□	□	□	□	□	

7) When choosing a product in the category of cereals, there is little to loose by choosing poorly. [Acceptable alternatives available]

Totally disagree	1	2	3	4	5	6	7	Totally agree
□	□	□	□	□	□	□	

e. Suppose that you have to select another product than your preferred one, which of the following characteristics is the most important for your choice?
  □ brand
  □ taste (e.g. choco, honey, muesli,...)
  □ I always purchase the same product and would not buy any other product

[If answer c is checked, go directly to question 3.a. Else go to question f]

f. How big is the difference in importance that you attach to brand or taste?
(1 = very small difference – brand and type are almost equally important, 7 = very large difference – brand or type is much more important)

Difference in importance between brand or taste

Small difference	1 □	2 □	3 □	4 □	5 □	6 □	7 □	Large difference

3. Assortment perceptions
Screen 4

a. Indicate how much you agree with each of the following statements. All statements concern the assortment of margarine in the online shop.
(1 = totally disagree, 4 = neutral, 7 = totally agree)

1) In this assortment, there were a lot of different products. [variety, # of products]

Totally disagree	1 □	2 □	3 □	4 □	5 □	6 □	7 □	Totally agree

2) I think that the shelf of margarine was clearly organized (products that belonged together, were grouped). [shelf organization]

Totally disagree	1 □	2 □	3 □	4 □	5 □	6 □	7 □	Totally agree

3) It was difficult to find a product in the assortment of margarine. [cost, find]

Totally disagree	1 □	2 □	3 □	4 □	5 □	6 □	7 □	Totally agree

4) There was a great deal of variety in this assortment. [variety, # of products]

Totally disagree	1 □	2 □	3 □	4 □	5 □	6 □	7 □	Totally agree

5) It was very easy to select a product in the assortment of margarine. [cost, choose]

Totally disagree	1 □	2 □	3 □	4 □	5 □	6 □	7 □	Totally agree

6) I would be happy to choose from the same assortment on my next purchase occasion. [variety, quality of products]

Totally disagree	1 □	2 □	3 □	4 □	5 □	6 □	7 □	Totally agree

7) I found the assortment of margarine so poorly organized that it was difficult to choose. [cost, choose]

Totally disagree	1 □	2 □	3 □	4 □	5 □	6 □	7 □	Totally agree

8) I had the possibility to try new and different brands and types of margarine in this assortment. [variety, # of products]

Totally disagree	1 □	2 □	3 □	4 □	5 □	6 □	7 □	Totally agree

9) The choice selection of margarine was very good. [variety, quality of products]

Totally disagree	1 □	2 □	3 □	4 □	5 □	6 □	7 □	Totally agree

10) I found the choice of margarine a tough decision. [cost, choose]

Totally disagree	1 □	2 □	3 □	4 □	5 □	6 □	7 □	Totally agree

11) The product of my choice was easy to find in the assortment of margarine. [cost, find]

Totally disagree	1 □	2 □	3 □	4 □	5 □	6 □	7 □	Totally agree

12) I lost a lot of time with searching a product in the assortment of margarine. [cost, find]

Totally disagree	1 ☐	2 ☐	3 ☐	4 ☐	5 ☐	6 ☐	7 ☐	Totally agree

13) I found that there were several good options available for me to choose between. [variety, quality of products]

Totally disagree	1 ☐	2 ☐	3 ☐	4 ☐	5 ☐	6 ☐	7 ☐	Totally agree

Repeat question 3 for cereals (replace "margarine" by "cereals")

4. Satisfaction with purchase decision
Screen 6

a. Indicate how much you agree with each of the following statements. All statements concern your purchase decisions in the online shop for margarine. (1 = totally disagree, 4 = neutral, 7 = totally agree)

1) I am very satisfied with the purchase decision in the product category of margarine.

Totally disagree	1 ☐	2 ☐	3 ☐	4 ☐	5 ☐	6 ☐	7 ☐	Totally agree

2) I am pretty certain that I made the best decision about which product to select in the product category of margarine.

Totally disagree	1 ☐	2 ☐	3 ☐	4 ☐	5 ☐	6 ☐	7 ☐	Totally agree

3) I am very satisfied with the products I selected in the product category of margarine.

Totally disagree	1 ☐	2 ☐	3 ☐	4 ☐	5 ☐	6 ☐	7 ☐	Totally agree

Repeat question 4 for cereals (replace "margarine" by "cereals")

5. Availability of (preferred) products
Screen 8

a. Were there products (brands and/or types) that your household normally purchases, missing in the online shop? (click here to see the products of margarine that were offered during your purchase simulation)

    ☐ yes

    ☐ no

(if you do not see a pop-up, you have a pop-up blocker activated. Please switch it of temporarily)

[If 'yes' is checked in question a, go to question b. Else go directly to question d]

b. Can you indicate this (these) product(s) in the next list?
[Insert a list of products that were not available in the online shop]

c. Using the scale below, please indicate how much you like the products that were not available above those that were available.
(1 = no preference at all, 4 = equal preference, 7 = very strong preference)
Product A

Very low preference	1 ☐	2 ☐	3 ☐	4 ☐	5 ☐	6 ☐	7 ☐	Very strong preference

[Repeat question c for all products that were not available in online shop but used before by the household]

d. Did you notice that several products were temporary unavailable in the category of margarine?

    □ yes

    □ no

Screen 9

e. Select below the products from the assortment of margarine that your household purchased during traditional shopping trips in the last 12 months. Click on the pictures to select them (they can but do not have to be different from those that you selected during the purchase occasion).

(if you do not see a pop-up, you have a pop-up blocker activated. Please switch it of temporarily)

f. How often do you normally purchase these products? Indicate (approximately) the % every product takes in the total shopping basket of margarine.

For example: suppose that you purchase 3 different products (margarine A, B and C) but that that you purchase most of the time margarine A (7 times in 10), sometimes margarine B (2 times in 10) and sporadically margarine C (1 times in 10). Adapt the percentages as follows:

Margarine A   70%

Margarine B   20%

Margarine C   10%

(total sum is 100)

Product A | 1/n % |

...

Product N | 1/n % |

Total sum is   100%

[List all the items (n) that were selected in question e (fill up the % a priori with 1/n, calculate automatically the sum)]

Repeat question 5 for cereals (replace "margarine" by "cereals")

APPENDIX 3.B: SHELF ORGANIZATION (BY BRAND OR BY FLAVOR)

In both the verbal as well as in the pictorial shelf, we started by grouping the products according to the focal organization attribute. Afterwards, if more than one possibility remained to position the products, other attributes came into play.

In a **verbal**, *brand*-organized list, products were alphabetically (based on brand name) listed. In a verbal, *flavor*-organized list, products of the same flavor were placed together. For instance, in a flavor-organized verbal shelf of the cereals category, alternatives were first organized by flavor. The flavors themselves were alphabetically listed. Each flavor typically comprises a number of different alternatives (e.g. the choco taste includes choco pops, chocos,…). Within this (flavor) sub-group, alternatives were alphabetically organized by brand name. When an alternative came into more than one package size (hence, more than one alternative of the same flavor and brand name), the small package preceded the large one.

In a **pictorial** shelf, products were organized in blocks. This practice is comparable to the procedures that are used in a traditional supermarket. When organizing products by *brand*, we started by first grouping alternatives of the same brand. For margarine, a brand may consist of more than one type (e.g. offer both margarine and minarine). Within the sub-group of alternatives with the same brand, alternatives of the same type were grouped. Finally, if necessary, we placed the large package size right from the small package size (cf. traditional practice). For cereals, after grouping brands, we grouped flavors. In the traditional stores, 2 main groups are distinguished, viz. adult-oriented cereals (such as muesli, health, cornflakes) and children-oriented cereals (such as choco, honey, sugar, variety). The former are typically located on the upper shelves (more in line with 'eye-level of adults'), the latter are typically located on the lower shelves (more in line with 'eye-level of children'). To continue this line of thinking, we placed products that are oriented to adults on the top shelves and products that are oriented to children on the bottom shelves. Within these two main sub-groups, alternatives were further divided by flavor and, consequently, by type (e.g. corn, wheat,…). Finally, for alternatives that came in two package sizes, the large package size was positioned to the left of the small package size (cf. traditional stores). In contrast, when organizing alternatives by *flavor*, we started by grouping types for margarine and flavors for cereals. Afterwards, if necessary, the other attributes were taken into consideration.

To conclude, the shelf organization was made as realistic as possible and there was no systematic link between the position/place of a product on the shelf and its success (e.g. market share).

APPENDIX 3.C: Drop-out Analysis

In the following section, we will conduct a drop out analysis in an attempt to better understand why people decided to cease the experiment. We first look at the distribution of respondents that dropped out during a shopping session across manipulations (section 3.C.1). Afterwards we compare the profile of respondents that dropped out throughout the experiment and respondents that completed the experiment (section 3.C.2).

3.C.1 Distribution of drop-outs (during shopping session) across manipulations

One possible reason that people dropped out during the (mainly first) shopping sessions might be related to the (default) manipulations. To check whether consumers ceased the experiment because of the out-of-stock policy, the assortment or the default layout (mode and shelf organization) they were assigned to, we computed the number of respondents that dropped out during a shopping session across manipulations (see table 3.C.1). Comparing this figure with the prior (expected) distribution revealed no significant difference. We can therefore conclude that drop-outs occurred equally over the sample, irrespective of the manipulations.

Table 3.C.1: Distribution of respondents that dropped out during <u>a shopping session</u> across manipulations

Stimuli	Level	#	%	prior %
Total number of respondents that dropped out during a shopping session				**401**
Out-of-stock policy	Visible, no replacement	108	26.93%	25%
	Non-visible	104	25.93%	25%
	Replacement, focal attribute brand	89	22.19%	25%
	Replacement, focal attribute flavor	100	24.93%	25%
Shelf layout – mode (default)	Verbal	127	31.67%	33.33%
	Pictorial	274	68.33%	66.67%
Shelf layout – organization (default)	Brand	211	52.62%	50%
	Flavor	190	47.38%	50%
Assortment	Limited	129	32.17%	33%
	Extended (flavor)	141	35.16%	33%
	Extended (brand)	131	32.68%	33%

3.C.2 Profile of drop-outs

In addition, we compared the profile of respondents that dropped out throughout the experiment with the profile of respondents that completed the purchase simulations. Table 3.C.2 gives an overview of the socio-demographic characteristics, the Internet experience and the (traditional) grocery shopping information for both sub-samples and indicates when there is a significant difference between the two groups (see appendix 3.A, pre-purchase questionnaire for the exact questions).

Table 3.C.2: Comparing the profile of respondents that did not drop out versus respondents that did drop out

A. Socio-demographic characteristics

		No drop out	Drop out	Significant difference?
Gender	- Female	60%	54%	√
	- Male	40%	46%	
Age	- < 25 years	13%	14%	-
	- 26-35 years	37%	34%	
	- 36-45 years	26%	26%	
	- 46-55 years	18%	18%	
	- > 55 years	6%	9%	
Education	- High school or less	34%	46%	√
	- College	30%	26%	
	- College graduate	25%	21%	
	- Post-graduate	11%	7%	
Occupation	Unemployed	15%	19%	√
	Civil Servant	17%	14%	
	Other	7%	6%	
	Workman	7%	11%	
	Employee	46%	41%	
	Executive	5%	4%	
	Profession	1%	1%	
	Self-employed	3%	3%	
Family type	Single	8%	8%	-
	Partner only	26%	26%	
	Partner & children	54%	51%	
	Children	5%	7%	
	Parents	6%	8%	
	Other	1%	1%	
Number of children	0	41%	43%	-
	1	22%	20%	
	2	27%	25%	
	3	9%	10%	
	4	2%	1%	
	>5	1%	2%	

B. Internet experience

		No drop out	Drop out	Significant difference
Internet use	- daily	73%	72%	-
	- 5 à 6 days per week	12%	11%	
	- 3 à 4 days per week	7%	8%	
	- 2 days per week	3%	3%	
	- weekly	3%	5%	
	- monthly	1%	0.5%	
	- never	0.5%	0.5%	

C. Grocery shopping information

		No drop out	Drop out	Significant difference
* _Grocery_	- less than once per week	37%	36%	-
shopping	- once per week	58%	60%	
experience	- more than once per week	5%	4%	
* _How often_	- often	27%	26%	√
purchase	- almost always	58%	51%	
yourself	- sometimes	15%	23%	
* _Store loyalty_		4.92	5.03	-
*_Time pressure_		4.06	3.96	-
* _Shopping_	- positive	4.05	4.05	-
attitude	- negative	3.65	3.69	

Table 3.C.2 reveals that, in general, the profile of respondents that dropped out and those that did not drop out is quite similar. There are only some marginal (albeit significant) differences between the two groups. Compared to the profile of the non-drop-outs, significantly more males, more low-educated and more blue-collar workers seem to cease the experiment. In addition, compared to respondents that did not drop out, respondents that did drop out are significantly less likely to purchase grocery products themselves. As such, there seems to be a self-controlling tendency: people less likely to be the main grocery shopper are more likely to drop out. Moreover, respondents that dropped out are also less likely to belong to an online grocery shopping population (see online grocery shopping profile, chapter 1).

APPENDIX 4.A: OVERVIEW OF THE VARIABLES USED IN MODEL ESTIMATION

In the following table, we give an overview of the variables used in the final model estimation. We describe the variable, specify where it is included in the model and give an indication of the order of magnitude.

Variable	Description	Model	Order of magnitude	
			Margarine	Cereals
OOS_{it}	Stock-out dummy variable (equal to 1 if item i is out-of-stock, 0 otherwise)	Two-stage choice*	1 or 0	1 or 0
$D_{A,1,i}$	Attribute-level dummy variable (equal to 1 if item i is characterized by level 1 on attribute A, 0 otherwise)	Two-stage choice (CH)	1 or 0	1 or 0
LOY_i^h	Loyalty or initial (LT) preference of household h for item i (equal to the item's choice share in the category purchases over the last 12 months) *(Q5, post-purchase questionnaire)*	Two-stage choice (CH)	Between 0 & 1	Between 0 & 1
LP_{it}^h	Last purchase dummy variable (equal to 1 when item i was last purchased by household h at time t, 0 otherwise)	Two-stage choice (CO)	1 or 0	1 or 0
$OOS_{A,it}$	Stock-out asymmetry variable for attribute A (equal to the number of alternatives similar to i on attribute A that are out-of-stock in t)	Two-stage choice (CO)	0, 1, 2, …	0, 1, 2, …
$SUGG_{it}^h$	Suggestion dummy variable (equal to 1 when alternative i is suggested as a replacement item to household h at t)	Two-stage choice (CO)	1 or 0	1 or 0
$HPSUGG_{it}^h$	Higher price suggestion dummy variable (equal to 1 when alternative i is suggested as a replacement item to household h at time t and when i is of a higher package-equivalent price than the stock-out alternative, 0 otherwise)	Two-stage choice (CO)	1 or 0	1 or 0
CR^h	Weekly consumption rate for household h *(Q4, pre-purchase questionnaire)*	Incidence	>0 Mean: 0.862 Medium: 0.5 Mode: 0.50	>0 Mean: 1.382 Medium: 0.9 Mode: 0.50
INV_t^h	In-home inventory level (mean-centered) for household h at time t: $INV_t^h = INV_{t-1}^h + N_{t-1}^h - CR^h$ INV_0^h = in-home inventory level at the start *(Q4, pre-purchase questionnaire)* N_{t-1}^h = # of units bought by h in t-1	Incidence	Mean: 0.223 Medium: 0.0833 Mode: 0.25	Mean: 0.028 Medium: -0.1093 Mode: 0.00
CV_t^h	Category value for household h at time t (based on the parameters of two-stage choice model)	Incidence	Mean: -1.85	Mean: 1.206
$NVPOL_t^h$	Non-visible out-of-stock policy dummy variable (equal to 1 when consumer h has been exposed to a policy where stock-outs are not visible at first sight and when there were stock-outs at t, 0 otherwise)	Incidence	1 or 0	1 or 0

*CO = consideration stage, CH = choice stage

APPENDIX 4.B: EFFECT OF STOCK-OUT POLICY ON ONLINE PURCHASE BEHAVIOR

1. The effect of the replacement stock-out policy on the choice probability

The choice probability for alternative i when no suggestions are made, is given by the following expression:

$$p_i | NS = \frac{A_i}{\sum_j A_j}$$

(4.B1)

with $A_i = \exp(u'_i)$ for a one-stage (MNL) choice model

$A_i = \pi_i \exp(u_i)$ for a two-stage (B&V) choice model

When only alternative i is suggested (and other alternatives not), its attractiveness (A_i) increases (with a suggestion factor $SF_i > 1$) while the attractiveness of the remaining alternatives ($A_j, j \neq i$) remains unaltered:

$$p_i | S = \frac{SF_i A_i}{\sum_{j \neq i} A_j + SF_i A_i}$$

(4.B2)

where the suggestion factor (SF_i) captures the increase in attraction when an item is suggested compared to when it is not.

Therefore, the change in choice probability can be written as:

$$\frac{p_i | S}{p_i | NS} = \frac{SF_i A_i}{\sum_{j \neq i} A_j + SF_i A_i} * \frac{\sum_j A_j}{A_i} = \frac{SF_i * \sum_j A_j}{\sum_j A_j - A_i(1 - SF_i)} = \frac{SF_i}{1 - \frac{A_i(1 - SF_i)}{\sum_j A_j}} =$$

$$\frac{SF_i}{1 - p_i | NS * (1 - SF_i)} = \frac{1}{SF_i^{-1} * (1 - p_i | NS) + p_i | NS}$$

(4.B3)

It is interesting to compare the increase in attractiveness of an alternative when it is suggested (the suggestion factor) between a one-stage and a two-stage choice model.

In a one-stage (MNL) choice model the increase in attractiveness can be captured by:

$$SF_i = \exp(\omega'_{sugg})$$

(4.B4)

In a two-stage choice model, the increase in attractiveness depends on the impact of the suggestion on the consideration probability and is captured by the following expression:

$$SF_i = \frac{\pi_i|S}{\pi_i|NS} = \frac{1+\exp(\theta-s_i)}{1+\exp(\theta-s_i-\omega_{Sugg})} = \frac{1}{1+\exp(\theta-s_i-\omega_{Sugg})} + \frac{\exp(\theta-s_i)}{1+\exp(\theta-s_i-\omega_{Sugg})}$$

$$= \pi_i|S + (1-\pi_i|S)*\exp(\omega_{Sugg})$$

(4.B5)

Hence, incorporating (4.B4) and (4.B5) in expression (4.B3) equals:

$$\frac{p_i|S}{p_i|NS} = \frac{1}{\left[\exp(\omega'_{Sugg})\right]^{-1}*(1-p_i|NS)+p_i|NS} \qquad \text{(one-stage model)}$$

(4.B6)

and

$$\frac{p_i|S}{p_i|NS} = \frac{1}{\left[\pi_i|S+(1-\pi_i|S)*\exp(\omega_{Sugg})\right]^{-1}*(1-p_i|NS)+p_i|NS} \qquad \text{(two-stage model) (4.B7)}$$

Because suggesting a replacement item has a positive effect, the suggestion coefficient is positive ($\omega_{Sugg}>0, \omega'_{Sugg}>0$) and, as a result, $\exp(\omega_{Sugg})>1$ and $\exp(\omega'_{Sugg})>1$.
The increase in attractiveness of an alternative when it is suggested in a two-stage choice model (4.B5) can be rewritten as:

$$\pi_i|S+(1-\pi_i|S)*\exp(\omega_{Sugg}) = \exp(\omega_{Sugg})+\pi_i|S*(1-\exp(\omega_{Sugg}))$$

(4.B8)

Because $\pi_i|S$ has a value between 0 and 1 and, given a positive suggestion effect, $(1-\exp(\omega_{Sugg}))$ is smaller than 0, $\exp(\omega_{Sugg})+\pi_i|S*(1-\exp(\omega_{Sugg})) < \exp(\omega_{Sugg})$. As a result, compared to a two-stage model, the one-stage model would lead to overestimation of the suggestion effect when:

$$\exp(\omega_{Sugg}) + \pi_i \big| S *(1 - \exp(\omega_{Sugg})) < \exp(\omega'_{Sugg})$$

and to underestimation when:

$$\exp(\omega_{Sugg}) + \pi_i \big| S *(1 - \exp(\omega_{Sugg})) > \exp(\omega'_{Sugg}).$$

In our empirical study, the (significant) coefficients of the suggestion effect of the one-stage model were always larger than the equivalent measures of the two-stage model, respectively 1.5448 versus 1.3789 for margarine and 0.6255 versus 0.5570 for cereals. As such, in our empirical study, using the one-stage model would lead to an overestimation of the suggestion effect, which is illustrated for margarine in table 4.B1 (the two-stage choice model in the first part was discussed in section 4.4.4).

Table 4.B1: Comparing the two-stage (see section 4.4.4) and one-stage model wrt changes in choice probabilities when a replacement item is suggested (hypothetical example)[1]

	Two-stage choice model				One-stage choice model			
	A	B	C	D	A	B	C	D
a) regular choice environment								
Degree of consideration	0.69	0.4	0.69	0.85	-	-	-	-
Choice utility	0.18	0.74	0.74	0.6	-0.19	-0.19	0.36	0.43
Choice probability	18%	18%	31%	33%	18%	18%	31%	33%
b) disrupted choice environment (stock-out of alternative D)								
Choice probability	27%	27%	47%	0%	27%	27%	47%	0%
c) suggesting replacement items for the out-of-stock alternative								
Degree of consideration if item is suggested	0.90	0.72	0.90	0	1.35	1.35	6.72	-
Choice utility	0.18	0.74	0.74	0.6				
Choice probability if item is suggested (others not)	32%	40%	53%	0%	63%	63%	80%	0%
d) Out-of-stock effects								
Δ in consideration probability if item is suggested (others not)	30.20%	81.72%	30.20%		135%	135%	73%	
Δ in choice probability if item is suggested (others not)	20.52%	48.97%	14.16%					

---

[1] In this example, we do not take the effects of asymmetric switching into account. As an example, we take the coefficient of the suggestion variable of segment 1, margarine (see table 4.3). 1.3789 (two-stage model) and 1.5448 (one-stage model).

Table 4.B1 indicates that, compared to a two-stage model, the one-stage model would lead to an overestimation of the suggestion effect. Indeed, in the one-stage model, items with the same prior choice probability (A and B) would obtain the same gain from being suggested (irrespective of the underlying consideration and intrinsic choice utility) while the two-stage model shows that the effect of the suggestion is more pronounced for the low consideration, high utility item (B).

2. The effect of the stock-out policy on the incidence probability

Changing the benchmark stock-out policy (visible, no replacement) ($PI|0$) to a more active stock-out policy (non-visible or replacement) ($PI|\Delta pol$) changes the purchase incidence probability with the following fraction:

$$\Delta PI = \frac{PI|0 - PI|\Delta pol}{PI|0} = \frac{\dfrac{e^W}{1+e^W} - \dfrac{e^{W'}}{1+e^{W'}}}{\dfrac{e^W}{1+e^W}} = 1 - \frac{e^{W'}}{e^W} * \frac{1}{\dfrac{1}{1+e^W} + \dfrac{e^{W'}}{1+e^W}} =$$

$$1 - \frac{e^{W'}}{e^W} * \frac{1}{(1-PI|0) + PI|0 * \dfrac{e^{W'}}{e^W}} = 1 - \frac{1}{e^{-(W'-W)} * (1-PI|0) + PI|0}$$

(4.B9)

a) The effect of the non-visible policy is captured by the coefficient of the non-visible policy: $W' - W = \gamma_{NV}$ $\rightarrow$ $\exp(W' - W) = \exp(\gamma_{NV})$

(4.B10)

b) The effect of the replacement policy is captured by the coefficient of the category value and by the difference in the category value:

$W' - W = \gamma_{CV} \Delta CV$ $\rightarrow$ $\exp(W' - W) = \exp(\gamma_{CV} \Delta CV)$

(4.B11)

The change in the category value can be expressed as:

$$\Delta CV = \ln\left(\sum_j \exp(u_j) * \pi_j \big| S \right) - \ln\left(\sum_j \exp(u_j) * \pi_j \big| NS \right)$$

(4.B12)

188

Using the denominator of (4.B2) and (4.B1), respectively and assuming that there is only a suggestion for alternative i gives:

$$\Delta CV = \ln\left(\sum_{j \neq i} A_j + SF_i A_i\right) - \ln\left(\sum_j A_j\right) = \ln\left(\frac{\sum_j A_j - A_i + SF_i A_i}{\sum_j A_j}\right) = \ln\left(1 - \frac{A_i * (1 - SF_i)}{\sum_j A_j}\right)$$

$$= \ln\left(1 - p_i \big| NS * (1 - SF_i)\right)$$

(4.B13)

Substituting in (4.B11) the change in category value with expression (4.B13) and the suggestion factor with expression (4.B5) gives:

$$\exp(W' - W) = \exp\left(\gamma_{CV} \ln\left(1 - p_i \big| NS * (1 - SF_i)\right)\right) = \left(1 - p_i \big| NS * (1 - SF_i)\right)^{\gamma_{CV}}$$

$$= \left(1 - p_i \big| NS * (1 - \pi_i \big| S - (1 - \pi_i \big| S) * \exp(\omega_{Sugg}))\right)^{\gamma_{CV}}$$

$$= \left(1 - p_i \big| NS * (1 - \pi_i \big| S)(1 - \exp(\omega_{Sugg}))\right)^{\gamma_{CV}}$$

$$= \left(1 + p_i \big| NS * (1 - \pi_i \big| S)(\exp(\omega_{Sugg}) - 1)\right)^{\gamma_{CV}}$$

(4.B14)

Note: We portray relative instead of absolute changes. An absolute change is defined as the value of the initial (base) setting minus the value of the other (focal) setting. A relative change is defined as the percentage change between two variables (settings) of interest and is calculated by dividing the absolute change with the value of the base setting. Both approaches are appropriate (as they compare the same numbers). Relative measures are especially valuable for our research as they allow to more easily and readily compare results between the two product categories.

APPENDIX 5.A: OVERVIEW OF THE VARIABLES USED IN MODEL ESTIMATION

In the following table, we give an overview of the variables used in the final model estimation. For each variable, we present a definition and give an indication of its order of magnitude.

Variable	Description	Order of magnitude	
		Margarine	Cereals
OOS_{it}	Stock-out dummy variable (equal to 1 if item i is out-of-stock, 0 otherwise)	1 or 0	1 or 0
$D_{A,l,i}$	Attribute-level dummy variable (equal to 1 if item i is characterized by level l on attribute A, 0 otherwise)	1 or 0	1 or 0
LOY_i^h	Loyalty or initial (LT) preference of household h for item i (equal to the item's choice share in the category purchases over the last 12 months) (Q5, post-purchase questionnaire)	Between 0 & 1	Between 0 & 1
LP_{it}^h	Last purchase dummy variable (equal to 1 when item i was last purchased by household h at time t, 0 otherwise)	1 or 0	1 or 0
$OOS_{A,it}$	Stock-out asymmetry variable for attribute A (equal to the number of alternatives similar to i on attribute A that are out-of-stock in t)	0, 1, 2, …	0, 1, 2, …
Vis_{it}^h	Visibility variable (equal to 1 if alternative i for household h is shown on the first screen at time t, 0 otherwise)	1 or 0	1 or 0
$Prox_{it}^h$	Proximity variable (equal to the weighted sum of the number of times alternative i is positioned next to an out-of-stock item (i_{oos}) at time t for household h, with weights equal to the preference of household h for the stock-out item ($Loy_{i_{oos}}^h$)) $$\rightarrow Prox_{it}^h = \sum_{i_{oos}} Loy_{i_{oos}}^h * Adj_{i-i_{oos},t}^h$$ with $Adj_{i-i_{oos},t}^h$ = adjacent dummy variable (equal to 1 if alternative i is adjacent to stock-out item i_{oos} for household h at time t, 0 otherwise)	> 0	> 0

APPENDIX 5.B: OVERVIEW OF ALTERNATIVE 'ON SCREEN' DEFINITIONS

Table 5.B1 describes a number of alternative definitions of 'on screen' variables that were, next to the first-screen variable, inserted in the model in an attempt to capture the effect of the placement/position of products *on* the virtual shelf/screen. By way of illustration, we incorporate a graphical representation of each of the different 'on screen' definitions.

Table 5.B1: Overview of different 'on screen' variable definitions

Name	Definition	Graphically (pictorial)[†]
Sequence*	Inverse of the sequence (column-order) of alternative i for household h at time t.	Inverse of $\quad$ 1st screen $\qquad\qquad\qquad$ Not 1st screen 1 $\quad$ ... $\quad$ 1 $\quad$ 1 $\quad$ No 1 2 3 4 5 6 7 8 $\quad$ No 1 2 3 4 5 6 7 8 $\quad$ No 1 2 3 4 5 6 7 8 $\quad$ No
Eye-level	Equal to 1 when alternative i is positioned on the middle rows (rows 2/3) for household h at time t, 0 otherwise.	1st screen $\qquad$ Not 1st screen 1 1 1 1 1 1 1 1 1 1 1 1
Top-left (a)	Equal to 1 when alternative i is positioned on the top left screen (see graphical representation of the delineation of top left) for household h at time t, 0 otherwise.	1st screen $\qquad$ Not 1st screen 1 1
Top-left (b)	Equal to 1 when alternative i is positioned on the top left screen (see graphical representation of the delineation of top left) for household h at time t, 0 otherwise.	1st screen $\qquad$ Not 1st screen 1 1 1 1 1 1
Top-rows (a)	Equal to 1 when alternative i is positioned on the first (top) row for household h at time t, 0 otherwise.	1st screen $\qquad$ Not 1st screen 1 1
Top-rows	Equal to 1 when alternative i is positioned on the first two	1st screen $\qquad$ Not 1st screen 1 1

(b)　　　(top) rows for household h at time t, 0 otherwise.

† Because it is not always straightforward to find a counterpart of each 'on screen' variable for the verbal shelf, we estimated for some of the operationalizations (eye-level, top-left a/b and top-rows a/b) a model based only on the dataset of respondents that never chose from the verbal shelf. For variables where the definition was appropriate/similar for the verbal and pictorial shelf (first screen and sequence), we (1) compared the results of the more extended dataset (including all the respondents) with the results of the more limited dataset (including only those respondent that never chose from the verbal list). The substantive results did not change. In addition, we (2) explicitly tested for interaction/moderating effects. In line with the former result, there was no improvement in fit and interaction terms were practically never significant. For these variables, we decided to continue with the more extended dataset.

* For this operationalization, we also tested a model where we 'replaced' the first-screen definition with the sequence definition (i.e. estimation of the model with only a sequence definition). Yet, using this alternative definition did not significantly improve model fit.

We estimated models incorporating, next to the first-screen variable, the above-mentioned on-screen variables, for both categories. Comparing the model fit and face validity for each of these alternative model estimations revealed that the model where only the first-screen definition was included, outperformed these alternative models. While some of the on-screen variables are possibly highly correlated with the first screen variable (such as the top-left definition where we were unable to define the top-left position per screen as result of the scrolling option), other definitions do not suffer from this caveat. Our results therefore might indicate that, in contrast to the traditional world where placement of products on the shelf (e.g. eye-level) is shown to have a strong effect, there is no such clear-cut effect of placement of products on the screen in the virtual store. This finding is confirmed by recent research of van der Lans (2002). His research reveals that consumers use different strategies to locate a target product on a (computer-simulated) supermarket shelf: horizontal zigzag, vertical zigzag, inward and upward spirals or even a random search strategy. As such, it is not straightforward which process consumers use during a search task and how placement of products on a computer screen might influence the outcome of this process.

APPENDIX 5.C: EFFECT OF VIRTUAL SHELF PLACEMENT ON ONLINE CHOICE BEHAVIOR

1. The effect of visibility on the choice probability

The choice probability for alternative i when visibility is not taken into account, is equal to:

$$p_i | NVis = \frac{\exp(u_{i|NVis})}{\sum_j \exp(u_{j|NVis})}$$

(5.C1)

with $u_{i|NVis}$ = choice probability when visibility effects are ignored

When the visibility is taken into account, the choice probability changes to:

$$p_i | Vis = \frac{\exp(\beta_{Vis} Vis_{it}^h) * \exp(u_{i|NVis})}{\sum_j \exp(\beta_{Vis} Vis_{jt}^h) * \exp(u_{j|NVis})}$$

(5.C2)

The change in choice probability for alternative i (Δp_i) when the visibility effect is taken into account ($p_i | Vis$) compared to a situation where this is not the case ($p_i | NVis$) can be written as:

$$\Delta p_i = \frac{p_i | Vis - p_i | NVis}{p_i | NVis} = \frac{p_i | Vis}{p_i | NVis} - 1$$

$$= \frac{\dfrac{\exp(\beta_{Vis} Vis_{it}^h) * \exp(u_{i|NVis})}{\sum_j \exp(\beta_{Vis} Vis_{jt}^h) * \exp(u_{j|NVis})}}{\dfrac{\exp(u_{i|NVis})}{\sum_j \exp(u_{j|NVis})}} - 1 = \frac{\exp(\beta_{Vis} Vis_{it}^h) * \sum_j \exp(u_{j|NVis})}{\sum_j \exp(\beta_{Vis} Vis_{jt}^h) * \exp(u_{j|NVis})} - 1$$

(5.C3)

2. The effect of proximity on the choice probability

The proximity-effect is particularly important in an out-of-stock situation. The change in choice probability for alternative i (Δp_i) when other alternatives are unavailable is equal to:

$$\Delta p_i = \frac{p_i|OOS - p_i|AV}{p_i|AV} = \frac{p_i|OOS}{p_i|AV} - 1 =$$

$$\frac{\dfrac{\exp(\sum_A \beta_{A,oos} OOS_{A,it} + \beta_{\mathrm{Prox}} \mathrm{Pr}\, ox_{it}^h) * \exp(u_{i|AV})}{\sum_j \exp(\sum_A \beta_{A,oos} OOS_{A,jt} + \beta_{\mathrm{Prox}} \mathrm{Pr}\, ox_{jt}^h) * \exp(u_{j|AV})}}{\dfrac{\exp(u_{i|AV})}{\sum_j \exp(u_{j|AV})}} - 1 =$$

$$\frac{\exp(\sum_A \beta_{A,oos} OOS_{A,it} + \beta_{\mathrm{Prox}} \mathrm{Pr}\, ox_{it}^h) * \sum_j \exp(u_{j|AV})}{\sum_j \exp(\sum_A \beta_{A,oos} OOS_{A,jt} + \beta_{\mathrm{Prox}} \mathrm{Pr}\, ox_{jt}^h) * \exp(u_{j|AV})} - 1$$

(5.C4)

where $p_i|AV$ is the choice probability and $u_{i|AV}$ the choice utility of alternative i when all alternatives are available and where $p_i|OOS$ is the choice probability when out-of-stocks (for other alternatives than i) occur.

Note: As indicated in appendix 4.B, we portray relative instead of absolute changes. Because a relative measure controls for the scale, it allows to compare results across the two product categories.

REFERENCES

AcNielsen (2004). Strong online grocery activity. *AcNielsen newsletter*. Available from http://www.factsfiguresfuture.com/archive/march_2004.

Ailawadi, K.L., Gedenk, K, & Neslin, S.A. (1999). Heterogeneity and purchase event feedback in choice models: An empirical analysis with implications for model building. *International Journal of Research in Marketing*, 16 (3), 177-198.

Ailawadi, K.L., Lehmann, D.R., & Neslin, S.A. (2003). Revenue premium as an outcome measure of brand equity. *Journal of Marketing*, 67 (4), 1-17.

Alba, J., Lynch, J., Weitz, B., Janiszewski, C., Lutz, R., Sawyer, A., & Wood, S. (1997). Interactive home shopping: Consumer, retailer, and manufacturer incentives to participate in electronic marketplaces. *Journal of Marketing*, 61 (3), 38-53.

Anckar, B., Walden, P., & Jelassi, T. (2002). Creating customer value in online grocery shopping. *International Journal of Retail and Distribution Management*, 30 (4), 211-220.

Anderson Consulting (1996). Where to look for incremental sales gains: The retail problem of out-of stock merchandise. *The Coca-Cola retailing research council*.

Anderson, E., Fitzsimons, G., & Simester, D. (2004). Measuring and mitigating the costs of stockouts. Working Paper. Cambridge: Sloan School of Management.

Andrews, R.L., Ainslie, A., & Currim, I. (2002). An empirical comparison of logit choice models with discrete and continuous representations of heterogeneity. *Journal of Marketing Research*, 39 (4), 479-487.

Andrews, R.L., & Currim, I.S. (2002). Identifying segments with identical choice behaviors across product categories: An intercategory logit mixture model. *International Journal of Research in Marketing*, 19 (1), 65-79.

Andrews, R.L., & Currim, I.S. (2004). Behavioral differences between consumers attracted to shopping online versus traditional supermarkets: Implications for enterprise design and marketing strategy. *International Journal of Internet Marketing and Advertising*, 1 (1), 38-61.

Andrews, R.L., & Srinivasan, T.C. (1995). Studying consideration effects in empirical choice models using scanner panel data. *Journal of Marketing Research*, 32 (1), 30-41.

Ansari, A. and Mela, C.F. (2003). E-customization. *Journal of Marketing*, 40 (2). 131-145.

Ariely, D. (2000). Controlling the information flow: Effects on consumers' decision making and preferences. *Journal of Consumer Research*, 27 (2), 233-248.

Asseal, H. (1998). *Consumer behaviour and marketing action*. Boston: Mass: PWS-Kent.

Babin, B.J., Darden, W.R., & Griffin, M. (1994). Work and/or fun: Measuring hedonic and utilitarian shopping value. *Journal of Consumer Research*, 20 (4), 644-656.

Baker, J., Parasuraman, A., Grewal, D. & Voss, G.B. (2002). The influence of multiple store environment cues on perceived merchandise value and patronage intentions. *Journal of Marketing,* 66 (2), 120-141.

Bakos, J.Y. (1997). Reducing buyer search costs: Implications for electronic marketplaces. *Management Science,* 43 (12), 1676-1693.

Bakos, J.Y. (2001). The emerging landscape for retail e-commerce. *Journal of Economic Perspectives*, 15 (1), 69-80.

Bell, D.R., & Fitzsimons, G.J. (1999). *An experimental and empirical analysis of consumer response to stockouts.* Working Paper. Philadelphia: The Wharton School.

Bellizzi, J.A., Crowley, A.E. & Hasty, R.W. (1983). The effects of color in store design. *Journal of Retailing*, 59 (1), 21-46.

Bellman, S., Lohse, G.L., & Johnson, E.J. (1999). Predictors of online buying behavior. *Communications of the ACM*, 42 (12), 32-38.

Ben-Akiva, M., & Lerman, S. (1985). *Discrete choice analysis. Theory and application to travel demand.* Cambridge (Mass).

Beuk, F. (2001). *Out-of-stock! Out-of-business?* Doctoral Dissertation. Rotterdam: Erasmus Food Management Institute (in Dutch).

Bhargava, H.K., Sun, D., & Xu, S.H. (2005). Stockout compensation: Joint inventory and price optimization in electronic retailing. Forthcoming in *INFORMS Journal of Computing.*

Bhat, C.R. (2001). Quasi-random maximum simulated likelihood estimation of the mixed multinomial logit model. *Transportation Research,* 35B (7), 677-695.

Biz.yahoo (2005). Kmart.com is ranked top site in best and worst of site design 2005. Available from http://biz.yahoo.com/prnews/050323/dew019_4.html

Boatwright, P., & Nunes, J.C. (2001). Reducing assortment: An attribute-based approach. *Journal of Marketing*, 65 (3), 50-63.

Borin, N., & Farris, P. (1995). A sensitivity analysis of retailer shelf management models. *Journal of Retailing*, 71 (2), 153-171.

Boyer, K.K., & Hult, G.T. (2005a). Customer behavioral intentions for online purchases: An examination of fulfillment method and customer experience level. Forthcoming in *Journal of Operations Management.*

Boyer, K.K., & Hult, G.T. (2005b). Extending the supply chain: Integrating operations and marketing in the online grocery industry. Forthcoming in *Journal of Operations Management*.

Brehm (1966). *A theory of psychological reactance*. New York: Academic Press.

Broere, Van Gensink, & Van Oostrom (1999). De relatie tussen looprichting en aankoopgedrag. *Erasmus Food Management Institute, EFMI 2001-05* (in Dutch).

Broniarczyk, S.M., Hoyer, W.D., & McAlister, L. (1998). Consumers' perceptions of the assortment offered in a grocery category: The impact of item reduction. *Journal of Marketing Research*, 35 (2), 166-176.

Bronnenberg, B.J., & Vanhonacker, W.R. (1996). Limited choice sets, local price response and implied measures of price competition. *Journal of Marketing Research*, 33 (2), 163-174.

Brynjolfsson, E., & Smith, M. (2000). Frictionless commerce? A comparison of Internet and conventional retailers. *Management Science*, 46 (4), 563-585.

Bucklin, R.E., & Gupta, S. (1992). Brand choice, purchase incidence and segmentation: An integrated modeling approach. *Journal of Marketing Research*, 29 (2), 201-215.

Bucklin, R.E., Gupta, S., & Siddarth, S. (1998). Determining segmentation in sales response across consumer purchase behaviors. *Journal of Marketing Research*, 35 (2), 189-197.

Bucklin, R.E., & Lattin, J.M. (1991). A two-state model of purchase incidence and brand choice. *Marketing Science*, 10 (1), 24-39.

Bultez, A., & Naert, P. (1988). SH.A.R.P.: Shelf allocation for retailers' profit. *Marketing Science*, 68 (7), 211-232.

Burke, R.R. (1996). Virtual shopping: Breakthrough in marketing research. *Harvard Business Review*, 74 (2), 120-131.

Burke, R.R. (1997). Do you see what I see? The future of virtual shopping. *Journal of the Academy of Marketing Science*, 25 (4), 352-360.

Burke, R.R., Harlam, B.A., Kahn, B., & Lodish, L.M. (1992). Comparing dynamic consumer choice in real and computer-simulated environments. *Journal of Consumer Research*, 19 (1), 71-82.

Buttle, F. (1984). Retail space allocation. *International Journal of Physics, Distribution and Material Management*, 14 (4), 3-23.

Campo, K. (1997). *Variety seeking and the sensitivity to in-store promotions*. Unpublished doctoral thesis, UFSIA (University of Antwerp), May.

Campo, K., & Gijsbrechts, E. (2005). Retail assortment, shelf and stockout management: Issues, interplay and future challenges. *Applied Stochastic Models in Business and Industry* (a special issue on "Bridging the gap between academic research in marketing and practitioners' concerns") edited by Bemmaor, A.C. & Franses, P.H., 21 (3).

Campo, K., Gijsbrechts, E., & Guerra, F. (1999). Computer simulated shopping experiments for analyzing dynamic purchasing patterns: validation and guidelines. *Journal of Empirical Generalisations in Marketing Science* 4, 22-61.

Campo, K., Gijsbrechts, E., & Nisol, P. (2000). Towards understanding consumer response to stock-outs. *Journal of Retailing*, 76 (2), 219-242.

Campo, K., Gijsbrechts, E., & Nisol, P. (2003). The impact of retailer stockouts on whether, how much and what to buy. *International Journal of Research in Marketing*, 20 (3), 273-286.

Campo, K., Gijsbrechts, E., & Nisol, P. (2004). Dynamics in consumer response to product unavailability: Do stock-out reactions signal response to permanent assortment reductions? *Journal of Business Research,* 57(8), 834-843.

Center for Competitive Analysis (2000). The soap and other detergents manufacturing industry: Trends and characteristics. *A Report of the Center for Competitive Analysis.*

Chandon, P.J., Hutchinson, J.W., & Young, S. (2001). Measuring the value of point-of-purchase marketing with commercial eye-tracking data. Working paper. Fontainebleau: INSEAD 2001/19/MKT.

Chandon, P.J., Hutchinson, J.W., & Young, S. (2002). Unseen is unsold: Asses visual equity with commercial eye-tracking data. Working paper. Fontainebleau: INSEAD 2002/85/MKT.

Charlton, P., & Ehrenberg, A.S.C. (1976). An experiment in brand choice. *Journal of Marketing Research*, 13 (2), 152-160.

Childers, T.L., Carr, C.L., Peck, J., & Carson, S. (2001). Hedonic and utilitarian motivations for online retail shopping behavior. *Journal of Retailing,* 77 (4), 511-536.

Chittaro L., & Ranon R. (2002). New directions for the design of virtual reality interfaces to e-commerce sites. *Proceedings of AVI 2002: 5th International Conference on Advanced Visual Interfaces*, ACM Press, New York, 308-315.

Clemmer, E.C., & Schneider, B. (1993). Managing customer dissatisfaction and waiting: Applying social-psychological theory in a service setting. *Advances in services marketing and management: research and practices*, 2: Greenwich, CT: JAI Press, 213-229.

Cohen, S., & Gadd, M. (1996). Virtual reality shopping simulation for the modern marketer. *Marketing and Research Today*, 26 (1), 18-26.

Cole, C.A., & Balsubramanian, S. (1993). Age differences in consumers' search for information: public policy implications. *Journal of Consumer Research*, 20 (1), 157-169.

Cook, T.D., & Campbell, D.T. (1979). *Quasi-experimentation: design and analysis issues for field settings*. Chicago.

Corsten, D., & Gruen, T. (2003). Desperately seeking shelf availability: an examination of the extent, the causes and the efforts to address retail out-of-stocks. *International Journal of Retail and Distribution Management*, 31 (12), 605-617.

Corstjens, J., & Corstjens, M. (1995). *Store wars: The battle for mindspace and shelfspace*. Wiley: Chichester.

Corstjens, M., & Doyle, P. (1981). A model for optimizing retail space allocations. *Management Science*, 27 (7), 822-833.

Cude, B.J., & Morganosky, M.A. (2000). Online grocery shopping: An analysis of current opportunities and future potential. *Consumer Interests Annual*, 46, 95-100.

Czarnowski, A. (2001). Current state of the multiples: how are consumers shopping these days? *Taylor Nelson Sofres Superpanel.*

Danaher, P.J., Wilson, I.W., & Davis, R.A. (2003). A comparison of online and offline consumer brand loyalty. *Marketing Science*, 22 (4), 461-476.

De Clerck, S., Gijsbrechts, E., Steenkamp, J-B. E.M., & Dekimpe, M. (2001). *The impact of assortment reductions and extensions on category sales*. Working paper. Belgium: Catholic University of Leuven.

Degeratu, A.M., Rangaswamy, A., & Wu, J. (2000). Consumer choice behavior in online and traditional supermarkets: The effects of brand name, price, and other search attributes. *International Journal of Research in Marketing*, 17 (1), 55-78.

Desmet, P. & Renaudin, V. (1998). Estimation of product category sales responsiveness to allocated shelf space. *International Journal of Research in Marketing*, 15 (5), 443-457.

Dhar, R. (1997). Consumer preference for a no-choice option. *Journal of Consumer Research*, 24 (2), 215-231.

Dickson, P.R., & Sawyer, A.G. (1990). The price knowledge and search of supermarket shoppers. *Journal of Marketing*, 54 (3), 42-53.

Djevizova, K., & Atanassova, Y. (2004). eStrategies for promotion of end-use efficiency products and services in the local market. Available from http://www.acadjournal.com/2004/V12/Part6/p1/ .

Donthu, N., & Gilliland, D. (1996). Observations: the infomercial shopper. *Journal of Advertising Research*, 36 (2), 69-76.

Drèze, X., Hoch, S.J. & Purk, M.E. (1994). Shelf management and space elasticity. *Journal of Retailing*, 70 (4), 301-326.

Ellen, P.S., Mohr, L.A., & Webb, D.J. (2000). Charitable programs and the retailer. Do they mix? *Journal of Retailing*, 76 (3), 393-406.

Emmelhainz, M.A., Stock, J.R., & Emmelhainz, L.W. (1991). Consumer response to retail stock-outs. *Journal of Retailing*, 67 (2), 138-147.

Eroglu, S.A., Machleit, K.A. & Davis, L.M. (2001). Atmospherics qualities of online retailing: A conceptual model and implications. *Journal of Business Research*, 54 (2), 177-184.

Fader, P.S., & Hardie, B.G.S. (1996). Modeling consumer choice among SKUs. *Journal of Marketing Research*, 33 (4), 442-452.

Fader, P.S., & McAlister, L. (1990). An elimination by aspects model of consumer response to promotion calibrated on UPC scanner data. *Journal of Marketing Research*, 27 (3), 322-332.

Fangfang, D., & Shyam, S. (2004). Orienting response and memory for web advertisements: exploring effects of pop-up window and animation. *Communication Research*, 31 (5), 537-567.

Farquhar, P.H., & Pratkanis, A.R. (1993). Decision structuring with phantom alternatives. *Management Science*, 39 (10), 1214-1226.

Finn, A. (1988). Print ad recognition leadership scores: An information processing perspective. *Journal of Marketing Research*, 25 (2) 168-177.

Fitzsimons, G.J. (2000). Consumer response to stockouts. *Journal of Consumer Research*, 27 (2), 249-266.

Fitzsimons, G.J., & Lehmann, D.R. (2004). Reactance to recommendations: When unsolicited advice yields contrary responses. *Marketing Science*, 23 (1) 82-94.

Floor, K., & van Raaij, F. (1998). *Marketing-communicatiestrategie*. Houten: Educatieve Partners Nederland.

Folkes, V.S. (1984). Consumer reaction to product failure: An attributional approach. *Journal of Consumer Research*, 10 (2), 398-409.

Forehand, M.R, & Grier, S. (2003). When is honesty the best policy? The effect of stated company intent on consumer skepticism. *Journal of Consumer Psychology*, 13 (3), 349-356.

Fortheringham, A.S. (1988). Consumer store choice and choice set definition. *Marketing Science*, 7 (3), 299-310.

Gallagher, K., Foster, K.D., & Parsons, J. (2001). The medium is not the message: comparing advertising effectiveness in print and on the web. *Journal of Advertising Research*, 41 (4), 57-70.

Gensch, D.H. (1987). A two-stage disaggregate attribute choice model. *Marketing Science*, 6 (3), 223-239.

Geuens, M., Brengman, M., & S'Jegers, R. (2003). Food retailing, now and in the future. A consumer perspective. *Journal of Retailing & Consumer Services*, 10 (4), 241-251

Gijsbrechts, E., Campo, K, & Goossens, T. (2003). The impact of store flyers on store sales and store traffic: a geomarketing approach. *Journal of Retailing*, 79 (1), 1-16.

Gilbride, T., & Allenby, G.M. (2004). A choice model with conjunctive, disjunctive, and compensatory screening rules. *Marketing Science*, 23 (3), 391-407.

Grewal, D., Iyer, G.R., & Levy, M. (2004). Internet retailing: Enablers, limiters and market consequences. *Journal of Business Research*, 57 (7), 703-713.

Gruen, T.W., Corsten, D., & Bharadwaj, S. (2002). Retail out-of-stocks: A worldwide examination of causes, rates and consumer responses. Washington D.C.: Grocery manufacturers of America.

Guadagni, P.M. and Little, J.D. (1983). A logit model of brand choice calibrated on scanner data. *Marketing Science*, 2 (3), 203-239.

Gupta, S. (1988). Impact of sales promotions on when, what and how much to buy. *Journal of Marketing Research*, 25 (4), 342-355.

Hansen, T. (2005). Understanding consumer online grocery behaviour: Results from a Swedish study. *Journal of Euromarketing*, 14 (3), 31-58.

Hanssens, D.M., & Weitz, B.A. (1980). The effectiveness of industrial print advertisements across product categories. *Journal of Marketing Research*, 17 (2) 294-306.

Häubl, G., Dellaert, B., Murray, K., & Trifts, V. (2004). Buyer behavior in personalized shopping environments: Insights from the institute of online consumer studies. In *Designing personalized user experiences in e-commerce*, edited by Karat, C., Karat, J., & Blom, J. (eds). New York, NY: Kluwer.

Häubl, G., & Trifts, V. (2000). Consumer decision making in online shopping environments: the effects of interactive decision aids. *Marketing Science*, 19 (1), 4-21.

Hess, J.D, & Gerstner, E. (1998). Yes, 'bait and switch' really benefits customers. *Marketing Science*, 17 (3), 283-289.

Ho, T.H., & Chong, J.K. (2003). A parsimonious model of stock keeping-unit choice. *Journal of Marketing Research*, 40 (3), 351-365.

Hoch, S.J., Bradlow, E.L., & Wansink, B. (1999). The variety of assortment. *Marketing Science*, 18 (4), 527-546.

Hoffman, D.L., & Novak, T.P. (1996). Marketing in hypermedia computer-mediated environments: Conceptual foundations. *Journal of Marketing*, 60 (3), 50-68.

Holbrook, M. B., & Lehmann, D.R. (1980). Form versus content in predicting starch scores. *Journal of Advertising Research*, 20 (3), 53-62.

Hotelmarketing (2004). Online spending more than doubles. *Hotelmarketing*. Available from http://www.hotelmarketing.com/index.php/content/article/online_spending_more_than_doubles/

Hoque, A.Y., & Lohse, G.L. (1999). An information search cost perspective for designing interfaces for electronic commerce. *Journal of Marketing Research*, 36 (3), 387-395.

Howard, J.A. (1989). *Consumer behaviour in marketing strategy*. Englewood Cliffs, N.J.: Prentice-Hall.

Howard, J.A., & Sheth, J.N. (1969). *The theory of buyer behavior*. New York, NY: Wiley.

Hoyer, W.D. (1984). An examination of consumer decision making for a common, repeat-purchase product. *Journal of Consumer Research*, 11 (3), 822-829.

Hoyer, W.D., & Cobb-Walgren, C.J. (1988). Consumer decision making across product categories: The influence of task environment. *Psychology and Marketing*, 5 (1), 45-69.

Huffman, C., & Kahn, B.E. (1998). Variety for sales: mass customization or mass confusion? *Journal of Retailing*, 74 (4), 491-513.

Internet Retailer (2005). Consumer data may be more vulnerable offline than online, expert says. Available from http://www.internetretailer.com/dailyNews.asp?id=14461

Jaccard, J., Turrisi, R., & Wan, C.K. (1990). *Interaction effects in multiple regression.* Sage: Newbury Park, California.

Jedidi, K., & Zhang, J. (2002). Augmenting conjoint analysis to estimate consumer reservation price. *Management Science*, 48 (10), 1350-1368.

Kahn, B.E., & McAlister, L. (1997). *Grocery revolution: The new focus on the consumer.* Addison-Wesley Pub. Co.

Kamakura, W.A., Kim, B.D., & Lee, J. (1996). Modeling preference and structural heterogeneity in consumer choice. *Marketing Science*, 15 (2), 152-172.

Kämäräinen, V., Saranen, J., & Holmström, J. (2001). The reception box impact on home delivery efficiency in the e-grocery business. *International Journal of Physical Distribution and Logistics Management*, 31 (6), 414-426.

Kämäräinen, V., Småros, J., Holmström, J., & Jaakola, T. (2001). Cost-effectiveness in the e-grocery business. *International Journal of Retail and Distribution Management*, 29 (1), 41-48.

Keh, H.T., & Shieh, E. (2001). Online grocery retailing: success factors and potential pitfalls. *Business Horizons,* 44 (4), 73-83.

Kelley, H.H. (1973). The process of causal attribution. *American Psychologist* , 28, 107-128.

Kempiak, M., & Fox, M. (2002). Online grocery shopping: consumer motives, concerns and business models. *First Monday*, 7 (9), Available from http://www.firstmonday.org/issues/issue7_9/kempiak/index.html

Key Findings (1999). Trends and insights into the business marketplace. Available from www.keyfindings.com.

Kolesar, M.B. & Galbraith, R.W. (2000). A services-marketing perspective on e-retailing: implications for e-retailers and directions for further research. *Internet Research: Electronic Networking Applications and Policy*, 10 (5), 424-438.

Kotler, P. (1991). *Marketing management: Analysis, planning, implementation and control.* London: Prentice-Hall International Editions.

Kucuk, S.U. (2004). Reducing the out-of-stock costs in a developing retailing sector. *Journal of International Consumer Marketing.* 16 (3), 75-105.

Kutz, K. (1998). Online grocery shopping on track for rapid growth. *Andersen Consulting Newsletter*, January 20.

Laroche, M., Kim, C., & Matsui T. (2003). Which decision heuristics are used in consideration set formation? *Journal of Consumer Marketing*, 20 (3), 192-209.

Leclerc, F., & Little, J.D.C. (1997). Can advertising copy make FSI coupons more effective? *Journal of Marketing Research*, 34 (4), 473-484.

Leeflang, P., Wittink, D., Wedel, M., & Naert, P. (2000). *Building models for marketing decisions.* Boston: Kluwer Academic Publishers.

Leong, S.M. (1993). Consumer decision making for common, repeat-purchase products: A dual replication. *Journal of Consumer Psychology*, 2 (2), 193-208.

Levy, M., & Weitz, B. (1995). *Retailing Management*, Second Edition, Burr Ridge, IL.: Irwin.

Lohse, G.L. (1997). Consumer eye movement patterns on yellow pages advertising. *Journal of Advertising*, 26 (1), 62-74.

Lohse, G.L., & Wu, D.J. (2001). Eye movement patterns on Chinese yellow pages advertising. *Electronic Markets*, 11 (2), 87-96.

Louvière, J.J., Hensher, D.A, & Swait, J.J. (2003). *Stated Choice Methods: Analysis and Application*, University Press, Cambridge, UK.

Lynch, J.G.Jr (1982). On the external validity of experiments in consumer research. *Journal of Consumer Research*, 9 (4), 225-239.

Lynch, J.G.Jr, & Ariely, D. (2000). Wine online: Search costs affect competition on price, quality and distribution. *Marketing Science,* 19 (1), 83-104.

Malhotra, N. (1999). *Marketing research : An applied orientation.* London: Prentice-Hall.

Mandel, N., & Johnson, E.J. (2002). Can web pages influence choice: Effects of visual primes on experts and novices. *Journal of Consumer Research,* 29 (2), 235-245.

Manrai, A.K. (1995). Mathematical models of brand choice behavior. *European Journal of Operational Research*, 82 (1), 1-17.

Manrai, A.K., & Andrews, R.L. (1998). Two-stage discrete choice models for scanner panel data: An assessment of process and assumptions. *European Journal of Operational Research*, 111 (2), 193-215.

Marketing Online (2003). De e-supermarkt heeft toekomst. *Marketing online.* Available from http://www.marketing-online.nl/nieuws/index2003-14.html (in Dutch).

Marketing Online (2004). Verzendkosten grootste ergernis internetwinkels. *Marketing online.* Available from http://www.marketing-online.nl/nieuws/moduleitem35372.html (in Dutch).

Marketing Online (2005). Koopgedrag verandert sterk. *Marketing online.* Available from http://www.marketing-online.nl/nieuws/moduleitem38149.html (in Dutch).

McAlister, L. (1982). A dynamic attribute satiation model of variety-seeking behavior. *Journal of Consumer Research,* 9 (2), 141-150.

McAlister, L., & Pessemier, E. (1982). Variety seeking behavior: An interdisciplinary review. *Journal of Consumer Research.* 9 (3), 311-322.

McFadden, D., & Train, K.E. (2000). Mixed MNL models for discrete response. *Journal of Applied Econometrics,* 15 (5), 447-470.

McGoldrick, P. (2002). *Retail Marketing (second edition).* New York: The McGraw-Hill Companies.

McGree, A., & Boyer, K. (2005). Online and in-store customers: Comparing loyalty and execution. In *Grocery E-commerce behavior and business strategy*, edited by Kornum, N., & Bjerre, M., Edward Elgar Publishing Limited, UK.

Mehta, N., Rajiv, S., & Srinivasan, K. (2003). Price uncertainty and consumer search: a structural model of consideration set formation. *Marketing Science*, 22 (1), 58-84.

Menon, S., & Kahn, B.E. (2002). Cross-category effects of induced arousal and pleasure on the Internet shopping experience. *Journal of Retailing*, 78 (1), 31-40.

Menon, G., Raghubir, P., & Schwarz, N. (1995). Behavioral frequency judgments: an accessibility-diagnosticity framework. *Journal of Consumer Research*, 22 (2), 212-228.

Mizerski, R.W., Golden, L.L., & Kernan, J.B. (1979). The attribution process in consumer decision making. *Journal of Marketing Research*, 16 (4), 552-559.

Morales, A., Kahn, B.E., McAlister, L., & Broniarczyk, S.M. (2005). Perceptions of assortment variety: the effects of congruency between consumer's internal and retailer's external organization. *Journal of Retailing,* 81 (2), 159-169.

Morganosky, M.A., & Cude, B.J. (2000). Consumer response to online grocery shopping. *International Journal of Retail and Distribution Management*, 28 (1), 451-458.

Morganosky, M.A., & Cude, B.J. (2001). Consumer response to online food retailing. *Journal of Food Distribution Research*, 32 (1), 5-17.

Morganosky, M.A., & Cude, B.J. (2002). Consumer demand for online food retailing: Is it really a supply side issue? *International Journal of Retail and Distribution Management*, 30 (10), 451-458.

Motes, W.H., & Castleberry, S.B. (1985). A longitudinal field test of stockout effects on multi-brand inventories. *Journal of the Academy of Marketing Science*, 13 (4), 54-68.

Murphy, A. (2003). (Re)solving space and time: fulfillment issues in online grocery retailing. *Environment and Planning A,* 35 (7), 1173-1200.

Nagle, T.T., & Holden, R.K. (1995). *The strategy and tactics of pricing: a guide to profitable decision making.* Englewood Cliffs, N.J.: Prentice Hall.

Nedungadi, P. (1990). Recall and consumer consideration sets: Influencing choice without altering brand evaluations. *Journal of Consumer Research.* 17 (2), 262-276.

Needel, S.P. (1995). Marrying market research and virtual reality: implications for consumer research. In *Information Technology: How can research keep up with the pace of change?* ESOMAR Conference, 25-27 January, Brussels, Belgium. 65-75

Palmer, A., Beggs, R., & Keown-McMullan, C. (2000). Equity and repurchase intention following service failure. *Journal of Services Marketing*, 14 (6), 513-528.

Parasuraman, A., Zeithaml, V.A., & Malhotra, A. (2005). E-S-QUAL: A multiple-item scale or assessing electronic service quality. *Journal of Service Research*, 7 (3) 213-233.

Peckman, J. (1963). The consumer speaks. *Journal of Marketing*, 27 (4), 21-26.

Pessemier, E.A. (1964). Forecasting brand performance through simulation experiments. *Journal of Marketing*, 28 (2), 41-46.

Petty, R.E., & Cacioppo, J.T. (1984). The effects of involvement on responses to argument quantity and quality: Central and peripheral routes to persuasion. *Journal of Personality and Social Psychology*, 46, 69-81.

Petty, R.E., & Cacioppo, J.T. (1986). The elaboration likelihood model of persuasion. *Advances in Experimental Social Psychology*, 19, 123-205.

Pieters, R.G.M., & Bijmolt, T.H.A. (1997). Consumer memory for television advertising: a field study of duration, serial position and competition effects. *Journal of Consumer Research*, 23 (4), 362-372.

Pieters, R.G.M., & Warlop, L. (1999). Visual attention during brand choice: The impact of time pressure and task motivation. *International Journal of Research in Marketing*, 16 (1), 1-16.

POPAI (2001). Consumer Buying Habits Study of Food in the Netherlands. *Point-of-purchase advertising International*.

Progressive Grocer (1968a). The out of stock study: Part I. October, S1-S16.

Progressive Grocer (1968b). The out of stock study: Part II. November, S17-S32.

Punakivi, M. (2003). Comparing alternative home delivery models for e-grocery business. *Doctoral Dissertation*, Helsinki University of Technology, Department of Industrial Engineering and Management.

Punakivi, M., & Tanskanen, K. (2002). Increasing the cost efficiency of e-fulfilment using shared reception boxes. *International Journal of Retail and Distribution Management*, 30 (10), 498-507.

Punakivi, M., Yrjölä, H., & Holmström, J. (2001). Solving the last mile issue: reception box or delivery box? *International Journal of Physical Distribution and Logistics Management*, 31 (6), 427-439.

Putrevu, S., & Ratchford, B.T. (1997). A model of search behaviour with an application to grocery shopping. *Journal of retailing*, 73 (4), 463-485.

Raijas, A., & Tuunainen, V.K. (2001). Critical factors in electronic grocery shopping. *The International Review of Retail, Distribution and Consumer Research*, 11 (3), 255-265.

Reibstein, D.J., Youngblood, S.A., & Fromklin, H.L. (1975). Number of choices and perceived decision freedom as a determinant of satisfaction and consumer behavior. *Journal of Applied Psychology*, 60 (4), 434-437

Ring, L.J., & Tigert, D.J. (2001). Viewpoint: the decline and fall of internet grocery retailers. *International Journal of Retail and Distribution Management*, 29 (6), 266-273.

Roberts, J.H., & Lattin, J.M. (1991). Development and testing of a model of consideration set composition. *Journal of Marketing Research*, 28 (4), 429-440.

Roberts, J.H., & Lattin, J.M. (1997). Consideration: Review of research and prospects for future insights. *Journal of Marketing Research*, 34(3), 406-410.

Roberts, M., Xu, X.M., & Mettos, N. (2003). Internet shopping – the supermarket model and customer perceptions. *Journal of Electronic Commerce in Organisations*, 1 (2), 33-44.

Rohm, A.J., & Swaminathan, V. (2004). A typology of online shoppers based on shopping motivations. *Journal of Business Research*, 57 (7), 748-757.

Rossiter, J.R., & Percy, L. (1997). *Advertising communications and promotion management*. New York: McGraw-Hill.

Ruud, P. (1996). Approximation and simulation of the multinomial probit model: An analysis of covariance matrix estimation. Working Paper. Berkeley: Department of economics, University of California.

Russo, J.E., & Leclerc, F. (1994). An eye-fixation analysis of choice processes for consumer nondurables. *Journal of Consumer Research*, 21 (2), 274-290.

Saranen, J., & Småros, J. (2001). An analytical model for home delivery in the new economy. Working paper. Helsinki: University of Technology.

Schary, P.B., & Becker, B.W. (1978). The impact of stock-out on market share: temporal effects. *Journal of Business Logistics*, 1 (1), 31-44.

Schary, P.B., & Christopher, M. (1979). The anatomy of a stock-out. *Journal of Retailing*, 55 (2), 59-70.

Senecal, S., & Nantel, J. (2004). The influence of online product recommendations on consumers' online choices. *Journal of Retailing*, 80 (2), 159-169.

Shankar, V., Smith, A.K., & Rangaswamy, A. (2003). Customer satisfaction and loyalty in online and offline environments. *International Journal of Marketing Research*, 20 (2), 153-175.

Shocker, A.D., Moshe, B.A., Boccara, B., & Nedungadi, P. (1991). Consideration set influences on consumer decision-making and choice: Issues, models and suggestions. *Marketing Letters*, 2 (3), 181-197.

Shycon, H.N., & Sprague, C.R. (1975). Put a price tag on your customer servicing levels. *Harvard Business Review*. 53 (4), 71-78.

Siddarth, S., Bucklin, R.E., & Morrison, D.G. (1995). Making the cut: Modeling and analyzing choice set restriction in scanner panel data. *Journal of Marketing Research*, 32 (3), 255-266.

Simonson, I. (1993). Get closer to your customers by understanding how they make choices. *California Management Review*, 39 (4), 68-84.

Simonson, I. (1999). The effect of product assortment on buyer preferences. *Journal of Retailing*, 75 (3), 347-370.

Simonson, I., Carmon, Z., & O'Curry, S. (1994). Experimental evidence on the negative effect of product features & sales promotions on brand choice, *Marketing Science*, 13 (1), 23-40.

Simonson, I., & Tversky, A. (1992). Choice in context: tradeoff contrast and extremeness aversion. *Journal of Marketing Research*, 29 (3), 281-296.

Simonson, I., & Winer, R.S. (1992). The influence of purchase quantity and display format on consumer preference for variety. *Journal of Consumer Research*, 19 (1), 133-138.

Sloot, L.M. (2001). In-store shopping behaviour: The in-store decision making process of shoppers in Dutch supermarkets. *Erasmus Food Management Institute, EFMI 2001-05*.

Sloot, L.M., Verhoef, P.C., & Franses, P.H. (2005). The impact of brand equity and the hedonic level of a product on consumer stock out reactions. *Journal of Retailing*, 81 (1), 14-35.

Småros, J., & Holmström, J. (2000). Viewpoints: reaching the consumer through e-grocery VMI. *International Journal of Retail and Distribution Management*, 28 (2), 55-61.

Smith, D.N., & Sivakumar, K. (2004). Flow and Internet shopping behaviour: A conceptual model and research propositions. *Journal of Business Research*, 57 (10), 1199-1209.

Smith, K., Bolton, R.N., & Wagner, J. (1999). A model of customer satisfaction with service encounters involving failure and recovery. *Journal of Marketing Research*, 36 (3), 356-372.

Smith, M. (2003, December 30). Bumps in the sales road, part 2. *Click-Z Today*.

Spangenberg, E.A., Crowley, A.E., & Henderson, P.W. (1996). Improving the store environment: Do olfactory cues affect evaluations and behaviors? *Journal of Marketing*, 60 (2), 67-81.

Straziuso, J. (2004, May 04). Clicking for groceries. *The Washington Times.* Available from http://washingtontimes.com/business/20040516-102450-4340r.htm

Swait, J., & Andrews, R.L. (2003). Enriching scanner panel models with choice experiments. *Marketing Science,* 22 (4), 442-460.

Swait, J., & Louvière, J. (1993). The role of the scale parameter in the estimation and comparison of multinomial logit models. *Journal of Marketing Research,* 30 (3), 305-315.

Tanskanen, K., Yrjölä, H., & Holmström, J. (2002). The way to profitable Internet grocery retailing – six lessons learned. *International Journal of Retail and Distribution Management,* 30 (4), 169-178.

Thaler, R. (1985). Mental accounting and consumer choice. *Marketing Science,* 4(3), 199-214.

Train, K.E. (1999). Halton sequences for mixed logit. Working paper. Berkeley

Train, K.E. (2001). A comparison of hierarchical bayes and maximum simulated likelihood for mixed logit. Working paper. Berkeley

Train, K.E. (2003). *Discrete choice methods with simulation.* Cambridge: University Press.

Tversky, A., & Simonson, I. (1993). Context-dependent preferences. *Management Science,* 39 (10), 1179-1190.

Urban, T.L. (1998). An inventory-theoretic approach to product assortment and shelf-space allocation. *Journal of Retailing,* 74 (1), 15-35.

Van den Poel, D., & J. Leunis (1999). Consumer acceptance of the Internet as a channel of distribution. *Journal of Business Research,* 45 (3), 249-256.

Van der Lans, R. (2002). *In search of the brand: A conceptual model and a first empirical study.* Working paper. Tilburg: Tilburg University.

Van Elburg, A. (2001, October 04). Kruidenier. *Emerce.* Available from http://www.emerce.nl/archives/magazine/oktober2001/interview/13051.html (in Dutch).

Van Elburg, A. (2005, April 05). Trendbox: Internetverkoop zal sterk toenemen. *Emerce.* Available from http://www.emerce.nl/nieuws.jsp?id=565467 (in Dutch).

Van Herpen, E., & Pieters, R. (2002). The variety of an assortment: An extension to the attribute-based approach. *Marketing Science,* 21 (3), 331-341.

Van Ketel, E., van Bruggen, G.H., & Smidts, A. (2003). *How assortment variety affects assortment attractiveness.* In Michael Saren (ed.), Marketing: responsible and relevant? Proceedings of the 32nd EMAC Conference, Glasgow, UK: University of Strathclyde.

Van Trijp, J.C.M., Hoyer, W.D., & Inman, J.J. (1996). Why switch? Variety seeking behaviour as a product x individual interaction. *Journal of Marketing Research*, 33 (3), 281-292.

van Waterschoot, W., & Gijsbrechts, E. (2003). Knowledge transfer through marketing textbooks – the Howard and Sheth typology as a case in point. In *The Future of Marketing*, Kitchen, Ph., Palgrave-MacMillan, Houndmills, Basingstoke.

Verbeke, W., Farris, P., & Thurik, R. (1998). Consumer response to the preferred brand out-of-stock situation. *European Journal of Marketing*, 32 (11/12), 1008-1028.

Verhoef, P., & Langerak, F. (2001). Possible determinants of consumers' adoption of electronic grocery shopping in The Netherlands. *Journal of Retailing and Consumer Services,* 8 (5), 275-285.

Verhoef, P., & Sloot, L.M. (2005). Out-of-stock: Reactions, antecedents, management solutions and a future perspective. In *Retailing in the 21st century: Current and future trends*, Krafft, M., & Mantrala, M., Springer Verslag.

Viswanathan, M. (2002). Comparison of measures of speech quality for listening tests of text-to-speech systems. *Proceedings of 2002 IEEE Workshop on Speech Synthesis,* p.11-14.

Walter, C., & Grabner, J. (1975). Stockout cost models: Empirical tests in a retail situation. *Journal of Marketing.* 39 (3), 56-60.

Wedel, M., & Pieters, R.G.M. (2000). Eye fixations on advertisements and memory for brands: a model and findings. *Marketing Science*, 19 (4), 297-312.

Wiersma, T. (2004a). Albert.nl zet opmars voort, omzetstijging 30 procent. *Emerce* Available from http://www.emerce.nl/nieuws.jsp?id=197130. (in Dutch).

Wiersma, T. (2004b). Tesco claimt titel grootste online kruidenier. *Emerce* Available from http://www.emerce.nl/nieuws.jsp?id=196728. (in Dutch).

Wiersma, T. (2005). Online bestedingen stijgen naar 1,68 miljard in 2004. *Emerce* Available from http://www.emerce.nl/nieuws.jsp?id=494378. (in Dutch).

Wilkie, W.L., Mela, C.F., & Gundlach, G.T. (1998). Does "bait and switch" really benefit consumers? *Marketing Science*, 17 (3), 273-282.

Winer, R.S. (1999). Experimentation in the 21st Century: the importance of external validity. *Journal of the Academy of Marketing Science*, 27 (3), 349-358.

Wu, J., & Rangaswamy, A. (2003). A fuzzy set model of search and consideration with an application to an online market. *Marketing Science*, 22 (3), 411-434.

Wydra, D., & Martin, S. (1997). Online vs in-line: Research implications of online grocery shopping, November.

Xia, L., Monroe, K.B., & Cox, J.L. (2004). The price is unfair! A conceptual framework of price fairness perceptions. *Journal of Marketing*, 68 (4), 1-15.

Yalch, R., & Spangenberg, E. (1990). Effects of store music on shopping behavior. *Journal of Consumer Marketing*, 7 (2), 55-64.

Yrölä, H. (2001). Physical distribution considerations for electronic grocery shopping. *International Journal of Physical Distribution and Logistics Management*, 31 (10), 746-761.

Zeithaml, V.A., Parasuraman, A., & Malhotra, A. (2002). Service quality delivery through web sites: A critical review of extant knowledge. *Journal of the Academy of Marketing Science*, 30 (4) 362-375.

Zhang, J. (2001). Comparing consumer purchase behavior on the Internet and in brick-and-mortar stores: An overview of recent research. In *Internet Marketing Research: Theory and Practice*, edited by Ook Lee et al., Hershey, PA: Idea Group Publishing, 218-230.

Zhang, J., & Dimitroff, A. (2005). The impact of webpage content characteristics on webpage visibility in search engine results. *Information Processing and Management*, 41 (3), 665-690.

Zinn, W., & Liu, P.C. (2001). Consumer response to retail stockouts. *Journal of Business Logistics*, 22 (1), 49-71.

NEDERLANDSE SAMENVATTING

Inleiding tot probleemstelling

De 'Internet revolutie' leidt een nieuw tijdperk in, waarin e-commerce een niet meer weg te denken fenomeen is. Voor consumenten opent ze een wereld van nieuwe mogelijkheden en laat ze toe om producten en diensten op een elektronische manier te bestellen. Op dit ogenblik wordt het aankopen via Internet ook meer en meer een algemeen aanvaarde manier om frequent aangekochte consumptiegoederen (voedingswaren en huishoudproducten) op een snelle en efficiënte wijze te bestellen. De elektronische winkelomgeving verschilt duidelijk op een aantal punten van de traditionele winkelomgeving. Deze typische online kenmerken beïnvloeden niet alleen het elektronisch aankoopgedrag, ze bieden tegelijkertijd meer flexibiliteit voor een virtuele detailhandelaar (retailer). Dit impliceert dat effecten die vrij goed in kaart gebracht zijn voor traditionele winkelpunten niet zonder meer transfereerbaar zijn naar de elektronische winkelomgeving.

Eén van de problemen waar een e-supermarkt mee geconfronteerd wordt, is het stock-out probleem (i.e. tijdelijke onbeschikbaarheid van producten). Stock-outs vormen voor nieuwe distributiekanalen zoals een online winkel zelfs een groter probleem dan voor traditionele kanalen omdat de vraag nog sterker fluctueert en voorspellingsproblemen bestaan (Fitzsimons, 2000). Bovendien heeft recent onderzoek aangetoond dat bij Internetconsumenten productonbeschikbaarheid op de tweede plaats staat in hun top 3 van irritaties (Marketing online, 9/11/2004). Ondanks het belang van stock-outs voor een e-supermarkt, is er nog bijzonder weinig bekend over de impact ervan op elektronisch aankoopgedrag (en in welke mate dit verschilt van offline reacties).

Daarenboven zijn, in vergelijking met een traditionele supermarkt, de 'merchandising kosten' (i.e. kosten die men oploopt bij het maken van fysische wijzigingen aan de winkelomgeving) veel lager in een virtuele supermarkt. De stijging in flexibiliteit die hieruit resulteert, biedt kansen aan de e-tailer om beleidsopties te implementeren die niet of veel moeilijker geïmplementeerd kunnen worden in een traditionele supermarkt. In dit doctoraat nemen we op de volgende twee beleidsmogelijkheden onder de loep:

(1) Opportuniteiten voor actief stock-out management in een online supermarkt: de impact van de gekozen stock-out beleidsoptie op online stock-out reacties *(stock-out policy)*;

(2) Opportuniteiten voor in-store, schap-gerelateerd management: de impact van virtuele schappositionering op keuzes in een online supermarkt *(virtual shelf placement)*.

De volgende onderzoeksvragen werden in dit doctoraat geformuleerd:

	Project 1: Stock-out policy	Project 2: Virtual shelf placement
Doelstelling	* *Hoe maken consumenten een aankoopbeslissing voor frequent aangekochte consumptiegoederen:*	

- *in een 'gewone' online winkelomgeving (regular)?*
- *in een online winkelomgeving die 'verstoord' wordt door stock-outs (disrupted)?*

* *Wat is het effect van verschillende stock-out beleidsopties:*	* *Wat is het effect van de plaats van producten op een virtueel schap:*
(1) stock-outs zichtbaar voor iedereen (visible policy) versus stock-outs enkel zichtbaar na een aankooppoging (non-visible policy)?	*(1) producten zichtbaar op het eerste scherm versus producten niet zichtbaar op het eerste scherm (visibility)?*
(2) niet suggereren van een substitutieproduct (no-replacement policy) versus het suggereren van een substitutieproduct (replacement policy)?	*(2) producten in de onmiddellijke omgeving van een geprefereerd out-of-stock product versus verder afgelegen producten (proximity)?*
(2a) het suggereren van een substitutieproduct van een hogere prijs versus het suggereren van een substitutieproduct van dezelfde of lagere prijs (modererend effect van een hogere-prijs suggestie)?	*(3) de kans dat consumenten meer vatbaar zijn voor de plaats van een product op een virtueel schap als ze geconfronteerd worden met een groot versus klein assortiment (modererend effect van assortimentsomvang)?*

Het onderzoeksdomein in dit doctoraat heeft zich beperkt tot de studie van het aankoopgedrag van frequent aangekochte consumptiegoederen in een virtuele winkelomgeving *(electronic grocery shopping services)*. De eerste, globale doelstelling van dit doctoraat bestond uit het in kaart brengen van de verschillen tussen een elektronische en traditionele winkelomgeving en aan te geven hoe deze verschillen een invloed uitoefenen op elektronisch aankoopgedrag. In dit onderzoek hebben we niet enkel gekeken naar aankoopgedrag in een 'gewone/normale' elektronische winkelomgeving maar hebben we ons in het bijzonder geconcentreerd op een omgeving die 'verstoord' werd door een stock-out situatie. Op basis van een overzicht van de belangrijkste verschillen tussen een elektronische en traditionele winkelomgeving (hoofdstuk 1) en een literatuuroverzicht mbt stock-outs in traditionele supermarkten (hoofdstuk 2) werd een conceptueel raamwerk opgesteld. Dit conceptueel raamwerk laat toe om na te gaan hoe consumenten een beslissing nemen in een 'normale' online winkelomgeving en in een online winkelomgeving die 'verstoord' wordt door een stock-out situatie.

De tweede doelstelling van dit doctoraat was na te gaan hoe elektronisch aankoopgedrag beïnvloed wordt door de gekozen beleidsopties (marketing acties) van een e-tailer. Meer specifiek hebben we onderzocht in welke mate consumenten beïnvloed worden door de gekozen out-of-stock politiek (project 1) en de plaats van producten op een virtuele schapruimte (project 2). Teneinde data voor zowel het eerste als het tweede onderzoeksproject te verzamelen, werd een experiment opgezet. Een bestaande online shopping service werd aangepast aan de noden van het experiment. In het experiment werden de out-of-stock politiek (3 versies) (onderzoeksproject 1), het assortiment (3 versies) en de schapindeling (2 versies) (onderzoeksproject 2) gemanipuleerd. Respondenten werden gevraagd om in de online winkel gesimuleerde aankopen te doen voor 2 productcategorieën (margarine en ontbijtgranen) voor 6 fictieve weken (*time-compressed setting*). Voor beide onderzoeksprojecten werden bestaande individuele aankoop-(incidence) en keuze(choice)modellen (bv. Bronnenberg & Vanhonacker, 1996; Bucklin, Gupta, & Siddarth, 1998; Bucklin & Lattin, 1991) aangepast zodat vooropgestelde hypothesen getest konden worden. Terwijl de gekozen stock-out beleidsoptie een invloed uitoefent op zowel de aankoopbeslissing (ja/nee) als de keuzebeslissing (welk product), heeft de plaats van producten op een schap vooral een effect op de keuzebeslissing. Daarom hebben we ons in het eerste project geconcentreerd op de aankoop- en keuzebeslissing, terwijl de aandacht in het tweede project beperkt werd tot enkel de keuzebeslissing. Hoofdstuk 3 beschrijft het online computergesimuleerde experiment. De twee projecten worden respectievelijk in hoofdstuk 4 en 5 besproken.

Dit doctoraat levert inzichten in hoe virtuele retailers (of fabrikanten in hun rol van *category captain*) via marketing mix acties elektronisch aankoopgedrag kunnen beïnvloeden. Terwijl het eerste project richtlijnen verschaft voor actief online stock-out management, worden in het tweede project de 'veelbelovende plaatsen' op een virtuele schapruimte geïdentificeerd. De resultaten stellen virtuele retailers (of fabrikanten) in staat om de meest gepaste stock-out beleidsoptie te implementeren en helpen hen

215

bestaande virtuele schapruimte beter te beheren. Uiteindelijk zullen onze resultaten helpen bij de verbetering van hun prestaties (*performance-enhancing*). Hierna zullen we eerst de belangrijkste bevindingen betreffende de algemene onderzoeksvraag samenvatten. Daarna worden de resultaten en implicaties van elk van de projecten belicht. We eindigen met de formulering van enkele algemene conclusies en geven de algemene beperkingen van dit onderzoek aan.

Globale onderzoeksvraag

Hoe nemen consumenten een aankoopbeslissing in een 'normale' online keuzeomgeving en in een online keuzeomgeving die 'verstoord' wordt door stock-outs?

Wanneer consumenten voedingswaren en huishoudproducten (*grocery products*) op een elektronische manier aankopen, hebben ze de neiging gebruik te maken van vereenvoudigende heuristieken, zowel in een 'normale' als in een 'verstoorde' online winkelomgeving. Het gebruik van deze vereenvoudigende tactieken laat hen toe om op een snelle en efficiënte manier tot een voldoeninggevende beslissing te komen. Deze bevinding wordt ondersteund vanuit het algemene aankoopbeslissingsproces van supermarktproducten. Bij dergelijke aankopen blijken consumenten immers weinig geneigd om veel aandacht te geven aan alle informatie/alternatieven (zgn. *peripheral-route processing*) en gebruiken ze typisch – hoewel niet exclusief – een routine besluitvorming in een 'normale' keuzeomgeving (zgn. *routinized response behavior*) en een beknopte besluitvorming wanneer ze geconfronteerd worden met een interruptie (zgn. *limited problem solving*). Ook de onderliggende motieven om voedingswaren en huishoudproducten via een e-supermarkt te bestellen, stimuleren het gebruik van vereenvoudigende tactieken. Uit de e-grocery literatuur blijkt immers dat winkelgemak (*convenience*) de belangrijkste motivatie is om voedingswaren en huishoudproducten via het Internet te bestellen (bv. Andrews and Currim, 2004; Morganosky and Cude, 2002; Raijas and Tuunainen, 2001). De tendens om vereenvoudigende heuristieken te gebruiken bij de aankoop van frequent aangekochte goederen in een e-supermarkt werd bevestigd in de empirische studie. Zo waren consumenten meer geneigd om gesuggereerde producten aan te kopen (1^e project, suggestie-effect) of om producten te kiezen die een opvallende plaats hadden op het virtuele schap (2^e project, visbility- en proximity-effect).

Bovendien blijkt, zowel vanuit een conceptueel standpunt (theoretisch raamwerk, hoofdstuk 2) als vanuit een empirisch standpunt (project 1, hoofdstuk 4), dat consumenten die geconfronteerd worden met een stock-out situatie in een e-supermarkt meer geneigd zijn in de online winkel te blijven en een ander product te kiezen. De tendens om naar een ander substitutieproduct te switchen ipv te beslissen geen aankoop in de categorie te doen, kan verklaard worden door een aantal typische kenmerken van de elektronische winkelomgeving. Zo is bijvoorbeeld het winkelgemak een belangrijke determinant bij het aankopen van producten via het Internet en geeft het ontbreken van fysieke verplaatsingen in een virtueel winkelpunt aanleiding tot een daling van de zoekkosten. Deze tendens werd wederom bevestigd in het empirisch onderzoek waar er slechts een klein of helemaal geen effect van stock-outs op de aankoopbeslissing gevonden werd (hoofdstuk 4).

Onderzoeksvraag van het eerste project
Op welke manier beïnvloedt een actief stock-out beleid de aankoop- en keuzebeslissing
van een consument in een e-supermarkt?

In het eerste onderzoeksproject werd onderzocht hoe een online retailer aan de hand van een actief stock-out beleid, negatieve effecten van stock-out reacties kan reduceren. In dit onderzoek werden de volgende 3 stock-out beleidsopties onder de loep genomen: (1) een beleid waar geen suggesties gedaan worden en stock-outs zichtbaar zijn voor iedereen (*no-replacement, visible policy*), (2) een beleid waar stock-outs enkel zichtbaar zijn wanneer men het desbetreffende product wil aankopen (*non-visible policy*) en (3) een beleid waar voor elk out-of-stock product een substitutieproduct wordt voorgesteld (*replacement policy*).

In traditionele supermarkten zijn stock-outs typisch zichtbaar (lege plaats op het schap) en worden er geen substitutieproducten voorgesteld. De visible, no-replacement optie werd daarom als benchmark gebruikt in dit onderzoek. De selectie van de andere beleidsopties was gebaseerd op (1) de huidige praktijken van e-supermarkten en (2) de mate waarin de virtuele retailer een duidelijk implementatievoordeel heeft tov een traditionele retailer. Ten eerste heeft men in een virtuele winkel, in tegenstelling tot een traditionele winkel waar stock-outs zichtbaar zijn voor alle klanten, de mogelijkheid om enkel de kopers van het stock-out product op de hoogte te brengen. Online retailers kunnen hun stock-out problemen minder zichtbaar maken door ze aan te kondigen via een pop-up die verschijnt wanneer men het desbetreffende product wil aankopen. Ten tweede kan een online retailer gemakkelijker een alternatief product voor elk out-of-stock product voorstellen. Een online retailer kan immers gebruik maken van een technologische procedure om onmiddellijk en bij elke stock-out gebeurtenis een suggestie te doen. Traditionele retailers daarentegen moeten eerst vaststellen dat er een stock-out probleem is waarna ze hun schapruimte fysisch moeten re-organiseren. Eén van de essentiële vragen bij de suggestiepolitiek is de selectie van een geschikt suggestie-item. In dit opzicht hebben we de modererende invloed van de prijs van het gesuggereerde item mee in rekening genomen. Resultaten uit het empirisch onderzoek tonen aan dat de gehanteerde beleidsoptie een significante invloed uitoefent op de aankoop- maar ook op de uiteindelijke keuzebeslissing.

Ten eerste blijkt uit de resultaten dat het gebruik van een typisch elektronisch kenmerk, de pop-up, om stock-out problemen te verbergen, de aankoopkans in een categorie doet dalen, vooral voor consumenten die de neiging hebben hetzelfde product te kopen. Voor deze 'gewoonte-kopers' (*habitual buyers)* versterkt de valse verwachting die de non-visible beleidsoptie schept (nl. de mogelijkheid om hun geprefereerd product te kunnen kopen), de negatieve ervaring die zij hebben wanneer ze vaststellen dat hun geprefereerd product toch niet beschikbaar is. Verder blijkt uit de resultaten dat consumenten zeer snel geïrriteerd en gefrustreerd zijn (i.e. hun '*point-of-frustration*' bereiken), zelfs na één of enkele klikken. Hoewel het dus a-priori aantrekkelijk lijkt voor online retailers om hun stock-out problemen te verbergen, tonen de resultaten dat consumenten negatief reageren en dat ze verkiezen om op voorhand het daadwerkelijke aanbod (de beschikbare producten) te kennen.

Ten tweede tonen de resultaten dat, in het algemeen, de kans dat een item in overweging (en dus gekozen) wordt significant stijgt wanneer het als substitutieproduct wordt gesuggereerd, vooral voor consumenten die niet veel belang hechten aan de productcategorie. In tegenstelling met het onderzoek van Beuk (2001) die geen effect van de suggestiepolitiek in een traditionele winkel vond, blijkt uit onze resultaten dat het suggereren van substitutieproducten een waardevolle beleidsoptie kan zijn voor online retailers. Echter, de resultaten tonen dat de suggestie van een substitutieproduct enkel in een sterk positief effect resulteert onder bepaalde voorwaarden. Zo worden positieve effecten geneutraliseerd wanneer substitutieproducten met een hogere prijs ('verdachte items') gesuggereed worden. Verder tonen de resultaten dat suggesties vooral gewaardeerd worden wanneer het gesuggereerde item aanvankelijk niet of weinig in overweging genomen werd maar toch aantrekkelijk is (zgn. *low consideration, high utility item*).

Hoewel het suggereren van substitutieproducten een sterke invloed uitoefent op het keuzegedrag van een groot segment van consumenten, is het effect op de aankoopbeslissing klein tot onbestaand. Het potentieel van de suggestiepolitiek om de kans dat men beslist niet aan te kopen in geval van een stock-out te reduceren, is daarom slechts beperkt aanwezig. De afwezigheid van sterke effecten op de aankoopbeslissing kan verklaard worden door elektronische winkelkenmerken (in het algemeen meer geneigd om in een online context een substitutieproduct aan te kopen ipv de winkel te verlaten zonder aankoop). Ook de productcategorie (een groot assortiment en de variety-seeking tendens voor ontbijtgranen) en/of de artificiële onderzoeksomgeving kunnen als verklaring aangehaald worden waarom effecten op de aankoopkans klein of afwezig zijn.

Globaal genomen duiden de resultaten aan dat online retailers (of fabrikanten in hun rol van *category captain*) door een substitutieproduct te suggereren een invloed kunnen uitoefenen op de keuze van consumenten die geconfronteerd worden met een stock-out situatie. Echter, ze dienen behoedzaam te zijn bij de selectie van het gesuggereerde substitutieproduct. Zo kunnen consumenten niet overtuigd worden om duurdere items aan te kopen. De resultaten duiden verder aan dat consumenten negatief reageren wanneer ze sceptisch staan tov de procedures die aan de grondslag liggen van de beleidsopties. Dit blijkt het geval wanneer stock-outs verborgen worden of wanneer hogere prijs items gesuggereerd worden. Consumenten waarderen en belonen een open en eerlijke retailer, i.e. een retailer die alle kaarten op de tafel legt en daadwerkelijk helpt om een eenvoudige en moeiteloze beslissing te maken. Retailers moeten dan ook bij voorkeur een open en consumentgeoriënteerde politiek nastreven (cf. de principes van *customer relationship marketing*).

<u>*Onderzoeksvraag van het tweede project*</u>

Op welke manier beïnvloedt de plaats van producten op een virtueel schap de keuzebeslissing van een consument in een e-supermarkt en hoe wordt dit gemodereerd door assortimentsomvang?

In het tweede onderzoekproject werd nagegaan hoe de plaats van een product op een virtueel schap, de keuzebeslissing van een consument beïnvloedt en of – en in welke mate – het assortiment een modererende invloed uitoefent. In dit onderzoek werd de invloed van (1) *'visibility'* (plaats als dusdanig) en (2) *'proximity'* (plaats relatief tov van andere producten) bestudeerd. Terwijl het *'visibility-effect'* kan spelen bij elke keuze-beslissing wordt het *'proximity-effect'* vooral belangrijk in een out-of-stock situatie. Consumenten die geconfronteerd worden met een out-of-stock moeten beslissen welke van de overblijvende alternatieven ze wensen aan te kopen (als ze al kopen). In een dergelijke situatie heeft de plaats van een product op een (virtueel) schap misschien nog een sterkere impact op de uiteindelijke keuze die men maakt. Dit onderzoek geeft inzicht in, of en hoe, online consumenten de positionering van producten op een virtueel schap gebruiken als een vereenvoudigende tactiek en hoe het gebruik ervan gemodereerd wordt door het aangeboden assortiment.

Bij de start van de Internet-hype werd gesuggereerd dat schapruimte-beheer (*shelf management*) niet of van zeer gering belang was voor een e-supermarkt. Zo is er in een virtueel winkelpunt in principe een onbeperkte schapruimte en geeft het ontbreken van fysieke verplaatsingen aanleiding tot een significante daling van de zoekkosten. Echter, recente (meer realistische) ontwikkelingen duiden aan dat een online retailer met (eigen) schapruimte-problemen geconfronteerd wordt. De hoeveelheid informatie die men per scherm kan voorstellen is begrensd en de volgorde/positie van producten op een virtueel schap is bepalend voor hun zichbaarheid en (als gevolg hiervan) hun aankoopkans. Bovendien hebben online retailers meer opportuniteiten om hun schapruimte aan te passen. Ze kunnen immers letterlijk via één knop de plaats van producten op een schap veranderen. De empirische resultaten uit dit onderzoek geven aan dat een e-supermarkt inderdaad geconfrontereerd wordt met het probleem van schaptruimte-allocatie over producten. Zowel de locatie van producten op een virtueel schap, als de nabijheid van producten in een out-of-stock situatie hebben een significant effect op online keuzebeslissingen.

Ten eerste wijzen resultaten op een significant effect van de positionering van producten *over* verschillende schermen. Producten die op het eerste scherm gepresenteerd worden, hebben een grotere kans om gekozen te worden (*visibility-effect*), vooral door consumenten die minder belang hechten aan de productcategorie. Eerste-scherm alternatieven springen niet enkel meer in het oog (*prominence*), consumenten beginnen typisch op het eerste scherm met het verwerven en verwerken van informatie (*primacy*). Omdat het onwaarschijnlijk is dat consumenten het volledige assortiment scannen, biedt het het eerste scherm van de default/start optie online retailers de mogelijkheid om specifieke alternatieven onder de aandacht te brengen (cf. in-store stimulus). Het is niet enkel het scherm dat alle consumenten eerst zien, veel consumenten blijven bij de start/default optie, ondanks het feit dat ze zelf de layout van het scherm kunnen wijzigen. In tegenstelling tot dit *across-screen* effect, werd er geen effect gevonden van de positionering van producten *op* een scherm. In contrast met bevindingen uit traditionele winkelpunten die het effect van de plaats van een product op een traditioneel schap onderstrepen (bv. oog/hand-hoogte), blijkt in een e-supermarkt geen uitgesproken *on-screen* effect te bestaan.

Ten tweede blijkt dat wanneer consumenten gefixeerd zijn op een bepaalde sectie van het schap (bv. wanneer ze hun geprefereerd item gevonden hebben en vaststellen dat het tijdelijk niet beschikbaar is), ze meer geneigd zijn op binnen deze sectie te blijven. Resultaten duiden aan dat consumenten die geconfronteerd worden met een stock-out situatie van een geprefereerd product meer geneigd zijn om een ander product uit de onmiddellijke omgeving te kiezen (*proximity-effect*). Online retailers hebben dus ook mogelijkheden om 'indirect' items te suggereren door consumenten te sturen naar specifieke items in de nabijheid van een stock-out item.

Ten slotte tonen de resultaten dat de tendens om visibility en proximity als heuristieken aan te wenden afhankelijk is van het assortiment dat aangeboden wordt. Beide heuristieken worden vooral belangrijk wanneer consumenten meer moeilijkheden ervaren met het vinden en kiezen van een alternatief in het assortiment. Deze *'ease of processing'* is niet enkel een functie van de omvang van het assortiment (*size*) maar wordt ook bepaald door de samenstelling, i.e. het aantal alternatieven met 'populaire' attributen (*composition*).

In het algemeen duidt dit project aan dat consumenten hun online keuzebeslissing vereenvoudigen door (onbewust) gebruik te maken van schap-gerelateerde heuristieken – vooral wanneer ze een *'difficult-to-process'* assortiment verwachten of vermoeden. Dit impliceert dat online retailers (of fabrikanten in hun rol van *category captain*) mogelijkheden hebben om het keuzegedrag van consumenten via efficiënt schapruimte-beheer te beïnvloeden.

Algemene conclusies, beperkingen en indicaties voor verder onderzoek

De resultaten van dit doctoraat geven aan dat online consumenten, o.m. gedreven vanuit de convenience-georiënteerde motivatie om frequent aangekochte producten via een elektronische supermarkt te bestellen, (onbewust) gebruik maken van heuristieken die hen toelaten om op een snelle en efficiënte manier een beslissing te nemen. Uit de resultaten blijkt dat vooral consumenten die minder belang hechten aan de productcategorie meer geneigd zijn om via deze heuristieken een beslissing te nemen. Dit impliceert dat vooral deze consumenten 'vatbaar' zijn voor invloeden van online retailers die het online zoekproces vergemakkelijken. De stijging in flexibiliteit van de elektronische winkelomgeving geeft online retailers dan ook de mogelijkheid om direct (via de suggestie van substitutieproducten) of indirect (via de plaats van producten op het schap) het gebruik van bepaalde heuristieken te stimuleren en hierdoor elektronisch aankoopgedrag te beïnvloeden (en uiteindelijk hun *performance* te verbeteren). Het zou interessant om ook andere manieren (bv. promo-etiket of een opvallende kleur) te bestuderen die aangewend kunnen worden om bepaalde producten meer te laten opvallen en hierdoor hun kans dat ze in overweging genomen/gekozen worden te laten stijgen.

De resultaten van dit onderzoek zijn onderhevig aan een aantal beperkingen. Ten eerste kunnen we niet uitsluiten dat het gebruik van een experimenteel design aanleiding heeft gegeven tot vertekeningen in de resultaten. Hoewel een experiment noodzakelijk was voor de vooropgestelde onderzoekvragen, bevat het steeds een aantal artificiële elementen (bv. geen budget- of tijdsbeperking, geen consumptie, vaste aankoopfrequentie,…). Het zou interessant zijn om dit onderzoek te doen in een reële virtuele winkel waarbij het daadwerkelijke aankoopgedrag van consumenten gevolgd kan worden. Een tweede beperking betreft het beperkte domein van dit onderzoek. De studie werd enkel gedaan voor twee categorieën (margarine en ontbijtgranen) uit de frequent aangekochte consumptiegoederen in één online supermarkt. Het uitbreiden van het onderzoeksdomein (bv. andere producten en/of duurzame goederen) biedt interessante mogelijkheden voor verder onderzoek. Verder werd slechts een beperkt aantal stock-out beleidsopties onder de loep genomen en werden enkel algemene schappositionering effecten bestudeerd. Het bestuderen van andere stock-out beleidsopties of meer gedetailleerde schappositionering effecten (o.a. via eye-tracking) vormt een interessante uitbreiding van dit onderzoek. Ten slotte was onze empirische studie beperkt tot één online supermarkt. Dit impliceert dat we niet empirisch kunnen achterhalen hoe online en offline aankoopgedrag verschillen en op welke manier een online winkel (of hieraan gerelateerd een computergesimuleerd experiment) betrouwbare voorspellingen kan doen voor traditionele marketing mix instrumenten.

Wissenschaftlicher Buchverlag bietet

kostenfreie

Publikation

von

wissenschaftlichen Arbeiten

Diplomarbeiten, Magisterarbeiten, Master und Bachelor Theses
sowie Dissertationen, Habilitationen und wissenschaftliche Monographien

Sie verfügen über eine wissenschaftliche Abschlußarbeit zu aktuellen oder zeitlosen
Fragestellungen, die hohen inhaltlichen und formalen Ansprüchen genügt,
und haben **Interesse an einer honorarvergüteten Publikation**?

Dann senden Sie bitte erste Informationen über Ihre Arbeit per Email
an info@vdm-verlag.de. Unser Außenlektorat meldet sich umgehend bei Ihnen.

VDM Verlag Dr. Müller Aktiengesellschaft & Co. KG
Dudweiler Landstraße 125a
D - 66123 Saarbrücken

www.vdm-verlag.de

www.ingramcontent.com/pod-product-compliance
Lightning Source LLC
La Vergne TN
LVHW022308060326
832902LV00020B/3333